PRAISE FOR

Don't miss a single word...
LONDON EVENING STANDARD

Relaxed, laconic, hilarious.
THE STAGE

A brilliant storyteller.
THE BOSTON PHOENIX

PRAISE FOR *C'EST LA VIE*

Ian Moore is a brilliant comedian whose wit is as sharp as his dress sense, and he has managed to take that on-stage storytelling brilliance and put it in his writing.
JOHN BISHOP

If Ian Moore writes this well in France, he should never be let back into the UK.
DANNY WALLACE

A delicious second helping of muck, mods and mayhem in rural France.
JULIA STAGG, AUTHOR OF *L'AUBERGE*

Easily the best Englishman-abroad memoir since Gerald Durrell was in short trousers and knocking around pre-war Corfu.
TONY PARSONS

Funny, charmingly grumpy. I loved this expat take on the ups and downs of life in rural France.
BEN HATCH, AUTHOR OF *ARE WE NEARLY THERE YET?*

C'EST LA VIE

This edition copyright © Ian Moore, 2025
First published as *C'est Modnifique!* in 2014

All rights reserved.

No part of this book may be reproduced by any means, nor transmitted, nor translated into a machine language, without the written permission of the publishers.

Ian Moore has asserted their right to be identified as the author of this work in accordance with sections 77 and 78 of the Copyright, Designs and Patents Act 1988.

Condition of Sale
This book is sold subject to the condition that it shall not, by way of trade or otherwise, be lent, resold, hired out or otherwise circulated in any form of binding or cover other than that in which it is published and without a similar condition including this condition being imposed on the subsequent purchaser.

An Hachette UK Company
www.hachette.co.uk

Summersdale Publishers
Part of Octopus Publishing Group Limited
Carmelite House
50 Victoria Embankment
LONDON
EC4Y 0DZ
UK

This FSC® label means that materials used for the product have been responsibly sourced

www.summersdale.com

The authorized representative in the EEA is Hachette Ireland, 8 Castlecourt Centre, Dublin 15, D15 XTP3, Ireland (email: info@hbgi.ie)

Printed and bound by Clays Ltd, Suffolk, NR35 1ED

ISBN: 978-1-83799-613-1

Substantial discounts on bulk quantities of Summersdale books are available to corporations, professional associations and other organizations. For details contact general enquiries: telephone: +44 (0) 1243 771107 or email: enquiries@summersdale.com.

IAN MOORE

C'EST LA *Vie*

Adventures of an English Grump in Rural France

summersdale

For Samuel, Maurice and Thérence
– mes petits gars

CONTENTS

1. School Daze 9
2. Adopt, Adapt and Improve 19
3. On the Hedge of Insanity 31
4. Getting My Goat 42
5. Unlucky for Some 53
6. *Août* of Sorts 64
7. New Rules, New Rulers 74
8. Mother in Loire 84
9. Camera Shy 94
10. Needing *Assurance* 103
11. *La Délivrance* 114
12. Harsh Treatments 124
13. Bullied Goat Grump 136
14. The Home Guard 147
15. *Seul* Man 157
16. Finding Your Voice 169
17. No *Pain*, No Gain 183
18. Cross Words 195
19. Beyond *Repas* 206
20. A Ticking Bomb 218
21. Acting Up 230
22. A Very Cordial *Entente* 241
23. Nice and Quiet 252
24. Pussy Whipped 265
25. Question Time 276
26. They Shift Horses, Don't They? 288
27. Just the Beginning... 299

Recipes..312
Acknowledgements...316
About the Author..318

SCHOOL DAZE

'Do you really live in France?'

Quite often I get asked this question in awe, with a barely concealed hint of jealousy. This was outright hostility, though. It was one of those gigs a comedian has nightmares about. One of those moments when no matter what you do, no matter what you try, no matter how much you turn on the comedic charm or, failing that, poke the wasp's nest with a metaphorical stick, the audience just isn't buying it. You've brought out the old infallible material, you've joked about your jokes not working, you've insulted the bloke with the nasty jumper on the front row... and no, nothing. It's the comedian's worst enemy: indifference.

The implication from the heckler's question was clear: how could I possibly be successful enough to commute from rural France when I was patently (on tonight's shambolic evidence at least) not good enough for a sparsely attended, poorly lit room above a pub with a cheap microphone and an even cheaper backdrop?

He had a point. I was exhausted, though; the constant travel had finally worn me down, so now, when I needed to dig in, when I really needed to work the room, there was nothing there. All I could think of, all that was running through my head was, 'But I shouldn't even be here...'

'Whereabouts in France?'

The heckler continued contemptuously, as if by testing my geographical knowledge the whole thinly constructed France charade would come tumbling down.

My half-French wife Natalie and I, together with our young son Samuel and old Jack Russell Eddie, had made the leap from small-town suburban England to the unfashionable end of the Loire Valley, where Natalie's family originates from, seven years previously. We'd bought a property that was far too big for us, in the middle of nowhere, and we loved it. It wasn't just home for us, it was paradise. The plan had been simple: fill the house with a large family and work towards the inevitable (in our eyes at least) time when Natalie would get a job locally and I would give up stand-up entirely and concentrate on writing. It was a plan painted in broad strokes and short on detail, but it didn't seem to matter; it was just obvious to us that one day it would happen.

And pretty quickly we got halfway there; we filled the place with a large family. Samuel, now 11 years old, had two younger brothers, Maurice (seven) and Thérence (three). Eddie had enjoyed her last few years as master of her domain and had died peacefully, only for Natalie, with the zeal of a nineteenth-century missionary, to replace her with two more dogs, two horses, two cats and two hens (not counting many other animal comings and goings), creating a menagerie which collectively had about as much idea of 'peace' as an excitable school trip on a car ferry.

SCHOOL DAZE

'Don't you miss England?'

A different heckler chirped up now, a woman who tragically – and fatally for a comedian trying to stamp his authority on the room – had apparently taken pity on me.

The truthful answer was a straight, unequivocal 'no', for the simple reason that I was spending more time in England than I was at home anyway. I was fast becoming history's most uncommitted *émigré*. A lot of expats – and I know because I've gigged for them all over the world – will give you a whole list of things they miss about 'home', from Marmite to pubs to *Antiques Roadshow*, to drinking in the street and swearing at traffic wardens. Well, I am an expat and all I was missing was the country that I'd ostensibly moved to in the first place! It didn't seem right. And I was missing my family, animals included if I was pushed. I just wasn't seeing them. Not just 'I wasn't seeing them often enough', but a more upsetting, far more hurtful and damaging, 'I wasn't seeing them much at all.'

'Why?' interrupted the angry heckler again.

The whole gig seemed to be descending into a good-cop, bad-cop heckle-off, while the rest of the audience either checked their watches or stared at the grubby, 1970s-style patterned carpet, all a little embarrassed.

'Why did you go there? Were you run out of the country?'

He laughed at his own joke, thankfully getting even less response than I was getting.

The plan (and that really is giving what was actually just 'a vague notion' far too much gravitas) concerning my retirement from live performance comedy was largely scuppered by the very real need to earn money. We live in a relatively poor area of France, an agricultural backwater, and any job that Natalie had previously been able to find was minimum-wage and necessitated being away from home all day – hardly possible when trying to care for a sizeable human family, alongside what had become a burgeoning and practically full-time animal rescue centre. In fact it was difficult enough trying to fit everything in even while she was, at this point, on maternity leave.

The only thing bringing in any regular money, therefore, was stand-up comedy and that, for a number of reasons – not least of which my brain's rank inability to remember anything other than a few stock French phrases – was happening everywhere in the world except France. Whereas when we had first moved abroad I would commute back to the UK to work on a Thursday, Friday and Saturday in metropolitan comedy clubs, I was now spending weeks away gigging in the Middle East, other parts of Europe, sometimes North America and especially, for some reason, India – basically anywhere in the world with an expat community, a microphone and a desire for some entertainment from 'the old country'. I was doing well on the corporate circuit in the UK, too, as an after-dinner speaker and awards host. So while the ambition may certainly have been to be at home more, in truth, financially speaking, we'd never been better off.

But we had also never been more apart – and, physically and emotionally, it was taking its toll.

About a year before this Natalie and I had hit upon an idea that we thought could help make our plan a reality, and on paper it looked bulletproof: why not turn our large property to our advantage, make it work for us? Not in a *gîte* or *chambres d'hôtes* way – that idea had been mooted but quickly discarded

SCHOOL DAZE

on the basis that my social skills, that is, my almost total lack of tolerance for other people, would be tested too quickly and possibly disastrously if people actually had to stay with us. Our idea was to use the space we have, in particular the number of outbuildings, to set up a kind of school – a holiday school – for paying adults to come and learn a skill: painting, writing, pottery; the kind of thing that you see advertised everywhere and that seems quite popular. The intention was to use local hotels and *chambres d'hôtes* to house our students, which meant that local businesses would benefit but also that we would still have our place largely to ourselves. We would call the school 'Les Champs Créatifs' – the 'Fields of Creativity'.

We had done a mountain of research, which had even included going to other places in France to try out courses for ourselves, and decided that as we had contacts in writing anyway we should start with writing courses. There had been a multitude of options obviously: Natalie had been away and done a course in needlecraft that seemed very popular and I had taken a two-day course in French cookery, but we settled on writing. Natalie had done some teaching and could easily have taught a course in languages; I suggested some kind of doctorate in animal rescue and chaos theory, with an extra module in soft furnishings, to which she responded swiftly with a barb of her own: 'Let's concentrate on your skills then, shall we? How about a course in Verbal Abuse of Equines or How Not to Dress in Rural France, or, here's one, a PhD in Moody Git.' Despite this extensive in-house expertise, however, we made the decision to 'hire in' the tutors.

We were genuinely excited by the prospect of what we were trying to create, and although the classic advice is that married couples should never work together, we were loving it. We decided not to do anything until the necessary building work had been completed, as we simply didn't want the stress. Suppose the building was delayed and it wasn't finished in time? It would mean cancelling the courses and notifying both the tutors and the pupils, and the enterprise would hardly recover from that kind of start. It also meant that we could take our time. It seemed to us that the most important thing was the tutors. Obviously we were providing a peaceful, hopefully creative, location in one of the most beautiful places in the world, but it was the tutors who had to be interesting enough and, to a certain extent, well known enough, to attract paying punters.

Another idea we had was that the writing courses shouldn't be just open-ended 'creative writing' but genre-specific. By appealing to genre enthusiasts we reckoned that we would get genuinely committed people on the courses; by narrowing our market, we thought, we would actually be increasing our chances of success. We chose crime fiction (a hugely popular genre), historical crime fiction (one of the fastest-growing genres and an obvious choice with the châteaux of the Loire Valley as our setting) and travel writing, again making use of our location.

Eventually, the building work was completed (late, naturally) and we began to get excited. I had gained an office, a bolthole where I could work on my writing, and Natalie had done wonders with the classroom itself, despite my mocking the process. A few months earlier it had been a damp storage room and she had transformed it into a shabby-chic, Laura Ashley Mecca with more cushions than there are balls in an IKEA soft-play area. We couldn't wait to get started. Over the course of our first summer we planned to run four courses (two for crime fiction, one for historical crime fiction and one for travel writing), all of five days each, and with enough space in-between for our students to learn, and hopefully, rest. We'd even left a space at the end of August for us all to take a well-earned holiday ourselves if we could persuade someone to house-sit the 'home-zoo', which wouldn't necessarily be that easy.

We put out an advertisement for potential tutors and couldn't believe the response: hundreds of authors replied, some household 'genre' names, and we went about matching people to dates and suitability. Our confidence grew as more than one friend told us that, on paper at least, we had a winner. The location was perfect, the courses were well thought out and, as we were paying above the going rate, the tutors were going to be first-class too. We were quietly confident; finally we thought we had hit upon something that meant, even if it was only for the summers to begin with, we would be together as a family. I gleefully and confidently left my gig diary blank for the two months that we would be doing the school and it felt good to know that I would be at home.

Now, I'm not one for portents – and for the most part everything had gone smoothly anyway – but, looking back, there were signs there if I had been inclined to look for them. The only time I had been nervous was when I was interviewing a famous crime writer in his local pub over a generously portioned ploughman's. We were very keen to acquire his services; he is a well-respected writer and an experienced 'writing school tutor', so we thought adding his name to the roster would give the opening year an added push. He also seemed enthusiastic and we were now getting down to the nitty-gritty of dates and finances.

We had just reached the point where I was explaining his fee when his face turned purple. He began to have difficulty breathing and started coughing violently, a hacking cough that tore apart the bucolic serenity of this quiet country pub.

'Were you expecting more?' I said uselessly, misreading his swift descent into a choking death as some kind of elaborate wages protest. 'Other people have said that it's quite generous...'

He loosened his tie with difficulty and staggered off towards the toilets. The few other customers in the bar stared at me as if I'd poisoned the man, and after 20 minutes the barmaid came over to me and quite rightly asked if I thought I shouldn't go in and check on him. My phone rang – it was Natalie.

'Well?' she asked, excitedly. (We had rather pinned our hopes on persuading this author to join us if we could arrange our diaries effectively, hence I was paying for lunch.)

'Erm, I'll call you back,' I replied nervously. 'I think I may have killed him.'

I hadn't, obviously, and he returned to the table a short while later looking flustered and apologetic – and just as I was very obviously writing the word 'INSURANCE' on a handy beer mat.

'It went down the wrong hole,' he offered, by way of explanation, but in the end we never could match our diaries up well enough for him to teach a course for us, which was possibly just as well if he nearly choked to death every time he ate cheese.

The first writing course was due to start at the end of May and advertising had begun the previous November. We weren't really sure when we should start our publicity campaign but it seemed best to cover all bases and just go for blanket coverage: the website was up and running, and looked warm and inviting; at the end of the year a well-known glossy magazine did a two-page spread on me as a stand-up and this, 'our new departure'. We began receiving magazines from all over the world, particularly North America and Australia, copies of publications where our full-colour, beautifully photographed and written adverts were featured. Everything was geared up and on time, all we had to do was wait for the enquiries...

Not one came.

Not one enquiry. Not one solitary spark of interest. It got to the point where I asked friends to test the website email link for us and then I would go to the inbox and all that would be there were emails from those friends jokingly asking if there were still any spaces going. It wasn't necessarily even that depressing at first, we were just dumbstruck, absolutely stunned. Every business has its setbacks and we'd even talked about the possibility of not filling 'all' the places on offer and maybe cutting one course out of the schedule if we needed to. But no-one?! Not even by mistake? No-one?

In early spring, when disaster seemed imminent, we had to make a decision. We hadn't banked on absolutely no-one signing up for the courses, but as this was clearly going to be the case our projected income for the entire summer was now a worrying 'nil'. Not only that, we had no savings left. A combination of building work, furniture, preparation, publicity costs and reams of Laura Ashley material meant that we had spent almost £30,000 on our school. We needed money quickly.

C'EST LA VIE

I have been in charge of booking my own live performances for years – it has its many advantages and is relatively straightforward, with my diary normally full of gigs at least six months in advance – but at this point I could have done with an aggressive agent standing by ready to fill my diary for me. I got on the phones, as they say, and did my best...

And so here I was. On stage in a room above a pub somewhere in the West Midlands, under a glaring, unforgiving light, the audience for the most part disinterested, as warm banter and genuine laughter filtered up from the bar below. I was lucky to be working at all and, not only that, I was going to be busy too. I would be away most of the summer, when I should have been at home for most of it. At least we were still, ostensibly, in France; me, Natalie, the boys and the flotsam and jetsam of the animal kingdom; we still had that.

What we also needed now, though, was a Plan B.

ADOPT, ADAPT AND IMPROVE

I don't like chaos. I don't like disorder, discombobulation, mess, clutter or muddle. I'll have no truck with bedlam, mayhem or turmoil. I like straight lines and order, bullet points and alphabetising. I like polished shoes, cutlery in the right drawer and trouser creases you could slice bread with. If personal organisation is my (admittedly low-wattage) superpower, then nihilistic, unruly and demanding puppies are my kryptonite.

'What do you think of Roxy?' Natalie said airily while sat at the computer one afternoon. When she's after something and laughably thinks she needs my approval, the conversations leave me reeling; to anyone else watching it's like a cat playing with a mouse. It was obvious from the computer monitor what she meant by 'Roxy'. Roxy was a Jack Russell cross, rescued by a local charity after being severely mistreated by her owners in Spain. Natalie had had a bee in her bonnet since the local dog groomer (never a phrase I'm happy with) started banging on about the plight of Spanish hunting dogs, how they're abused and discarded, or worse, once they have served their purpose. It's gruesome stuff and heartbreaking to read some of the stories but really, a line has to be drawn.

'We're full up here!' I said. 'The new rule is this: from now on this place operates along the same lines as the still-touring Four Tops; it doesn't matter if there are no original members left, but there's a number limit – so it's one out, one in.'

Natalie turned back to the screen and the picture of Roxy looking needy.

'She's a pretty little thing who needs a home,' she said.

'But she's not right for us anyway,' I continued, needlessly, feeling like I had to say something.

'How do you mean?' Natalie said, without turning around.

I should have left it there. I should have just walked away, quit while I wasn't that far behind. Idiot.

'Well, she's a *ratier*,' I began; keen to use any French I had for the purpose of gravitas. 'Their instinct is to hunt.'

Natalie nodded sagely.

'We have cats and hens; they wouldn't be safe,' I blathered. 'Plus,' I added, unknowingly drawing the lid over my own coffin, 'she's a couple of years old; she's already learned to hunt. You'd need a younger dog and then you could train it.'

'You're absolutely right, Ian,' she said, using my first name the way parents do to draw a line under things and swivelling round on the office chair. 'You're right. We should get a puppy instead.'

I think at that point my mouth may have fallen open in classic cartoon style; I certainly didn't say anything. I went to my office and just sat in stunned silence, leaving Natalie to her office-chair victory swivels. I went back in, a few hours later, hoping the dust had settled, only to be greeted with a voice from upstairs: 'I think I've found the puppy you're looking for!'

'Excellent,' I said, sarcastically, and downed a glass of wine. 'That's Plan B sorted, then. More animals, eh? Who'd have thought that'd be the answer to our problems?'

It's one thing to be so comprehensively outplayed in the parlour game of 'new puppy vs no puppy', but quite another to then be required to do the eight-hour round-trip drive to pick up 'my' puppy. To my mind we had enough on our plate, and it wasn't as if the animals we had already were maintenance-free. The two dogs were polar opposites. Toby, a spaniel–border collie cross is delightful but mentally limited, like an over-friendly village idiot; Pierrot, an elderly King Charles spaniel, was by now deaf and partially blind, but had settled into a routine of personal sexual gratification that caused visitors' jaws to drop while they simultaneously tried to cover up the eyes of their children. Junior was the first horse to arrive and immediately took a dislike to what he considered to be his natural challenger for leader of the pack – me. He subjected me to physical and – to my mind at least, though I'm no horse whisperer – verbal abuse. If he were human he would probably be in solitary confinement somewhere; however Natalie had decided to reward his behaviour by getting him a concubine, Ultime, who was flighty, frisky and full of youthful vigour, especially, much to Junior's initial delight, in the 'stable department'.

Our two cats, Vespa and Flame, had been half of a litter found abandoned in the hayloft. The hens, my lovely hens, Tallulah and Lola, scratch about the place like a pair of old fussbudgety spinsters visiting a stately home, and bustle about with a look on their faces that's part admiration and part 'wiping a finger along the mantelpiece' superiority.

Nonetheless, we all set off early one morning, all of them singing made-up 'We're Off to Get a Puppy' songs while I was feeling more like the wretched Sydney Carton in *A Tale of Two Cities* – and utterly resigned to my fate.

If you look on a map, the Loire Valley doesn't seem that far from the Dordogne, but it bloody is, so by the time we got there most tempers were almost as frayed as mine. Even when we were no more than a few kilometres away I was still blithely issuing 'I'll turn this thing around and we'll go straight home' threats, with ever-decreasing effectiveness. The thing was, we weren't going to 'see' a puppy; this wasn't like an interview process to check our compatibility; this was a pick-up, a done deal, a *fait accompli* and I felt like I'd been bounced into it.

We had agreed to meet our contact from the Phoenix Association rescue centre and then drive to the foster home where the puppy had been living for the past few days. The foster carer, a harassed-looking woman living in the middle of nowhere, had six dogs and six cats which had the run of the place and, laudable though her vocation is, it was chaos in there. Fortunately, it was a nice day so the animals could be outside, but then they were in one minute and out the next: all over the furniture, on the kitchen surfaces, chasing each other through open windows and jumping on the dining table. While Natalie chatted dogs and general animal cruelty with the woman, I stood in a corner, keeping myself as still as possible to avoid being covered in hair (or worse), occasionally hissing in Natalie's direction that there was 'no way our house would ever be like this, no way at all'.

ADOPT, ADAPT AND IMPROVE

And then Gigi appeared. She had been playing with the other dogs, and even at just 12 weeks old was standing her ground against older and rougher animals. Gigi is a cross between a dachshund and a Chihuahua, and though she obviously had a bit of spunk about her she would have fitted into one of my slippers. Far from worrying about her chasing the hens or fighting with the cats, our main concern would be to avoid stepping on her or being on our guard against circling buzzards mistaking her for a baby rabbit.

It never occurred to me that at some point in my life I would be carrying around a small dog in a bag and introducing my 'chiweenie' which, crushingly, is what this cross-breed is known as. But she was charming; full of character and spirit and a loving little thing. She was also feisty, mischievous, ignored any instructions I might give and had me immediately wrapped around her little finger. She therefore fitted in perfectly.

If I'd hoped that the acquisition of Gigi would somehow satisfy Natalie's insatiable craving, I was wrong. At first I'd thought this new bout of mass animal-collecting was somehow a displacement therapy, a comforting fallback to make up for what, even in early spring, was looking like the financial and emotional disaster of the school. Maybe it was in part, but it had also developed into a full-blown addiction. People living with a partner's addiction may have warning bells and emergency measures: a lock on the drinks cabinet maybe, a ban on chocolate. We had to ban some of the animal-based documentary channels, skip TV adverts when a charity ad came on, avoid magazines. And once you've started collecting animals of course there is bound to be a natural, and inevitable, drop off in numbers – as much as you care for your pets, they are susceptible to old age, ill health, etc. – and though mourning is heartfelt, in our case it is also brief and swiftly replaced by a new search.

Most families develop their own holiday time traditions sooner or later – whether it be an acrimonious Christmas Day game of Trivial Pursuit or putting 'amusing' hats on a sleeping elderly relative. They are bookmarks, part *Groundhog Day*, part collective familial nervous tic. Easter is much the same and we had by now developed our own Easter tradition in France: we bury one of the pets. A macabre twist on the general idea, granted, but one that had unfortunately now become something of an early-spring regularity.

Lola, one of our hens, died on Easter Sunday, and it cast something of a pall on the day. She hadn't been herself for a week or so and had begun to stay in the coop rather than get up in the morning. She had started attacking the spring tulips like they were a reminder of something evil in her past and then, frustratingly, took to laying her eggs wherever she felt like it, as though she was mocking the traditional Easter egg hunt. She then started laying eggs with no shell on at all, which sounds like some evolution of convenience cooking but was actually a very messy business indeed. It was tempting to put the whole thing down to a temporary mood swing or the behaviour of a hormonal teenage hen, but the truth is hens are inscrutable creatures and very obvious signs of ill health are pretty thin on the ground. Also, there was no point in asking the vet, who would probably just laugh at us and suggest a nice sauce, some rosemary and a large pot.

She was definitely alive in the morning when I opened up their coop, though she remained in her nest. I thought nothing of it at first and went about the serious business of hiding the boys' Easter eggs in the garden, which was proving harder than I'd imagined. After hiding a few of the eggs it became clear that Toby, Pierrot and Gigi were following at a discreet distance and systematically eating what I'd hidden. So I started again, before realising that while leaving the things out of canine reach they were also directly in the sunlight and liable to be mere chocolate puddles by the time the boys found them. I started a third time, taking dog behaviour and sun trajectory into account. I finally settled back as the big hunt began, only to realise half an hour later, when only half of the eggs had been found, that I couldn't remember where I'd hidden most of the damn things, at which point Natalie took over and I was retired from my position.

Later on that day we upheld another one of our Easter Sunday traditions by attending the *foire aux ânes* ('donkey fair'), which takes place locally and which, frankly, I dread every year. I've got nothing against donkeys; I quite like the creatures. We even had one, briefly, before it was repeatedly sodomised by our horse, Junior. Personally, I'm pleased that their role is recognised so much that they get their own *foire*, but when confronted by any group of animals my morale sinks and my patience wears thin; the rest of the family go running around like the kids in *Charlie and the Chocolate Factory*, while I have to repeat myself, saying, 'No', 'Don't be silly' and 'It won't fit in the car'.

Not only is the *foire aux ânes* an Easter celebration of all things donkey, there is the inevitable *brocante* with its stalls and stalls of tat where Natalie will, every year, buy some metal ornamental jug-type thing and the boys will splurge their pocket money on small toys exactly like the ones they already have and don't play with anymore. I will be left to queue for an outrageously over-priced lunch while the rest of them are off bartering with Romanies and then they'll return and complain that I bought the wrong thing. Again, it's an Easter Sunday tradition, as is the strop that goes with it.

'You're so moody, Daddy!' Samuel said as we drove back home afterwards, to the noisy accompaniment of various types of garden ironmongery rolling about in the boot. I tried to argue my case, but apparently the only way to prove that I'm not moody would have been to turn the car around and stuff it full of hooved, herbivorous mammals or – as I like to call them – 'Junior fodder'.

'Yes, son; yes I am. Very moody.' I was resigned, and after a week's travelling and working away I was too tired to argue my case. The poor boys were sensing the pressure we were under more and more and I was behaving like a grumpy mod zombie.

When we got back home it was obvious that Tallulah, our other hen, was on her own. The hens always go around together, so Natalie went off in search of poor Lola; she didn't have to look very far. Lola hadn't made it out of the coop and was already stiff from rigor mortis, her eyes glazed and her head at an odd, questioning angle like a horrible parody of those terracotta oven dishes you see in fancy cook shops.

Lola was Maurice's hen and he didn't take the news well. Up until that point he'd always taken the death of a pet phlegmatically; sad and quiet, certainly, but not tearful. This time though he was distraught, utterly inconsolable, obviously having reached an age where he's aware that death is very much the end and that Lola wasn't coming back. We buried Lola while little Maurice's sobs continued unabated and Tallulah clucked and fussed plaintively in the background. I know she was just a hen, but despite where we live we are not hard-nosed country folk and these things do affect us. We all felt saddened by her death, maybe because we hadn't seen it coming and also because exactly this time last year we were burying the short-lived rabbit, something that preyed very heavily on both Samuel's and Maurice's minds.

I don't know whether haste helps the grieving process, but Natalie was determined to give it a go; a replacement was immediately sought and duly arrived from the market the following Thursday. Victoria (it had become policy now that all new hens were to be named after songs by The Kinks) was a handsome girl and more tame than either Lola or Tallulah, allowing herself to be stroked and immediately strutting about the place with some confidence. Tallulah however, who had obviously begun to pine for her absent friend, wasn't keen. They eyed each other suspiciously like two old women at a tea dance who've both taken a fancy to the same man; there was no outright hostility, but rather a coolness, and so to start with they kept their distance. Tallulah had taken to hanging around the bird feeders with the cats, waiting for some stray bread to fall, but Victoria was happy to explore and even lay eggs in the flowerbeds, which, convenience aside, was amazing for such a young hen and one so new to her surroundings.

In short, although Lola's death was a shock, we felt we'd quickly got things back on an even keel and everything animal-wise was fine again – but we were wrong.

Toby, the spaniel–collie cross, is a follower, not a leader. One minute he's chasing mice because he's seen the cats do it and the next he's chasing the cats because he's seen Gigi – who may only be a chiweenie but has the attitude of a lairy Rottweiler – do it. Occasionally we'll give Toby a bone to chew on, though not very often. It may be good for a dog's teeth, but can play havoc with their digestive system – and although as a mod I have a hankering for nostalgia, that doesn't stretch to white dog poo.

I sat under the lime tree enjoying the spring sunshine; a brief window of tranquillity had opened and I was determined to take full advantage. Maurice had scored two goals in his football match earlier and was now revelling in delight; Samuel was buried deep in the world of Harry Potter and Thérence had taken himself off for an afternoon nap on the sofa; Natalie was, as usual, doing something unfathomable in the garden somewhere, while the animals all did their thing. The hens were pacing up and down; the cats were lying languidly in the sun; Gigi and Pierrot were lazing on the terrace while the horses took the opportunity to hump without being barked at, as Toby was distracted by his bone. It was as peaceful as it gets; a hazy, soft-focus, bucolic dreamscape which lasted about five minutes.

I'd just begun to drift off when the violence of Natalie's screams scared me clean out of the hammock and on to the ground. I picked myself up to see her angrily chasing Toby around the place. There were feathers everywhere, which may be a good sign in a pillow fight but not in a hen-and-dog combo. Victoria, it seems, had wandered too close to Toby who, although usually a very placid animal, likes a bit of space when chewing on a bone. He had taken exception to her proximity and lashed out taking a sizeable chunk of plumage and worse, half of one of her feet. There was blood everywhere.

ADOPT, ADAPT AND IMPROVE

It's no use arguing that it was out of character, bones are apparently Toby's equivalent of strong lager. They change his personality and the lovable beast becomes like a repressed husband who starts throwing his weight around after a few pints of Stella.

All hell broke loose. Every animal seemed to want to get involved and take sides. Gigi took exception to Toby being shouted at and kept hanging off the back of my trousers; the cats took advantage of the distraction and jumped on to the bird feeder; Pierrot, now almost totally blind and deaf, knew something was amiss and started rubbing himself furiously against a handy table leg; while Tallulah literally took Victoria under her wing and walked her away from the scene with a judgemental look on her face. The horses, seeing chaos as a new turn-on, continued humping noisily, adding to the bedlam of the scene.

We bathed and bandaged the damaged foot; it hadn't been completely severed, but Victoria was clearly traumatised by what had happened and steadfastly refused to leave the coop for weeks afterwards. I was surprised at this, frankly; I thought chickens still ran around if you chopped their heads off, but this one just sulked and stayed in bed all day. A decree was passed and Toby had all bone privileges removed, although he seemed to have no recollection of what he had done and therefore no remorse, so it all smacked of an uneasy truce.

Most people may have been tempted to conclude that the cat–hen–dog–horse nature of our home life was actually a pretty fragile existence, and that maybe a period of rest to let the animals find their level would be wise before introducing any newcomers to the mix. Natalie isn't most people. The strength of will she needed to turn down the offer of two more kittens during the following week only lasted a couple of days and so, on a trip to the market for fruit and veg, she returned with two more hens.

I was away by this point and had been for over a week – as if my being there would have prevented the new arrivals. The phone conversations I'd had indicated that the brittle dog–hen truce appeared to be holding, but that the hens themselves seemed to be divided. Tallulah, after showing brief concern for Victoria, was now having very little to do with her at all, which added to Victoria's isolation and lack of verve. The new hens however, Monica and Anaïs, (Monica kept The Kinks theme going but Anaïs was more like a name for a 1920s Parisian courtesan to me) had given Victoria a new confidence while simultaneously ruffling Tallulah's feathers in the process. Are hens political?

Questions, questions.

The real point was that after ten days on the road I was now sitting in my hotel room, staring at dank, grey Birmingham, and my thoughts were dominated, admittedly happily, by the potential in-fighting of a group of young hens. If I'd been at home all that time I would have tutted and sulked and railed against the increased mayhem of the place, pleaded with Natalie and the boys for a bit of peace and quiet, sought solace somewhere away from the animal anarchy. I wasn't at home, though, and I missed the whole feather-and-fur merry-go-round. The circus was driving me potty when I was there but it seemed, precariously at least, to be keeping me sane when I wasn't. Can't live with 'em, can't live without 'em.

ON THE HEDGE OF INSANITY

Without consciously realising it, we had slipped straight back into our old routine. Natalie was happily collecting animals, those animals were rewriting the rules on acceptable behaviour and the boys were growing up in a Narnia-like animal–countryside–fantasy existence. For a while we were in a kind of daze about the initial failure of Les Champs Créatifs and were almost too nervous to discuss alternatives. At some point we would have to sit down together and talk about the future again, but for now it was impossible – and not just because we'd had our fingers burned.

So much of my life is spent not just travelling but planning the travelling. I have to dedicate whole afternoons to booking a block of journeys, trying to find the best deal, matching up bus, train and plane connections, working out months in advance if I can do a particular weekend with hand luggage only, while remembering to avoid Paris during the school holidays for fear of being stuck on a budget airline surrounded by wailing infants who have somehow earned the right to go to Disneyland.

It's a complicated business and it requires clarity of thought, order and no small amount of patience, and I have, I think, got it down to a fine art. Sadly, it means that I've now become an expert on Ryanair timetables and destinations; I can quote prices and the best times to travel on Eurostar; and I know the night-time links for National Express. If I were on *Mastermind*, 'Travel between France and the UK' would be my specialist subject. But even I occasionally get it wrong. Badly wrong.

We'd only been living in France for a month when I was flown out to Tokyo to do some shows there. The gigs were OK, as I remember, but what set the trip apart was that the head of Virgin Japan was in the audience one night – he liked what he saw, so he bumped me and my fellow performers all up to Virgin Upper Class. It was a beautiful way to travel and I fell asleep immediately, which while on the one hand meant that I didn't have to talk to my fellow comedians, also meant that there was limited opportunity to feel really smug. As it was, however, I arrived back at Heathrow feeling refreshed and ready to meet my more mundane connection to Paris.

'You're a little early to be checking in, Mr Moore,' said the British Airways crew member behind the desk, trying hard to hide the smirk on her lips. 'A year early.'

In those early days I booked these trips with genuine excitement, I was jet-setting around the world – OK, I was mostly just flying to London Stansted, but it felt almost exhilarating to be travelling like that. The thrill soon wears off, however, when you try to add up just how many hours you've spent pacing up and down airport terminals or trying to keep warm on exposed railway platforms. It's especially upsetting when you're a whole year early for your flight and being charged a fortune to change it. I vowed there and then that I would not make that mistake again, that no matter how long I spent planning the journeys

I would take more care. It wasn't just about the money, it was about dignity. No-one likes to be made to look that stupid and in the seven years since, despite taking hundreds of flights and thousands of trains, I'd had a screw-up-free record.

As I was scrabbling around for short-notice gigs I didn't have the luxury of well-researched pre-planning – decisions had to be made in haste, travel plans concocted on the backs of envelopes without due care and attention, and it had a disastrous effect. I was feeling pretty jaunty, which is fatal for me, and had made the drive to Calais in record time, meaning that I could jump on an earlier Eurotunnel train and arrive in England just in time to turn on the car radio and listen to the football. It had all been beautifully worked out.

'You're a little early to be checking in, Monsieur,' said the petite French lady in the ticket booth.

'Really?' I replied, probably a little cocksure. 'Surely it's only a couple of hours.'

'It's a week, Monsieur. Today is the twenty-first, this booking is for the twenty-eighth.'

In the end I felt quite sorry for the poor girl in the booth as she had to listen to such a heartfelt volley of Anglo-Saxon profanities which, although not directed at her, were very much aimed in the direction of the universe in general, of which she no doubt felt a part.

I bought a new ticket at twice the price of the old one and drove slowly on to join the boarding queue. Oh well, I thought, it could be worse: at least this kind of thing only happens once every seven years…

The following day I had to fly to Belfast for a corporate event and I was travelling from Gatwick. I used to like Gatwick

C'EST LA VIE

Airport – I spent my teenage years living not far from it and it always seemed so impossibly romantic that somewhere so close to my home could be a hub from which to go anywhere in the world. The glamour has largely gone from international travel and Gatwick in particular seems to be less of an airport these days and more a holding station for every stag party in the world. When I arrived to check in there were at least three large groups of Mario Brothers stags, two sets of nuns and a dozen overweight blokes wearing comedy breasts, though they may have just been shirtless. Clearly, if you dress up like that for a stag party you should consider yourself very fortunate indeed that you've found someone sympathetic enough to want to share their life with you, but the rest of us don't care. Grow up.

To be fair, my romantic view of Gatwick didn't last past the time I had a summer job there. I worked shifts in the cafe after passport control and it was miserable; you could see how stressed people got just by being in an airport: the constant noise of screaming children, bickering adults and assorted drunks was horrendous, and I hated the job. I remember Terence Trent D'Arby coming through the cafe one morning and being appallingly impolite as we tried to serve him but, and I offer this up as an apology, that in no way excused how many times his sausage roll was dropped on the floor before it was handed to him on an equally grubby paper plate.

I had tried to check in online for my return flight to Belfast, but as usual couldn't do it; I could get the outbound OK, but the return wasn't happening. Budget airlines are notorious for this; you need the computer skills of a Pentagon hacker to get around their websites at the best of times, but I'd allowed myself some space so I enquired at the desk.

'I couldn't print out my return online,' I said, to a frankly orange-skinned creature behind the desk.

'That's because it's not open yet,' she replied.

'Really?' I asked. 'But I'm coming back tomorrow morning, first thing.'

'No, sir, this booking is for a return on Saturday morning.'

Twice! Twice in a bloody week! Had I become so blasé about the whole travel business that I barely even looked at the computer screen anymore, just blithely confirming whatever's thrown up in front of me like some diffident Roman emperor? Or, and in my fragile, paranoid state this was my favoured option, was my subconscious basically telling me, 'Enough is enough. Stop all this travelling malarkey; it's doing you no good.' If only.

It was with a sense of weariness, then, that I eventually got to Belfast and to the reception desk at the Europa Hotel.

'Hi there, you should have a reservation for me? Mr Moore?'

'Ach, no, Mr Moore. According to our records you checked in yesterday.'

It seemed that the disaster of our writing school was having a knock-on effect on everything else; it was casting a dark shadow. It wasn't simply a case of saying, 'Oh well, we'll just carry on doing what we've done before', and switch straight back into gigs/being away/travel/Natalie-on-her-own mode. Everything seemed to be getting harder. Even the weather seemed to be against us as spring, for the second year running, decided that biblical downpours were the way forward.

The wet weather had serious repercussions: Natalie's grand spring garden plans were once again being scuppered, leaving her angrily tutting at the heavens from the dry of the lounge.

It was also a blow to my plans too – not in terms of travel but something far more important: chutney. For the second year in a row my fruit trees were barren. I would be chutney-less and my passion, my get-away-from-it-all safety net of standing in the kitchen and boiling the goodness out of fresh fruit would be denied me once again. This really was turning out to be a tough year indeed.

'Well, there's plenty of other things you can do,' Natalie said, quite reasonably, while I was grouching my way around my fruitless orchard on a rare dry afternoon. 'All those hedge trimmings need piling up and burning for one thing.'

More than two-thirds of the property, approximately 200 metres, has a thick leylandii hedge; the previous owners planted that species of leylandii specifically because of its apparently famous ability to remain immune to disease. Mother Nature, though, obviously in one of her more capricious moods, had seen fit to pooh-pooh such claims and the thing was now dying of the very diseases it's not supposed to catch. It still needs trimming every year, however, which means I rub my back, affect a limp and get someone else in to do it, citing a not wholly inaccurate physical frailty. This year, although the hedge got trimmed, all the trimmings were left where they fell, partly because we thought we could save money by not employing our intimidating Portuguese gardener, Manuel, who we had inherited from the previous owners of the house, to do the whole job, and partly because it was felt that I could do with the exercise – a decision taken in my absence.

Initially we had thought about not trimming the hedge at all, again partly for financial reasons but also in the hope that just letting it run wild would help the struggling patches find some enthusiasm for life and begin to regrow. Manuel was having none of it.

'What?' he asked, incensed. 'You want it to look like nobody lives here?'

And off he went to get the industrial hedge trimmers, overriding our decision entirely and looking at me over his shoulder like I'd obviously bullied Natalie into such folly. The horses had played a hand in the verdict too.

While largely unaffected by noise, low-flying French fighter jets, the incessant barrage of hunters, etc., the horses do get quite flustered if another equine body happens to wander past the gate. Usually they start running around and neighing loudly – but not this time. This time they got themselves stuck in the hedge. The hedge runs around most of the property and there's a gap of about half a metre between it and the wire-mesh fence on the other side. I'd blocked off any access to this gap, knowing that if they went behind the hedge they would either cut themselves badly or destroy the fence. What I hadn't banked on was Junior getting so aerated at the sight of a strange horse or that Ultime would follow him up this narrow, potentially dangerous alley and that both of them would get stuck.

I only realised there was a problem when I was washing the dishes after lunch and couldn't help noticing that Junior was staring at me from the other side of the kitchen window. He needed my help, definitely, but the look on his face was the usual mix of belligerence and arrogant aggression, like he would rather stay stuck there for the rest of his life than rely on me for assistance.

Horses it seems, like aeroplanes, sharks and Margaret Thatcher, don't do reverse. Believe me I tried. I squeezed into the gap and stood facing Junior, Ultime right behind him, and I began pushing. We went slowly backwards for a couple of metres and then something spooked the skittish Ultime, so they both began moving forward, putting me in some danger, forcing me to dive into the hedge to avoid being crushed. We played this game for an hour, each time with the same result, as I ended up on the floor trying not to get stamped on.

I wanted to avoid the nuclear option, which was to take a chainsaw to the hedge and cut them a gap, but it really couldn't be avoided. It was a delicate operation as I began to cut a hole inches from Junior's face. This is the horse that eyes me with disdain if I approach him with an apple – the look I was getting now as I began noisily chainsawing close enough to give him a shave was one of outright hostility. I'd hoped that the noise of the chainsaw would spook him into reversing but, no, this horse would stand up to a tsunami.

I cut a gap just big enough for him to squeeze through, and as soon as it was done he charged at me, again sending me flying as he went angrily by, snorting like the devil horse I genuinely believe him to be. Then he stopped, his head high and his mane flowing in the breeze; a handsome beast, no doubt, but an angry, angry individual. This time, however, his anger wasn't directed at me but at Ultime, who for once hadn't followed him and remained stuck behind the hedge. He went trotting back to the gap and seemed to bellow at the poor creature – it wasn't a neigh or a snort; it sounded more like an irate, domineering husband shouting at his wife that for Christ's sake would she get a move on, they were going to be late. Whatever it was, it did the trick and Ultime came darting out and charged dangerously about the place while she got her composure back, seemingly apologetic and looking for her earrings.

I stared at Natalie and then at the tonnes and tonnes of hedge trimmings that Manuel had left for me to collect. I'm not completely against physical labour – I can see the benefits – but this is the kind of back-breaking toil that not only crushes you physically but leaves you questioning the sanity of your decision to live where you do. It took me seven hours. Seven hours of piling the things on to a tarpaulin and moving said heavily laden tarpaulin halfway across the field to the fire. It was so heavy I had to drag it, walking at an acute angle to get any purchase on the ground. I looked like an Arctic explorer walking into a violent headwind and I was not happy.

But being on the road for a long stretch means that you begin to romanticise even about the things you don't like. And although even the mere thought of dragging that stuff around brings me out in a sweat and cramps, there were upsides. Gigi, as puppies are wont to do, would jump on to the tarpaulin and hitch a ride, adding to the weight, and Junior, Devil Horse, sauntered past at one point and deliberately, I tell you, trod on the end of the tarpaulin, which sent me hurtling ignominiously to the ground. Natalie, the children and, seemingly, all the animals thought this was hilarious. Even I, lying on the ground and spitting grass indignantly out of my mouth, saw the funny side of that, though vowed to get my own back on 'that bloody horse'.

Victoria, our battered and assaulted hen, seemed more animated than usual by my plight – and so in one moment of slapstick I had united the entire family, animals and all. Even Toby, who'd been laying low for a while and who, to avoid further tellings-off, had taken to carrying Gigi about on his back – presumably his version of the 'human shield' logic. Amazingly, Victoria's apparent recovery was, in fact, due to cannibalism. Natalie had searched the internet hen forums to seek advice on how to deal with an injured chicken and, one can only presume, some unthinking wag had jokingly posted on one of these unchecked areas of expounding madness and said 'feed the thing scrambled eggs'! So what did we do with the first egg Victoria laid? Scramble it up and feed the bloody thing back to her! We fed a sick hen her own eggs! Her own spawn and progeny! I'm no expert but that's how BSE started, isn't it? This is how epidemics and animal panics begin, surely? It's so wrong and if it's not wrong it surely can't be right, if you get my drift.

The absurdity continued as, taking advantage of my testosterone-fuelled physical endeavours, Natalie despatched me straight away to cut the grass at the front of the house which, because of the monsoon-like spring weather, had got too tall to be mowed. Neither of us felt confident about taking the horses out to do the job as they seemed more concerned with aggressive, noisy horse sex than anything else and we feared for the safety of passing motorists, however seldom. I was handed my father-in-law's petrol strimmer, a vicious piece of equipment with a rotating metal blade, good enough to do the job, certainly, but a dangerous weapon in the wrong hands; it looks like a cross between a flamethrower and a circular saw, and like most machines has a novelty factor that swiftly wears off.

Things went well for the first 20 minutes, which may have been responsible for my dip in concentration. I got too close to the fence. The violently rotating blade hit the wire, but rather than cut it, it just twisted around the thing which caused the blade to seize up. All this happened in the blink of an eye, so rather than have time to release the 'trigger', I was still holding on to it and was flipped over like I was performing a rather ostentatious goal-scoring celebration, a purely gymnastic backflip or an Olympic somersault, but with a poorly judged landing…

I lay there on the ground, unable to move, dazed but physically unharmed and wondering quite frankly what the hell had happened. I'd banged my head, certainly, and was maybe even a little concussed as the family gathered around me.

'Are you OK?' Thérence asked. To be fair there wasn't a great deal of concern in his toddler voice, more a tone of acute condescension.

'Fine. Absolutely fine,' I replied and began frantically gathering up the grass that I had managed to cut and adding it to the burgeoning fire pile.

Eventually it was over. 'There you go!' I said, as I dumped the last hedge trimming and grass-laden tarpaulin on to the fire pile. *'C'est fini!'*

Natalie and the boys gathered around me again, recognising the brutal physical nature of the tasks undertaken and pleased to see them finally completed with me mostly in one piece.

'Over seven hours,' I said, milking the moment for what it was worth. 'Over seven hours I've been at all this.' I swayed my arm, indicating what actually looked like a fairly meagre fire pile. 'That would have cost us a fair bit if we'd got Manuel to do all that!' I added triumphantly and took a victory swig from a cold beer gratefully accepted from Maurice.

'Not really,' Natalie said, as the throng dispersed. 'He'd have done it in three.'

GETTING MY GOAT

'That's enough for me,' I said, stretching my arms and trying to pull myself off the sofa. *'Je suis fatigué.'*

'Yes Daddy,' Samuel replied, 'you are fat and gay.' He looked at me nervously, secretly knowing that he'd probably gone too far with this bilingual pun, but with a hint of pride in his eyes too as deep down he knew he'd delivered a brilliant line. I suppose that I should have been annoyed at his cheekiness – this is the twenty-first century, so I could hardly consider 'gay' to be much of an insult – but fat? That hurt, especially for a mod.

My little boy was growing up and as a comedian I just had to stand back and admire the joke, even if I was the butt of it. We'd come a long way in the seven years since we'd both stood in our living room one night watching a late-night performance of me in some television show or other. I can't normally watch myself on television, but Samuel was transfixed by it, and what the hell, I was getting big laughs. No harm in letting him know the old man can work a room.

After my performance was over, tiny four-year-old Samuel stood watching the blank screen for a couple of minutes, with a serious, determined look in his eye.

'I'm coming to work with you next time, Daddy,' he said eventually, and with some gravity. 'I'll stop those people laughing at you.'

I looked at him – he still didn't know which way I'd go on the *'fatigué'* thing, largely because I'm a moody sod, but also because the atmosphere had been pretty tetchy at home since we'd realised that the school was a non-starter. I gave him a big hug, but told him that he shouldn't really talk like that and that 'gay' isn't a pejorative word. He looked a little crestfallen.

'Sorry, Daddy,' he said.

'Also,' I continued, 'could you write it down for me? I'm definitely going to use that on stage next week.'

Relieved, he gave me a huge beaming smile and ran off to get a pen and paper. He had been laid low with a virus for a while and to suddenly see such animation was quite uplifting.

Samuel is frequently likened to me. People will quite often say, generally out of my earshot, 'Oh, he's just like his dad, isn't he?' They don't mean it in a good way, but Samuel is, at 11 years old, still young enough to see this as a compliment. He is the only one. A serious-minded boy, he can be moody, argumentative, obsessive, prone to prolonged bouts of physical inactivity and occasionally high-handed. He is, in essence, a 'mini me' and I watch him proudly as his levels of disdain and sarcasm reach a precocious maturity, and he lashes out unnecessarily at fools he will not suffer gladly. There are, however, rays of sunshine breaking through the clouds and my protégé in the darker arts of irritability is having his head turned by those cosy imps 'contentment' and 'enthusiasm'.

I blame his mother.

Maurice and Thérence are both very much in their mother's mould, with their sunny dispositions and zest for life. They run around at full speed laughing and playing without a care in the world, pausing sporadically only to pick flowers for their mummy or to check the chicken coop for fresh eggs. They have both taken to life with old-fashioned gusto and vim, and are determined to enjoy the experience. Of course, as a parent it's partly my job to ensure that they can do just that, but it's also nice to have an ally in the house – someone who'll join me in a sneer once in a while; a comrade in the fight against unrealistic optimism. I was beginning to fear that Samuel, however, was gradually being lost to the 'light' side.

My fear, it seems, was well-founded...

Zoos aren't for everyone and that's fair enough. I remember going to zoos as a child and they were miserable places with the saddest looking animals all suffering from varying degrees of neglect. I'm sure that those zoos still exist, but some have genuinely improved. Our local zoo, ZooParc de Beauval, is a conservation zoo and specialises in breeding endangered animals – for instance, white tigers, tree kangaroos, mountain gorillas and, sadly, hundreds of other species of animals and birds whose existence in the wild is threatened. We've taken friends to Beauval previously and they've been upset at the prospect, wandering around morosely, shaking their heads and repeating the mantra 'But it's just not right, is it?' And, of course, it isn't right. In an ideal world there would be no need for conservation zoos at all, but as man persists in treating the world like a cross between an ashtray and a giant car park then these places do an invaluable job and are to be applauded. Besides which, where else are you going to see an elderly chimpanzee masturbate in front of a group of terrified schoolchildren?

We go to Beauval regularly and have seen it change over the years and grow according to the needs of new species that need housing. A 10-hectare enclosure was built for elephants, which spreads the zoo out until it now incongruously borders a small vineyard; penguins threatened by a change in currents arrived from South America; anteaters, white rhinos, lemurs, tapirs, okapis, orangutans – the list goes on. They've even got giant pandas, which they 'rent' from a zoo in China at an exorbitant rate. Frankly, I didn't know that you could hire pandas and maybe that's the way forward for endangered species generally; get yourself out there for parties and social functions, open a few supermarkets and the like. I was once drinking alone in a pub when a stripper arrived for someone's birthday and it was one of the grimmest spectacles I have ever witnessed; imagine how much more fun it would have been if a panda had shown up instead. Although, to be honest, there wouldn't have been a whole lot of difference in appearance, as one pot-bellied mammal with black eyes pretty much resembles another.

Pandas notwithstanding, I can spend hours in the zoo, sitting back to back with the great apes separated by, one hopes, sturdy glass. I can watch the orangutan family play and socialise all afternoon – and watch them watch us too, which is just as fascinating. The one bugbear I have with the place is the 'petting zoo'. Petting always seemed to be frowned upon when I was growing up, certainly in swimming pools, but here it's positively encouraged. There's a farmyard section to wander through that has donkeys, chickens, pigs, sheep and goats. Frankly, it's all a bit like home to me and I'm constantly telling everyone to get a move on: 'Why are you playing with farmyard animals?' I'll ask incredulously. 'We have them at home! Come on! Let's go and stare at a tiger!'

The *'mini-ferme'*, literally 'mini-farm', is also the one place in the zoo where you are allowed to feed the animals and you can buy huge bags of popcorn to feed the goats. This is not for the faint hearted or the well dressed. The first time we went there I was holding two bags of popcorn and wandered into the farm area not realising that goats in particular can spot a bag of popcorn a mile away. They all came rushing at me, a dozen of them, jumping up at me with their muddy hooves all over my beige Sta-Prest trousers and trying to nibble my suede Chelsea boots. It felt like some kind of horrible set-up, like I was taking my first scuba dive in shark-infested waters and with a load of raw meat strapped to me. I barely made it out in one piece and haven't been back in the farm enclosure since, preferring to observe from relative safety.

Samuel too had been knocked over on his first foray into goat world and had subsequently always joined me – we would both shake our heads as we watched other poor saps get beaten up by uncouth, hungry goats. On this visit he decided to venture back in, leaving me alone on the other side of the fence. He was in there for a full half an hour just playing with one baby goat in particular. It was moving stuff, like an old episode of *Belle and Sebastian*, and when eventually he got bored of me looking at my watch he re-emerged. He was very quiet, though, very content but with a determined look on his face. I lost him after that, literally I mean, and eventually found him at the main gate talking to the office staff. Sensible boy, I thought, make your way to staff if you get lost.

'*Merci!*' I said to them waving and they waved back, clearly not knowing why.

'Daddy,' Samuel began, 'they sell the baby goats, you know?'

So that's why he'd made his way to the office! To ask about taking a bloody goat home!

'Oh Samuel,' Natalie began, clearly proud of her son for following in her footsteps, 'you can't just get a goat…'

'Your mum's right,' I said, though shocked at Natalie's uncharacteristic reaction.

'You have to get a couple or they'll be lonely.'

I stopped pushing the buggy in which Thérence was sleeping, Maurice having run off into the distance, and watched as Natalie and Samuel held hands crossing the car park. A new, deeper alliance was forged right there and then, and I didn't stand a chance.

They were at it immediately. It's inevitable that if you spend as much time away from home as I do that it will take time to acclimatise when you return – things may have changed, furniture moved, a new cushion here, a new picture there; but really, invisible fences?

I was playing football with Maurice one afternoon when, as I went chasing after the ball into the orchard, I was almost scythed in half by a fence I didn't know was there but that had apparently appeared out of thin air. I picked myself up and, utterly bewildered, reached out to touch the thing like I'd been hit by an invisible force field. I could see it now – obviously the beginnings of a new enclosure. It was made of thin green wire, camouflaged against a green-hedge background, but it had been erected in my absence and didn't seem to have any purpose whatsoever. It didn't go all the way around the orchard, so nothing was being kept out or in.

'It's for the goats,' said Samuel matter-of-factly. 'Mummy and I put it up last week.'

'Yep... look,' I said, remaining on the ground where I'd been cut down, 'firstly we don't know yet if we're getting goats and secondly you're not fencing them into my bloody orchard!'

He stared at me with a look of huge disappointment. Samuel had excelled this year, coming top of the whole school in his exams, and had therefore been promised a reward.

'But goats? Really?' I pleaded with him. 'Don't you want a laptop or something? Some new trainers? A flick knife?'

No. He had his heart set on goats and he had a powerful ally in Natalie.

It's fair to say that the whole goat saga had been a cause of family dissension, since the idea was first mooted that evening after the zoo visit. In short, my feelings were they would be more of a handful than any other of our animals, the fencing would have to be reworked to stop them getting out (and dogs and hens getting in) and that Samuel, though very keen and making all the right noises about cleaning and grooming, etc., had promised exactly the same when we took the cats on. For their part, Natalie and the boys – Maurice and Thérence were goat-keen too – took my misgivings on board, ignored them but stored them at the back of their minds anyway so as to rub my nose in it when the whole venture proved to be a startling success.

Obviously I was expected to muck in, which meant a whole lot of swearing and the kind of bad-tempered attitude that makes teenagers working on a supermarket checkout seem friendly and loquacious. The first bone of contention was the size of the goats. I had been told that they were 'pygmy' goats, but as I began to partition some space for them in the stable, so that they had access and the horses didn't, I was told that they wouldn't stay that size; that they were in fact baby pygmy goats. 'So they grow into proper goats, then?' I asked in a state of some confusion. No, I was told, they grow into adult pygmy goats. 'Which are how big?' I asked, gamely plugging away at this seemingly most difficult of concepts. 'Goat size' was the reply.

I set up their stable, frankly guessing at the size of the beasts, bought a *mangeoire* (feeding tray) so that their hay didn't touch the floor (goats apparently, and surely against all stereotypes, are fussy about how their food is presented), made them a bed and ensured easy access for us, so that we didn't have to go via the horses to clean the goats out. All of this was done under the watchful supervision of Natalie, as was the erecting of the new fence, which we did together in searing heat over two days. This itself was back-breaking work, as the sharp, metallic fence would quite often ping back and cut one of us, leaving us both looking like we had been mugged by Zorro. We didn't quite complete the fence, as a gate would be put in before the goats arrived.

'Are you sure it will be done on time?' I asked sceptically, knowing full well that very little is actually 'done on time'.

'Yes, of course,' Natalie replied as if my question had been a stupid one. 'Monsieur Valentin promised me.' Monsieur Valentin being a *menuisier* (carpenter) friend of Manuel's and therefore presumably subject to the same levels of silent fear as the rest of us.

However, the gate didn't materialise in time and so on Sunday and early Monday Natalie put the finishing touches to the thing herself. It had been hard work, but at the end it looked pretty good and very secure, so just maybe, I thought, allowing myself to enjoy the ride briefly, just maybe this would work.

And when I saw the little things as we picked them up from the zoo it was hard not to want it to work – two brothers, each three months old, with brown and white markings. Samuel had named them Toffee and Popcorn. They looked shy and quite unsure of what was going on as we deposited them into their comfy new home, but adorable nonetheless. Really adorable. That's when the trouble began.

We had been advised by neighbours, not the zoo we got them from, to keep them locked up for a couple of days so that they could get used to us, but that meant keeping Junior and Ultime out of their stable, which was nigh-on impossible. Junior immediately started breaking the door down, so we let him in and the goats made a dash for the open field where they proceeded to eat the brambles behind the hedge. Gigi found a gap in our new fence small enough to squeeze through and went charging after the goats, hoping they would play with her. The goats scattered and Gigi went berserk, sending Ultime on to her hind legs and chasing after the goats too, whereupon Junior, not one to shy away from a ruck, also went mad and starting bucking at me! I narrowly avoided having my head kicked off, and as Toffee and Popcorn found safety under the old caravan in their field, I caught Gigi and plugged the fence gap she had come through.

Thankfully, there was relative calm after that; the goats would occasionally emerge from underneath the caravan covered in oil like they'd been working in the motor trade for a while, but any sign of movement would send them scurrying back for cover. Which was all well and good until it came to time to put them to bed. Maurice and I managed to trap Popcorn relatively easily, but Toffee was proving to be more difficult: every time he was cornered he found a way past one of us and dived back into the bushes or back under the caravan. So Maurice and I developed a plan: as Toffee emerged from the hedge, one of us would herd him towards the gate where he'd then be cornered and couldn't escape. A foolproof plan.

Maurice chased him behind the hedge as I waited around the corner and then – pow! – he jumped through the gates! Through the gates! He had defied the laws of physics by putting his body through an opening it had no right to go through.

'Alien goat!' I said, staring at Maurice in disbelief.

And then both of us ended up chasing the bloody thing. Natalie and Samuel joined us, but it was practically impossible; all of the surrounding fields were full of crops at least 5 feet tall, so there was no way of seeing where Toffee was hiding. We flushed him out once and chased him, cornered him, chased him again and cornered him again. By this time we had been joined by a neighbouring farmer, Monsieur Girresse, who was more concerned about us running around in his field than any spooked goat. It was hopeless. The last we saw of Toffee that night was as he was trotting away, clearly spooked, clearly exhausted but determined not to be caught.

Four hours we had been trying to catch him, and although the whole thing had started off as a bit of a lark, it quickly became apparent that this was actually serious. Toffee had run off and we had no idea where to. As the sun sank I went off to look for a distraught Samuel, who had stubbornly refused to call off the search.

I found him crouched down in the same sunflower field where we had last spotted Toffee and he was utterly inconsolable, weeping so hard that he was out of breath. I heard him wail, 'Why me?' I might have said the same thing. It seems, as parents, we have one job and that is to protect our children from the harsh realities of the world; 'real life' will inevitably claim them one day and introduce them to cynicism, injustice and violence, but while I watched him and held him tight I could almost feel his little heart breaking, along with mine – his for Toffee and mine for him. I really felt that we'd let him down.

UNLUCKY FOR SOME

Almost two weeks later and there was still no news of Toffee, not a flicker; no sightings, no decimated crops, no forlorn midnight bleating. Monsieur Girresse, after first implying that Toffee had been caught and eaten by Gypsies softened his stance and, perhaps trying to make up for his accusation, seemed suddenly convinced that Toffee would reappear when the sunflowers and the corn were harvested later in the summer; that his massive combine harvester would rip up the crops to reveal an embarrassed baby pygmy goat with a startled look on its face, like a shopper disturbed in a fitting-room cubicle.

The day after Toffee's disappearance Monsieur Rousseau, our other neighbouring farmer – we live between the Rousseau and Girresse farms – had woken us up early with a telephone call to triumphantly reveal that he'd found Toffee standing nervously in the middle of the road and that he would be round in five minutes. It was a huge surprise and relief, and Natalie hurried to get Samuel up and dressed so he could thank the farmer himself and be reunited with his pet goat.

Victoriously Rousseau opened the boot of his jeep and with a flourish presented... Popcorn!

It seems that at some time during the night Popcorn had decided to make a bid for freedom too and while we were grateful to our neighbour it was something of a shock to the system to realise that our efforts to goat-proof the fence even further had been in vain. We thanked the slightly dejected farmer, put Popcorn back in his pen and immediately began raising the level of the gate, again.

The gate, as it was, stood about four feet high; Popcorn, at three months old, was just about a quarter of that and yet had apparently managed to leap over the gate. I'm not entirely sure that there isn't a bit of kangaroo in him – after all, the goats live very close to the kangaroo enclosure at the zoo, so who knows? There might be a bit of late night mammal–marsupial swinging action going on, where they throw their metaphorical car keys into the water trough and off they go.

We nervously contacted the zoo to report Toffee's escape and were expecting a backlash, or at least some sort of dressing down and admonishment, but they didn't seem surprised at all. They said that it wasn't exactly a rare occurrence; which makes me think that somewhere in the Loire Valley there's a rogue goat army massing, ready to pounce and mount a campaign against their erstwhile captors. The *soigneurs* (keepers) at the zoo also thought, somewhat against all the evidence, that Toffee would one day turn up.

'Really?' Natalie asked them sceptically. 'Our neighbour seems to think he may have been eaten.'

'Ah,' the zookeeper said, 'I hadn't thought of that.'

UNLUCKY FOR SOME

It struck me that there was an awful lot of unwarranted and unfounded speculation regarding the involvement of the local Romany in this matter. Like many other itinerant ethnic social groups, the Romany population in our local area are often the first port of call in the blame game, whether there's evidence or not. And personally I think it's a bit rich for the French to go around criticising people for outré food preferences, goats or otherwise. Two words my French friends: 'frog's legs'. Besides which, the Romany tend to shop in the supermarkets like most people, occasionally the *boucherie* as well – they're not wandering the fields dressed in fur loincloths and brandishing spears. It seemed like an overwrought reaction to me.

All this idle and pejorative conjecture wasn't much help to Samuel either. Poor lad – it's one thing to have your pet disappear but quite another to suspect he may have been eaten too! Maybe it was unwise to name them both after foodstuffs in the first place; not a mistake we were going to make again.

We were a little unsure what to do next. Samuel was still grieving for Toffee but it was also obvious that Popcorn was pining for his companion and needed company. The zoo, despite our shortcomings thus far, were more than happy to entrust us with another goat though and so, contritely, we had made our way back there just as they were bringing some of the other animals back in for the evening. The zoo goats share their night-time quarters with the takin, which are 'goat-antelopes' found in the Eastern Himalayas. As the first of the takin entered their indoor pen for the night the zookeepers warned us to stand back as they are 'nervous' animals. They might also have added that they are bloody angry beasts too. This weird-looking creature took one look at me and threw itself against its bars like a violent prisoner on a psychiatric ward. They are angry, angry animals, and I reckon would give even Junior a run for his money in a 'World's Most Short-Tempered Beasts' pageant. Even their offspring were spiteful, behaving like the little bloke egging on the school bully – little balls of nastiness hiding behind their mother's legs.

The zookeeping team quite rightly concentrated on getting these plainly livid beasts into their pens before dealing with us, and it was clear that they didn't feel comfortable herding the things either, especially as they all had to be separated for the night. The noises they made echoed off the walls of the vast 'stable' and it seemed entirely incongruous that right opposite these creatures were the pygmy goat pens, where all the goats were huddled in a corner obviously frightened by the sound of their neighbours from hell.

Relieved that the takin were now in and shut away for the night, the zookeeper was able to concentrate on us. The keeper proceeded to pluck out a bold little goat, standing aside from the others, which, we were told, was Popcorn's half-brother. He was placed gingerly in the travel cage in the back of the car and off we went, hoping that this time we wouldn't be so incompetent and that he would stay for more than four hours.

The journey home was spent trying to come up with a name, none of which Thérence approved of. He insisted the new arrival be called Toffee as well, but in the end we all agreed on Chewbacca. His all-brown coat and his mid-pitch bleating seemed to fit perfectly. He also seemed to enjoy being reunited with Popcorn too.

The search for Toffee still went on, but with ever-diminishing optimism. We began to look across a larger area which included a kind of goat farm itself, some kind of shanty-town affair a couple of kilometres away where a man lives in an old caravan at weekends and keeps geese, turkeys and goats in makeshift pens.

'You haven't seen our goat, have you?' Natalie asked him, not with any real hope of success.

'No,' the man replied. 'But if you want a goat, you can have these three females.'

'No, I don't think so...'

'They don't produce as much meat as male ones,' he interrupted.

'You're going to eat them?' Natalie asked incredulously, suddenly thinking that maybe we were the only people that didn't.

I shepherded her away before she took on his entire stock. The simple, harsh reality of French country living was once again something of a shock to all of us, and our hopes for a returning Toffee took a further tumble.

But if there is one thing guaranteed to take your mind off a lost pet then it's another lost pet. Vespa was missing too. In many ways Vespa had started the whole thing off. Natalie had found her abandoned under a hay bale almost exactly two years previously, a tiny kitten only a few days old, and Natalie had bottle-fed and nurtured her into adulthood. I had never really got on with cats, but Vespa was different; she was affectionate for a start and had gone a long way to replacing my old Jack Russell, Eddie. She had been gone ten days though and it was most unlike her to stay away for as long as that –

she would disappear for a couple of days, most cats do, but by now Natalie was frantic and leading a regular evening search team that was calling out not just for Toffee, but for Vespa too. Again, the poor Romanies and their eating habits were raised, ridiculously, as a potential explanation.

It was clearly going to be a long, hard summer for us all.

Samuel in particular was finding things very tough – not just because of Toffee and Vespa, but because he was due to start *collège* (secondary school) in September and we had been invited to go and see the headmaster, a nervous-looking individual who looked like a furtive rodent, before this school year ended. Now, Natalie does most of the talking in these situations, for obvious reasons, but this time I was even more silent than usual: I hadn't bargained on posters for 'contraceptive awareness' being all over the school walls, for starters. Just the week before we had watched Samuel's end-of-year school production – an innocent, joyous affair performed with *joie de vivre* by assorted 10- and 11-year olds, as yet unburdened with sexual responsibility. Now here I was thinking I'd have to kit the lad out for his first day at big school with a *préservatif* (condom) hidden in his satchel. I've got nothing against the posters being up – it's a good thing – and I'm sure he's a good few years off making them relevant, but it just struck me all of a sudden that life was about to get even more complicated, my hair was sure to get greyer and that elusive 'quiet life' was moving even further away.

Not that there was any chance of a quiet life now that the school holidays had started anyway. We live remotely enough for there not to be many other children around, but the children there are seemed to be permanently camped out at our place. I have never found French children to be anything other than respectful and well-mannered, but they are still children and therefore prone to bouts of noise and messy activity. This has the added effect of setting the animals off, as the hens flap about apparently complaining about the brouhaha, the dogs start chasing each other and the horses start charging around angrily. The whole place descends into total bedlam and I am constantly at the beck and call of gangs of kids.

'Monsieur Ian, can you turn on the pool pump?'

'Daddy, can we have a snack?'

'Monsieur Ian, can you kill a horsefly?'

'Daddy, can you do a backflip, juggle torches of fire, build a new goat pen and relax before you go back to work please?'

I know there are far worse things to be moaning about, but at the risk of sounding like some retired landowner who's been forced to take in evacuees, it is endlessly taxing.

In France, there is a tradition of sending your children off to holiday camp (or *colonie*) for a couple of weeks over the summer, to teach them a bit of independence, give them a bit of outdoor exercise and so on. Well, apparently *we* had become the local *colonie*. And it was an irony that wasn't lost on any of the neighbours, whose children descended on us each afternoon and who know me well enough by now to know that 'patience', 'good humour' and 'child-minding' are not on my list of strengths. Not only do they think it's ironic, they think it's bloody hilarious. Look at the funny Englishman, he came here for peace and quiet and now he's running a youth club!

One time Natalie actually discussed this idea with a couple of other mums, to the extent that instead of running writing schools it was suggested that we should take in teenage 'waifs and strays' from the big cities – you know, just for the summer.

'It's well paid!' Natalie explained, as if that were the clincher.

'So is selling your own kidneys,' I retorted. 'And I'd rather try that first! Look,' I added, 'we can't even keep hold of a goat for more than a few hours; who would trust us with some mixed up youth from the *banlieue* [suburbs]?'

The discussion was violently interrupted by the screams of one of the children. 'A rat!' shrieked the terrified child, and she was right too – huge, it was, and it had come scurrying out from under a large barrel of flowers next to the pool and was generally running about enjoying itself like it had had enough of being left out. The three women present, along with the suddenly-quiet children all turned and looked at me: 'Well?' they seemed to say. 'Don't just stand there!'

I couldn't honestly see what harm the thing was doing, and anyway I strongly feel that Natalie is very much responsible for this. Around this time last year she had found three newborn mice and in a gesture as futile as it was doomed had attempted to bottle-feed two of them to health. The third had somehow scrambled under the aforementioned flower barrel, where I couldn't rescue it, and then Maurice had pointed out that 'that's where snakes live' thus ending my search. Leave it to its fate, I thought, there's nothing I can do for it now. You read about these things don't you? People who flushed a baby lizard down the toilet only to find years later that a man-eating crocodile is terrorising the city through the sewage network. This was the same thing, maybe they hadn't been baby mice after all but baby rats, and the third had survived and was mighty pissed off that it hadn't got the shoebox–bottle treatment.

A real man of the country, especially a Frenchman, would have simply grabbed a shovel and beaten the monster into some kind of interesting *pâté* before everybody's eyes, but I prefer to delegate, rarely having the wardrobe to cope with such violence. I fetched Flame, now the sole remaining cat, figuring that this was more his department than mine but he just stared languidly at the flower barrel, clearly disinterested. Toby, trained as a hunting dog but just not up to the mark mentally, was currently having some kind of breakdown and was off whimpering at his own reflection somewhere; Gigi, as a tiny chiweenie puppy, was about the same size as the rat, so I didn't fancy her chances, and Pierrot would probably just try to hump it. Then, suddenly, it just disappeared back down its bolthole and didn't resurface. Clearly clever enough not to overplay its cards, it was going to spend the summer making cameos at socially awkward moments just to embarrass me. However, it would be the least of my problems.

They say that bad things happen in threes. I don't know who 'they' are or whether 'they' were particularly prone to misfortune, but it's an oft-repeated idiom and we nervously awaited the third prong of bitter fate, the rat not being serious enough to justify qualification. There was still no sign of Toffee the goat or Vespa the cat. I desperately wanted both, or at least one, to come wandering back.

I was away for work more and more, but on my return the first thing I would do was go for a walk and scour the fields as best I could. More often than not I would still be in my stage suit from the night before, usually a 1960s Italian-cut double-breasted affair with a matching shirt and tie, and add to that that I was shouting 'Vespa!' at the top of my voice. I must have looked like a befuddled mod who couldn't remember where he'd left his anthropomorphised scooter. Either way, there was no trace of either of them, but until bodies were found there was still a glimmer of hope, or a lack of closure, depending on your viewpoint.

Supposed 'Gypsy' animal-snatchers aside, Natalie had another explanation for all these sudden disappearances and frankly it was just as batty as the farmers'. According to Natalie, when the goats arrived it took the number of 'pets' to 13. Three dogs, two cats, two horses, four hens and two goats equals 13 and so, according to myth and legend (whose exactly I have no idea), one had to go – and so Toffee threw himself on his sword, as it were, and scarpered. Toffee's replacement, Chewbacca, had brought the animal count back up to thirteen, and lo and behold, Vespa disappeared.

To be honest, I've seen more meat on the bones in a plot of *Scooby Doo* and though, at a push, the facts fitted the theory, I wasn't buying it. It's just coincidence, I kept saying; bad luck maybe, but still just coincidence. And then Natalie's theory was quite brutally shot down when, despite us having only 12 animals at that point, poor, elderly Pierrot passed away.

It had been on the cards for months really. He had had a series of strokes before Christmas, and his eyesight and hearing had deteriorated so much that he was practically blind and deaf. When I had returned home one Sunday evening I could see that he was pretty near the end. I just had a feeling. He looked very doleful and utterly bewildered by everything and, not only did he not eat his dinner, he was also not bothering to gratify himself sexually using any of the garden furniture – a sure sign that the old boy was not well at all.

When Natalie came down the following morning she found Toby crying by Pierrot's bed, and Pierrot himself lying in a pool of blood after suffering what looked like a massive internal haemorrhage. The vet said it was unlikely that he had suffered and that it was a relatively peaceful ending for the old fellow; but although we had been expecting it for some time, when the end came it was still a shock.

Add Pierrot's death to the disappearances of Toffee and Vespa, and it just felt like we were being picked off one by one. We were terrified to let any of the other animals out of our sight; it was like an old-fashioned, Gothic murder mystery where all the remaining characters decide to stay in the same room of the big house so that they have safety in numbers.

Then the lights go out…

AOÛT OF SORTS

August is a strange month in France; famously the country shuts down as everybody heads off for their holidays, but this isn't the result of some late-July winding down, the first of August arrives and – pfft! – people just disappear into thin air. We've had builders at work on the place in the summer before – there was an apologetic flurry of activity towards the end of July, and then came the first of August and they vanished, leaving their tools, their stoves and half-smoked *Gauloises* as if they'd been kidnapped.

Granted, it's the holiday season, but the strangest things shut down – a local hotel and restaurant always closes in August for their *congés annuel* (annual leave). A hotel/restaurant in the Loire Valley! Shutting down! In August! That's like Lapland taking Christmas off. Even the local cinema, instead of packing the schedule with family-friendly films for the summer holidays, closes, just confirming what I've always suspected about the owners of the place, that they are rampant misanthropes with a particular dislike of children.

AOÛT OF SORTS

It's all very strange. The pace of life in France is part of its attraction for me, but it does take some getting used to. When we first moved, on the very first day, I wanted to put some shelves up so that we could begin to unpack. (I have to work myself up to DIY, so if the moment for action comes it has to be grasped before it passes.) I jumped into the car and headed off to the local French equivalent of B&Q, forgetting that it was lunchtime and that the place was closed for a couple of hours. This was in the days before I was properly attuned to the French way of life (well, as much as I am now, anyway), so I just angrily paced up and down outside the shop chuntering on about countersunk woodscrews. Coming from a country that pointlessly allows me to do my weekly shopping at three in the morning, I just couldn't comprehend any retail business closing for lunch. I gave up smoking a few years ago, not because of the ban or that I'd had enough, but because I couldn't buy any bloody tabs locally after six o'clock. Or any time on a Sunday!

August may be one of the many times the French like to take a bit of time off, but Natalie and I had decided that for logistical and financial reasons we wouldn't be having a holiday this year. Logistically, because I had to be available for any work going at the shortest notice and financially, because we were determined to build up our savings again and not have the Les Champs Créatifs debacle hanging over us for any longer than was necessary. It was hard on the boys, though; their friends had stopped coming round because they were all on holiday themselves and Natalie needed a break too; because of various deaths and disappearances she was becoming paranoid about letting any remaining animal out of her sight and very obviously needed to get away, even if just for a few days.

They had one day away at a local Center Parcs with some friends, but it was never going to be enough for them, though personally a whole day at a 'fun park', with its forced jollity and incessant insistence on 'activity', would have been more than enough for me. I could have gone with them – I was invited – but I'm a man of principle and having sworn years ago never, ever to set foot in such a place again I declined the invitation and set up my orchard hammock instead. Just the thought of the place brought me out in a cold sweat; the unremitting noise, the high-season crowds, the three-quarter-length luminous shorts covering bulging middle-aged midriffs, the 'muscle' T-shirts with their aggressive, sawn-off sleeves... If that's your thing then good luck to you, it's unlikely our paths will ever cross.

It was decided that Natalie and the boys would go away for a few days and stay with family in the Limousin a couple of hours south; I would babysit the place and they would have, albeit briefly, some respite from doing an animal headcount twice a day. Before they left, though, we hosted the annual family *fête* for the *Quinze Août*. The *Quinze Août*, literally August 15, is a bank holiday in France, ostensibly a religious festival commemorating the 'Assumption of Mary', but also I suspect because, by mid-August, they haven't had a bank holiday for just over a month and sparkly wine won't drink itself.

I do love a family *fête*. About thirty or so of Natalie's huge family turned up and, as always, there was bickering, laughter, food, singing, games and then more food – it's like a wedding, but where people actually get on, bickering being a good thing

AOÛT OF SORTS

in a French family, showing a healthy interaction. The culinary plan on these occasions is always pretty much the same in that everybody chips in: someone will buy the bread, another the cheese; people will bring a selection of starters and salads, etc., and, of course, someone else will bring the wine. The hosts, us on this occasion, will sort out the main course and in this I surpassed myself by offering up my new speciality: smoking lumps of charcoal, each with a delicate hint of dried-out meat.

I am a good cook, but I don't like barbecues. Every man thinks he can cook on a barbecue – it must be something in the hunter–gatherer DNA – but very few actually can and I certainly can't. I had brought a load of different types of sausage back with me from England and the plan was to showcase these 'speciality' meat products to the French; just as a gentle reminder that they're not the only culinary nation in the world. I failed. I failed miserably. Each blackened stump was followed by another blackened stump as we all sat down around various tables and tried to ignore the fact that what we were eating resembled burnt driftwood. I fear when Christmas rolls around this year and we are once again hosts I have some ground to make up; or I'll just brass it out, serve them charred kindling and try and make out that they are in the wrong and that, actually, gum splinters are an essential by-product of this English delicacy.

We needed a diversion from my barbecue efforts and, unsurprisingly, this was provided by our circus of performing animals. The satanic Junior gamely stepped up to the plate and tried to eat one of the goats. Samuel was feeding the goats at the time and, seemingly in a fit of jealousy, Junior picked one of them up in his mouth and swung the poor beast about, like a terrier with a rag doll. Samuel, quite rightly traumatised by this event, insisted that from then on the goats and the horses must be kept apart, and Natalie agreed. I believe that the US penal system has tried the same thing in some prisons by trying to keep apart members of the Bloods and the Crips gangs, but with very little success, and I feared the same outcome; all they've done is merely 'ghettoised' the opposing groups and added to the rancour.

The discussion on what to do was thrown open to the wider family, and the conclusion was a typically botched effort and the result of too much wine. The plan, from now on and according to family diktat, was to lock the goats up, which seemed a little harsh to me, and then to buy them collars and leads and take them for a daily walk. As usual, I sat through all of this in disbelief, with images of me walking my goats into town with my chiweenie in a handbag sending chills down my spine. Occasionally I offered up, in my best stuttering French, an opinion that was just ignored, solely, as far as I could see, on the basis that I'd made a right old mess of lunch. The initial and still staggering assumption that Junior would not at some point attack the goats was naive at best – he sexually assaulted our donkey – but to then try and keep them apart when they share the same stable was always destined to fail.

So as we all sat chiselling away at our carbonised lunch it was no surprise, and indeed a welcome distraction, to find that the goats weren't taking their new incarceration lying down and had, just an hour later, somehow escaped their confines and were quite happily gambolling about in the field, giving Junior two fingers and refusing to be cowed by the violent old sod.

AOÛT OF SORTS

Natalie and the boys left for the Limousin with family immediately after the *fête*, leaving me to clear up, which is, and I am deadly serious about this, a job I love. The best bit of a party is getting your house back in order; turn the music up loud, put your apron back on, finish whatever's left of the wine and have a right good tidy. I'm rarely as content as that; you could hire me out for the job. They were all partly relieved to be getting away, possibly just to eat something that didn't look like it had died in a house fire, but also nervous about leaving me with the remaining, and warring, animals, and I was left with strict instructions to 'keep an eye on the goats', like some peasant shepherd boy. Well, I did keep an eye on the goats and I wasn't all that keen on what I saw.

My goat knowledge is pretty thin, I admit, but is incestuous homosexuality a goat trait? These young goat brothers seemed to be mounting each other like there aren't any rules about these kind of things. Maybe it was a ruse to disgust Junior into leaving them alone – if so it definitely worked as he kept his distance with a look of horror and contempt on his face. This rampant debauchery was also having an unfortunate effect on Toby, who was now trying to mount Gigi. Considering the differences in size and breed, the actual mechanics of this operation posed something of a problem for them. The thing is, all this started the minute Natalie and the others had gone, the very minute, leaving me with the distinct impression that the animals save these moments of insanity for the rare occasions when Natalie isn't here, just to make my job harder. Nevertheless I was going out every hour, on the hour, and making sure everybody was safe and behaving themselves, like a nightwatchman in an animal mental institution, just checking the premises and trying not to get too involved.

It wasn't just the presence of the goats that was upsetting Junior, though; it was the fact that a third of his stable had been given over to these newcomers and he wasn't best pleased about it. In fact, Junior had treated this 'slight' with his usual good humour and equanimity, and had taken to trying to kick the door to the annexe down while Ultime stood just behind him, by turn encouraging him and also, it seemed, admonishing him like a wife standing behind her irate husband at a hotel reception, nudging him occasionally and saying, 'Tell them we booked, Geoffrey.' It's a comical sight, but even Junior's permanent level of ire has its limits and after a while he would just give up and slope off, Ultime at his side giving it the full nagging wife, 'Is that it, then? Just going to let them get away with it, are you?'

The goats were only allowed out of their pen under strict observation; their ability to escape and to provoke Junior into violence meant that until everybody was more attuned to their presence we couldn't risk leaving them all alone in the field together. We had every intention of letting the goats out permanently when everybody returned, but in truth none of us was looking forward to it. We had goat-proofed the fence as much as we could, we just had to hope that they didn't spot a gap before we did. I never realised just how high goats could jump but then I still wasn't sure what size Popcorn and Chewbacca would be fully grown anyway. Though we had secured the fence to quite a height, Natalie still had her doubts about it and the discussions took a predictable turn when they arrived home after a few days, refreshed, happy and, let's be honest, frankly surprised that I'd managed to maintain a full company.

Apparently, Natalie and the boys' short week in the Limousin had been the refreshing tonic that they all needed, but the truth was that on her return it was Natalie who was seeing gaps. She had really suffered since Vespa's disappearance; she was trying to cover it up, but very obviously pining, while at the same time Toby was in mourning for Pierrot. There was an atmosphere to the place, a sadness that was largely unspoken and difficult to resolve.

'But you said these were pygmy goats?' I said for the umpteenth time while we stood by the gate. 'Just how tall will they be?'

She thought for a minute and then levelled her hand at what she presumed would be adult-goat level. 'But that's goat size, surely?' I said, exasperated.

'It's adult pygmy goat size,' she said, as if that made any sense at all.

'No. Look…'

We had had this same conversation so often in recent weeks that both of us had now got to the point where we were treating each other like imbeciles.

'That,' I pointed at her hand still hovering, 'that is goat size. Adult. Goat. Size. These aren't pygmy goats, they are baby goats.'

'No,' Natalie countered, 'these,' she pointed at the goats as if I were a foreigner asking for directions, 'these are baby *pygmy* goats.'

'But,' I stretched the word out and rounded my vowels as if making it easier to lip-read would bring her around to my point of view, 'these baby "pygmy" goats,' I did the annoying international-speech-marks hand signal, 'are the same size as baby "non-pygmy" goats.'

'Yes,' she conceded, 'but they are baby "pygmy" goats.'

The conversation just went round in circles, until eventually it just disintegrated into childish name-calling and immature and insulting hand gestures. It ended when I tried to imply that, although a petite woman, I wouldn't call her a 'pygmy' wife – and she responded that unless I lose some weight sharpish, pretty much everything would be 'pygmy' in comparison with me anyway.

I stormed off to my office while she found solace and support in the company of Junior.

'Ian, can you come here?'

Natalie was at the foot of my office stairs. An entreaty like this was usually bad news: either I've done something wrong or I'm about to do something wrong. Neither is good.

'Is it important? I'm at a tricky bit,' I said, the implication being that I was writing. (I was actually alphabetising my old vinyl LPs.)

'Yes,' she said. 'It is.'

I stomped down the stairs like a stroppy teenager. What had I done now? I thought, they'd been away a week and she was still in the middle of post-break full-on inspection. There was bound to be a dried-up house plant somewhere.

'Well?' I began, but cut myself off halfway down the stairs, because there she was on the bottom step, tears in her eyes and cuddling Vespa. It was such a lovely sight.

We had no idea where the cat had been, she'd just sauntered back as only a cat can. She was a little thinner and certainly dehydrated, but she was even more affectionate than she had been before she'd left and clearly as relieved as we were that she was home again. We kept her in for the first couple of days but eventually, and nervously, let her out again, though she came back promptly when called, accompanied by a guard of honour from the dogs.

Samuel, Maurice and Thérence were obviously thrilled to bits when they saw Vespa again. Though the disappearance of Toffee had left its mark, we now felt like the ship had been steadied somewhat. Despite financial and various other pressures, I had decided that the last week of the summer holidays would be spent all together, and that we would do things as a family. Enough of separate holidays and goat babysitting; this last week would be our 'family' holiday, our 'staycation' as I believe it's rather tragically called.

The boys were delighted by the idea and gleefully pointed out the posters that were up all over town showing that 'This weekend! For two days only!' there would be a 'MONSTER TRUCK DERBY!' Thrills, spills, crashes, etc., etc.

'You can forget that, kids!' I said, to a not totally surprised reaction. 'Worse than Center Parcs!'

Things were getting back to normal.

NEW RULES, NEW RULERS

And so, all good things must come to an end.

Natalie's maternity leave, with Thérence now on the cusp of university education (I may be exaggerating), was finally over. Maternity leave in France is – as you would expect it to be from a country that still puts family first (as opposed to the Victorian 'family' rhetoric that governs UK politics) – extensive. It lasts up to three years, is paid and, for those who would prefer to go back to work, childcare is reasonably priced and state-subsidised.

But now it was over and whereas we'd expected Les Champs Créatifs to fill the gap and still allow Natalie to be at home full time, that was now obviously not going to happen – certainly not for the foreseeable future anyway.

Natalie had quite rightly decided that she wouldn't be going back to work for the despicable Monsieur Norbert at the local estate agency. By law he was obliged to offer Natalie her old job back, but he'd made it clear that once she came back her hours would change, the commission and salary structure would change – in fact, everything would change. Norbert wasn't very good at subtlety, so even without reading between the lines it was clear he didn't actually want her back, certainly not part-time.

It was no great blow, as working for him had been confidence-sapping and hardly rewarding for Natalie, and she'd already decided that a change of tack was needed, a new direction. There are not a whole lot of options around the agricultural end of the Loire Valley, but by using her obviously fluent French language skills she felt she might be able to get some work as an English assistant in a local school. She had done something similar back in England before we'd come to France and enjoyed it immensely.

She arranged an interview at the middle school that Samuel had just left which, like everything in France, was initially informal followed by an avalanche of bureaucracy and attendant *fonctionnaires* (officials). The school was very keen to take her on in some capacity – and even though at this point they could not offer any paid work, Natalie's employment had to be approved by the head of language education and recruitment for the entire *département* (county), who would conduct her own interview. It seemed like quite a stringent process for what was basically just a couple of hours a week volunteering in a junior school, but Natalie was keen to do it and here, especially here, contrary to how most outsiders see the French, the due process must always be followed.

In the meantime, while presumably the President himself was making sure 'i's were dotted and 't's were crossed in every tiny, rural educational establishment, we had to get the boys ready for the new school year and the French phenomenon that is *la rentrée*. As the summer holidays finally draw to a close everywhere, shops, TV, newspapers are full of *la rentrée*, which ostensibly is about the start of the school year, but actually equates to the country as a whole; the holidays are over, back to work.

Samuel's *collège* had given him a long list of things he/we had to buy: notebooks, textbooks, paper, pens, protractors – the basics really, but also textbooks and reading books as well. I don't know if this happens in the UK, obviously parents provide the pens and the mathematical stuff, but here you have to sort out the right kind of paper (small-squared and large-squared, never lined), subject dividers, folders and the like for each student, and you are given a grant by the government to do so, a hefty one too. All of which, according to Natalie, means that the pupil will take greater care of their stuff as they have had to go out and get it, but also, according to me, will mean if you do your shopping early enough you can buy the cheaper stuff and have money left over for other essentials like trainers, which are even more expensive here than they are in England.

I was not, unsurprisingly, the only spendthrift parent to have had this in mind.

The five of us, Natalie, myself and the boys, looked at the chaos in the Carrefour supermarket as the four aisles devoted solely to the school element of *la rentrée* resembled a particularly vicious prison riot, or when you see food parcels thrown out of the back of UN trucks to the desperate and the starving. Either way, it was a vicious spectacle.

'Mmm,' said Natalie. 'I'll take Maurice and Thérence to the swings while you and Samuel sort this out, I think.'

It was absolute pandemonium. We managed to get a few cheap things early on, but there were clearly some underhand

NEW RULES, NEW RULERS

shenanigans occurring. Every time we dropped the hard-fought-for cheaper notebooks into our trolley someone else would have them away while we were off looking for the next thing on the list. It was dog eat dog, and we needed a strategy.

'Right,' I said to Samuel and we got into a sporting huddle, 'you go and get a ring binder and I'll wait here. When you're back I'll go and get some highlighter pens while you guard the trolley.'

And off he went, diving into a particularly ferocious melee at the ring binder section, where he got swallowed up into the crowd.

'Samuel! Samuel!' I cried forlornly, like he'd fallen overboard on a car ferry and was somewhere in the icy depths below.

'Daddy, I'm OK…' came the reply, but then there was silence until he emerged again, battered, but able to shout, 'I'll meet you in Crayons and Paints!' And then he disappeared once more, warming to his task.

Crayons and Paints was worse, if anything, as it was this section that offered the widest price margins. People were merciless in their desire to pick up own-brand merchandise rather than the pricey Swiss varieties. I got there just as Samuel seemed to be in a tug of war with another child over a set of coloured pencils.

'I've got your back, son!' I shouted, as I went freewheeling past with the trolley and grabbing the pencil set from both of them.

'Nearly done! See you in Dividers.' And so it went on, Samuel using his skill and bravery to outwit opponents, and even showing some hitherto unknown rugby skills as he handed off other shoppers in pursuit of paintbrushes, erasers, compasses and other assorted paraphernalia. It took us half an hour to get the lot, but we managed it and finally made it to the checkout, miraculously unscathed and with the list completed.

We high-fived as we reached the till, a genuine bonding moment that sticks with a father and son, when you know that not only have you grown closer, you've done so through the crushing defeat of others. I was proud of him – his guile and courage had won the day and I could tell he was pleased with himself too as he puffed his chest out, having shown great fortitude in battle. Some of our beaten opponents hadn't fared so well and there were abandoned trollies, half-filled with stationery, left by frightened and exhausted shoppers who not only hadn't got the stomach for the fight but whose interest in education as a whole had just taken a pounding. And this was just the preparation! Imagine what trauma was to be endured when they actually got to school! They were going to hate it. Hate it like a small kid who didn't want to be there, suddenly thrust into a foreign world; hate it like a small kid suddenly without his mum for the first time in three years. Hate it like Thérence, for example.

All summer long we had been talking up the school experience to Thérence – and his brothers, who both love school (although Maurice does far more), had been doing the same. However, it's fair to say that Thérence was never entirely convinced and remained sceptical to the end. So when the big day came we were expecting a little trouble. Samuel and Maurice were starting on the same day, but Samuel insisted on taking the bus rather than one of us dropping him off. He was the only one on the bus, though, as every other child had insisted on being dropped off, rather sensibly realising that they could 'guilt' their parents into carrying their absurdly heavy school bags. Samuel was adamant, though, as a *collégien* he was looking forward to his elevation to the back seat of the bus, he'd earned the right, he said. But what happens when the bigger boys get on the bus and they want their seats back, his friends had asked. I won't move, he said, it's my right. They'll punch you, his friends said – he was recounting this conversation to us on the eve of the first day back – I won't move, he repeated, it's my right.

I'd never considered Samuel to be a kind of Rosa Parks figure and I wished him well. I've always taught him to fight the big battles and let others win the meaningless ones, but if he wants to make a stand for all the 'small-for-their-age 11-year-olds with a *Star Wars* fixation and glasses' in the face of bullying then all power to him. Eventually, if Thérence could be persuaded, there would be three Moore boys on the school bus and surely numbers must count for something. Maurice is less belligerent than Samuel, though, and far from provocatively sitting in someone else's seat he instead got on the wrong bus entirely on the way home and so, for an hour or more, was missing.

The plan had been for me to cycle up to the bus stop, a couple of kilometres away, and for Natalie to follow with Maurice's bike in the boot so that we could cycle home together. About halfway there I got a puncture, which is a sign that either I shouldn't bother exercising and that it's just way too late, or that I have so little regard for exercise I'd spent the bare minimum on an old bike at a *brocante* rather than invest in one that was up to the mark. I limped home, as it were, and Natalie continued on to the bus stop. All the other kids had already got off and were on their way but there was no sign of

Maurice. Natalie was told not to worry, as there was another bus coming.

It didn't seem very likely, however, and 20 minutes later Natalie rang the school. There was some confusion it seemed and Maurice was currently on one of the school buses – but they weren't sure which one. Some people would pay good money for an impromptu bus tour of the Loire Valley, but this was something we hadn't bargained on.

The first day back at school was, therefore, proving even more stressful than normal. Thérence, who only went for half a day, had only just calmed down, so traumatised was he by his morning surrounded by screaming, snotty three-year-olds. 'I'm never going back,' he had declared at lunchtime, and this was despite Natalie staying an extra half an hour in the classroom with him, leaving me loitering suspiciously outside the school gate making a mess of my nicely ironed Fred Perry polo shirt with a particularly crumbly croissant. Samuel's bus home was to arrive later and I had images of him emerging from it bloodied, limping and with only one shoe on, trying to maintain his pride and dignity like Alec Guinness in *The Bridge on the River Kwai*.

Meanwhile, the calls between Natalie, the school and the *mairie* (town hall) continued. The *mairie* is responsible for organising the school bus timetable and route; it seemed that there was some confusion and Maurice had been placed on the wrong bus. It later turned out Maurice had been placed on the *right* bus, but the driver had said that Maurice wasn't supposed to be on his route. Unfortunately, we have a history with this driver, a surly so-and-so who clearly feels that whatever life choices he had made to end

NEW RULES, NEW RULERS

up ferrying a load of schoolchildren about the place were clearly influenced by the devil himself, and he was therefore determined to be as unpleasant as possible. The previous year he had told Samuel to sit down and not walk about when the bus was moving. A reasonable request no doubt, though Samuel, probably mid-stream in some civil rights oratory, responded with 'I will sit down if you stop talking and swearing on your mobile phone while you're driving.' Cheeky definitely, but no less reasonable and, as other parents got wind of this power struggle, complaints were made to the *mairie* as to what the bloody hell was going on when one of the bus drivers was chatting on a phone for Heaven's sake. He was reprimanded and given a warning as to his future conduct.

Having presumably spent the summer then harbouring a grudge against the Moore boys, he simply couldn't help himself and upon seeing Maurice he just wanted him off his bus. Eventually Maurice was dropped off back at the *collège* and was told to wait for another bus, the one that Samuel was due to make his stand on, before finally arriving home. Samuel's bus has the added bonus of stopping right at our gate and Natalie and I were waiting, just glad that we would finally have everyone home, as it came to a dusty halt.

Samuel and Maurice were at the glass door, tired and hot, though not unduly stressed – but the door wouldn't open. This driver, having been made aware of the earlier confusion was quite rightly pleased to be delivering home the missing child, and the door was ruining his moment of delivery. You could see his mood darkening as he angrily and repeatedly stabbed at the door-release button. Samuel tried pulling the doors apart but was so weakened by his school bag that he was barely able to stay upright. Finally the doors gave way.

'It's a mess!' the driver said. 'My bus has a capacity of fifty-seven and they want me to take seventy-one. I don't even have seat belts.'

While we digested this bombshell and hugged the returning boys, we watched the driver as he tried and failed to close the doors before speeding off loudly, cursing the indignity of it all. Maurice, as befits his sunny disposition, thought the whole thing highly amusing; Samuel, however, was convinced that there was some kind of conspiracy and, as befits his less-than-sunny disposition, wanted answers and heads to roll. Thérence just looked at us all with a kind of 'You mean, I've got another fifteen years of this fiasco?' look on his face.

Madame Joubert, the impeccably dressed yet obviously harassed, middle-aged woman who was to interview Natalie for her school position agreed to meet locally to discuss, ostensibly, Natalie's role, her background, her qualifications and – laughably – 'test' her English. It was clear, however, that Madame Joubert had an ulterior motive. Every year, she explained, after the formalities and 'test' were over, the school recruits people from English-speaking countries to work as *assistantes*, but every year – and at this she shook her head and rolled her eyes – every year at least one of those recruits will just not turn up! It had happened again this year, she said – a girl from Canada this time, booked to start work at the beginning of the school year but who had ceased communication a week ago and had subsequently failed to show up.

'I mean, obviously I hope nothing untoward has happened...' she said, betraying her true annoyance, though like a delayed commuter expressing sympathy through gritted teeth for 'someone on the line'. She trailed off, 'But I'm in a spot.'

In short, the poor woman, Madame Joubert that is, was in desperate need of an English–French teaching assistant in Châteauroux to cover four infant and junior schools for three days a week (paid), and not only would Natalie be interested, could she start next week?

It was the stroke of luck we'd been hoping for. It wasn't just the financial boost for both of us; it wasn't just that it was a confidence boost for Natalie, who would be back teaching in Châteauroux 20 years after she had done so as a student; but more than that. Her new job as an English teaching assistant was spread across four primary schools and was over an hour's drive away, meaning that she would now have little time, if any, for further animal recruitment. It bordered on that rare thing then, a win–win situation.

8

MOTHER IN LOIRE

Of course, three years honing and being paid for mothering had turned Natalie's maternal instinct almost into a superpower. If she had been part of the X-Men team, she'd have ignored wanton criminality and swooped instead on suspected orphans, with her superpower weapons of choice, a bottle of Calpol and a bedtime story. And this state-sponsored maternal instinct was by now very much cross-species and it had rubbed off on every other female on the plot; it had become like one of those Sunday-night period dramas, all-domineering women bossing the menfolk around. Ultime, Vespa and the hens were all affected – even Gigi, a relative newcomer and still a puppy, was now wafting her scent around like a heavily made-up shop assistant on a department store make-up counter.

Now ten months old, Gigi was technically ready to be spayed, but every time we tried to book an appointment to have her sterilised she came back into season again. This had the added effect of sending Toby loopy; he's a socially baffled animal at the best of times, but whenever Gigi emitted her oestrogen wafts in his direction he looked like a confused teenage boy unsure of his new 'feelings'. Natalie and the boys would naturally have preferred to leave her intact, perhaps to breed a whole army of chiweenies, but the voice of reason, or 'grumpy Daddy' as I was apparently now known, even to the vaguest of school playground acquaintances, wouldn't have it.

I know that Natalie, in her weaker moments, regrets having had Vespa sterilised and would have loved more kittens, but there was a period when it was just me against the four of them as they tried to break me into some kind of puppy/kitten climbdown. I'm made of stern stuff and not widely known for my flexibility, but there were times when it just would have been easier to say 'Oh, do what you want then!' rather than put up with the incessant bleating about baby animals. Just as I was beginning to waver after what seemed like months of this whiny torture, salvation was at hand, and under doctor's orders too.

One would have thought that being surrounded by animals from an early age our children wouldn't be susceptible to allergies, and that being born in the middle of the remote, agriculturally intensive rural French countryside would mean hay fever was just a myth perpetuated by lily-livered city folk who had strayed too far from their lattés. Unfortunately not. Maurice is to all intents and purposes a strong boy, constantly charging around at speed, picking up and enjoying any sport he can and is therefore a constant fidget if cooped up indoors. But he's always fighting something or other. He had a slight heart murmur that was picked up when he was very small and a series of tests were run on him; I don't know how parents find the strength to cope when their child is seriously ill, I really don't. I watched as they rigged my little, 18-month-old Maurice up to a load of machines and I couldn't deal with it; I tried desperately to remain stiff-upper-lipped for the little man, but immediately broke down the minute we left the clinic. There was nothing wrong with him of course, 'heart murmur' I suspect is a modern medical euphemism that actually means 'we have some expensive machines that need an MOT.'

Maurice does, however, have hay fever and asthma, which of course can be controlled by medication and inhalers, but he's also become allergic to cats. And dogs. Cats and dogs. In fact, cats, dogs, horses and hens, though not the goats. I'm surprised he's not allergic to mods the list seems so comprehensive.

He had had more tests done at the start of the new school year (I waited outside, obviously) to determine just how severe these allergies were. The results suggested that he was least allergic to the cats, which Natalie put down to him cuddling the cats a lot and letting them sleep on his bed during the day, which is her 'feed a baby peanuts and it won't get a nut allergy' logic. The results also showed that he's most allergic to the horses, but we weren't planning on testing Natalie's cat-cuddle-bed theory to that extent, at least not yet.

The severity of allergy was, to be honest, pretty mild in all cases but it meant new rules, new doctor-led rules; no cats in the bedrooms for instance, no horse-hugging or goat-play. All the animals needed to be kept cleaner; nothing, absolutely nothing, was now to be kept under beds and even his favourite pre-school job, egg-collecting from the chicken coop, was off limits. And certainly, under no circumstances, said the doctor after learning the full extent of the menagerie, should we think of adding to our numbers.

MOTHER IN LOIRE

Maurice's hay fever was shown to be his most severe allergy, so from now on he must be kept out of long grasses too and away from haystacks and goat pens. Our house, it seems, our lifestyle even, was actively making Maurice unwell: the animals, the location, the temperatures – everything. And yet to watch him run around, exhausting himself and everyone around him you'd have to conclude that, really? Is he really suffering at all?

When he was about two, Maurice had chicken pox. He was covered from head to toe – the pustules were everywhere: in his ears, on his eyelids, under his hair. He had spots in his bottom and so severely between his legs that he couldn't walk without it being agony. Everyone said it was the worst dose of chicken pox they had ever seen, and it was painful just to look at him. Yet he never cried, never felt sorry for himself, never complained; he just got on with it. He's Maurice and that's what he does. Of course, it wasn't as bad as *my* chicken pox when I was young, but this hay fever seemed a cruel blow.

'What if he has to give up football because of the grass?' Natalie asked feverishly, briefly adopting my role as chief overreactor.

'Yes. And what if he never gets to compete in all four tennis Grand Slams because of Wimbledon and their anachronistic court surfaces?' I replied mockingly, though you never know.

Even if she wasn't under strict medical instructions not to add to the animal fur burden, Natalie would have been hard-pressed to have found the time for new additions – not just because of the new timetable of travel and her job, but because the existing members were proving even harder work than usual.

C'EST LA VIE

To my mind, it was a measure of just how content Junior had been over the past 18 months or so that he hadn't tried to escape in that time. And when I say 'content', I mean content in the way that a particularly violent US Border guard in a room full of cowering travellers is content, the way a watching snake is content – 'assassin content'. His relationship with Ultime had blossomed and he was the undisputed king of his patch, so why try to escape anymore? He was on top of the world.

But the goats had other ideas. To describe Junior as irritable would be ridiculous, like describing Pol Pot as cranky, but what at the time just seemed like an irritated nip at one of the goats had escalated, and the relationship was now teetering on the brink. Ultime, far from backing Junior up in his goat-bullying antics – or at the very least ignoring them – had taken to actively protecting Popcorn and Chewbacca like they were her very own. And this wasn't some kind of domestic, 'Oh, just leave the kids alone, will you?' type row; this was angry stuff. She regularly kicked Junior in the face, constantly chasing after him trying to bite him and, like any bully who is challenged, Junior was now completely at sea, his world turned upside down.

In the blink of an eye Ultime had gone from submissive concubine to queen of all she surveyed. She had obviously got it into her head that the two goats weren't goats at all, but were in fact her very own offspring; the foals to her mare and, as such, she was guarding them jealously from Junior. The goats, it has to be said, were playing up to this quite brilliantly and following Ultime wherever she went, especially at feeding time; whereas Junior had always approached his feed deliberately via the goats just to give them a shove, he was now getting a right-hoofer from Ultime at every meal. A few weeks of this and he was now so completely under the thumb that he had to wait for Ultime to finish her meal before he could eat at all.

He tried to fight back initially, he wasn't going to give up his throne easily, but Ultime, who was younger and fitter, was more than determined to give back a little of what she'd been getting for the past couple of years. Any brief sign of insubordination the old boy might show was therefore met with a swift roundhouse kick to the chops. If this was one of those TV documentaries about chimpanzees or something that always end with the battered old leader sent packing by a youthful upstart, you'd be inclined to feel sorry for him, but this is Junior, raised in the Devil's own Satanic stables with a score of victims behind him and at least one donkey quivering in a stable somewhere. You reap what you sow, old fruit. The king is dead, long live the queen. Of course he'd only gone down one peg and was still treating *me* like something he'd picked up on the sole of his hoof, but his powers were clearly waning.

I must admit, I did have some sympathy for him at the start – he was behaving like a deposed leader and he was obviously hurting; sulkily standing alone in a corner of the paddock that he now looked unable or unwilling to defend. He looked a spent force. But – and not for the first time – I'd underestimated him.

Toby and Gigi had started barking at what appeared to be nothing, always around dusk and always in a westerly direction. It was strange, obviously, but seeing as Toby would bark at a change in atmospheric pressure it was hardly a major concern, and Gigi had become such a bossy boots that her joining in wasn't a great surprise either. It was a warning, though, and it went unheeded. Natalie rang me one Friday night when I was in a Nottingham dressing room about to go on stage.

'The animals have escaped!' she said frantically.

'What? All of them?' I asked, astonished.

It seemed inconceivable to me that they had broken out en masse, besides which the hens, after a systematic destruction of Natalie's rose gardens were now not as free range as they once had been and were fenced into the orchard area.

Natalie explained that the horses and the goats had escaped, that clearly, over a period of a couple of weeks or so, Junior had been destroying the perimeter fence behind the leylandii hedge. The dogs had sensed it and I, like the naive commandant in *The Great Escape*, had been too complacent to take any notice and that every evening, around dusk, Junior would look around furtively and disappear behind the hedge to quietly destroy the fence, but also to leave it in a way that meant we didn't notice a thing.

Monsieur Rousseau, one of the neighbouring farmers, had rung Natalie on the Friday evening to ask if everything was OK. It was a strange question. We are on good terms with him, but not to the extent of him ringing up out of the blue and checking on our welfare. Natalie responded cautiously: everything's fine, she said, suspecting that because this conversation was actually taking place, maybe things weren't all that fine at all. 'Right,' said Rousseau. 'Good.' He paused. 'It's just that your horses and goats are in the road.'

Much to Junior's anger and disappointment, Ultime, Popcorn and Chewbacca were easily rounded up and happy to be back in the paddock. Junior, though far more reluctant, recognised defeat and skulked back in too. He had a look in his eyes, Natalie said, that suggested that may have been the last stand and he just came in quietly. Again, I did feel an element of sympathy for him – he doesn't like me and has made that abundantly clear over the past few years, but in a way I admire him. There was something noble about it even. It was a desperate attempt to regain control, break out, have his 'flock' follow him, be the leader again, the main man and, boy, can I empathise with the futility of that.

Junior's timing wasn't great, but to pick the Friday evening at the end of Natalie's first week at work was unfortunate to say the least. Her new job had got off to a tricky start. On her way across town to one of the other schools Natalie received a phone call from Samuel's *collège*. There had been an accident and Samuel had been taken to hospital. It wasn't serious, but...

It's one of those calls all parents dread obviously and with me being in England working she drove the hour back from work to our local hospital. Samuel had apparently been indulging in what I'm afraid all male Moores indulge in: winding up the big kid. Only this big kid had responded by tripping Samuel up in the playground, sending him flying down some stone steps, and subsequently into an ambulance and casualty. Natalie arrived to find Samuel feeling sorry for himself with his arm in a sling and his neck in a brace, being fussed over by nurses. And again, like all male Moores, he was hamming it up and loving it.

I spoke to him when he got home, though, and he sounded dreadful. I asked him if he was all right and the reply was a croaky, barely audible but heartbreaking 'I'm OK, Daddy.' I asked him what had happened and he struggled through the story like it was physically taxing for him; I gave him the same lecture I'd had at his age about picking the right targets or running away bloody quickly and he responded in all the right places while actually managing to sound worse as the conversation went on.

'It's a shame,' I said, 'but you're not going to be able to go to drama class tonight if you're like this.'

Drama was his new big interest and so the response was immediate and markedly less croaky, 'No, I'll be fine, Daddy. I really want to go!' I knew he would and he did, drama class being possibly the most apposite place for him to get over his 'injuries'. It turned out that he had possibly got off more lightly than the big kid as well, who was not only threatened with suspension but was also physically sick when told that his dad was on his way to deal with things. I felt quite sorry for him; it can't have been easy the following week at school when Samuel limped in still wearing his neck brace and arm sling, playing up to it massively. And the self-control of the big kid, or perhaps the fear of a paternal backlash, must have been almost Gandhi-esque as Samuel unselfconsciously removed his neck brace and arm sling, threw himself around in the PE lesson and then put his bandages back on again!

I suspected that it was just a stormy playground relationship that would need monitoring over the next few weeks. I'd already warned Samuel, who is small for his age, not to be alone near his locker, for instance, as I still have back spasms from the time I was shoved in my own locker at school – and also to skip any metalwork lessons, again painful memories are the result of a rather one-sided altercation with someone who went on to a short-lived career in armed robbery.

We were discussing this at dinner a few weeks later and after yet another school injury when Thérence revealed that he'd also been hit at school by some kid who hits everyone else as well, so he's not exactly picking on Thérence.

'You must tell the teacher immediately,' said Natalie, quite rightly.

'Punch him in the face,' said Maurice.

'Kick him,' said Samuel.

'I hit him on the bottom,' said Thérence as angelically as possible.

'What *have* you been teaching them?' Natalie asked angrily, as I tried not to catch her eye. 'I hope you're not all going to behave like this next week when the cameras are here!' Ah yes, the cameras. I'd forgotten about them – and deliberately so.

CAMERA SHY

I have often been asked, by fellow comedians, other assorted show business types and generally anyone who expresses surprise at my 'double life', if I had ever considered turning my bizarre existence into a reality TV show. An access-all-areas documentary based on my chaotic, animal-governed French home life, my job as a comedian and all the endless travel that goes on between the two. I'd be lying if I said that I hadn't considered it. I had. For about four seconds.

I simply do not understand the prurient appeal of so-called 'reality television'. Firstly, it's not real! This is no earth-shattering observation, but the whiny, self-regarding 'look at me-ism' of this modern TV phenomenon doesn't leave me cold, it actually makes me angry. D-list celebrities eating insects in a fake jungle–prison or drug-addled rock stars and their fictional home life or, to my mind worse, the ambushed anonymous of the lower reaches of society held up for public ridicule by middle-class TV executives because of whatever makes them slightly different from the rest of society, be it a hobby, a body shape or an addiction to dogging. These people and the programmes they're in all have one thing in common: you stick a camera in front of them and it is very much not real, it is unreality TV, the worst kind of fake.

There was no way I would countenance cameras at home, no way at all. I would consider it a gross invasion of privacy, I thundered regularly, a violation of 'home'. A disturbing, no-holds-barred, 'I have no secrets, come look at us' freak show with my lovely family as the exhibits. Well, I'd rather die. I'd always said that I wouldn't do it and I meant it; definitely not, no way. Hell on wheels, I would implore self-righteously, 'What do you think I am?'

Weak is what I am. Pathetically weak.

I had a new agent, and within five minutes I was saying, 'Wow, cameras? At home? What a great idea…'

In my defence, I thought it would be a good way to publicise Les Champs Créatifs in the future, if in the end we decided that we wanted to give it another go. Vanity never came into it. Not once. Never.

Natalie was reluctant from the start, though I wasn't exactly overjoyed either. I had sold it to her in the same way as I'd sold it to myself – as a way of us marketing the school – and she could see the logic in that. To be honest, what small new business wouldn't cry out for free prime-time advertising on a major television channel? But she was never happy with the idea at all. The boys on the other hand thought it was a fantastic turn of events and began planning how they would play their roles.

'You don't play a role,' I pointed out to Samuel. 'You just be yourself. They'll just watch us – er – well, being us.'

'Why?' he asked, quite rightly and genuinely bemused by the concept.

The nearer the time came for a pilot run of filming to take place, the more nervous Natalie and I became. We had decided, again, that we definitely would not be trying to do the school the following summer, an ever-changing decision, but which for now neutered any immediate advantages (that we could see) of taking part in a TV documentary at all. Also, the upheaval seemed unnecessary and potentially upsetting as all the boys were at important stages of school. They might be keen but it was also a difficult thing to justify inflicting on them and other people and, of course, the schools themselves.

'Don't worry,' we were told. 'This pilot run will be one handheld camera, that's all – not a whole crew. You won't even know we're there.'

I'd met the producer a couple of weeks before, ostensibly to iron out a few details but also, in my mind, to try and lay down a few parameters, some rules, at least some things that I felt should be off-limits and he was fine about that. It struck me afterwards that as an extremely successful 'Reality TV' producer he must have been through exactly the same kind of conversation a hundred times before; some publicity-hungry sap walks in, lays down the law of just how far the cameras were allowed to go before actually laying bare every foible and previously locked-away skeleton as soon as they start filming. Also you see people complain, after they're held up for public ridicule that they were 'misled', but I had no reason not to trust him. Quite by chance, we had known each other before when we were post-production runners in Soho nearly 20 years previously; Ed was also a very decent man and so – for the time being at least – my fears were somewhat allayed.

CAMERA SHY

The thing is, though, the phrase, 'You won't even know we're there' is utterly ludicrous. There's a bloke with a camera on his shoulder following you about your kitchen asking if you could 'just do that again' and 'could you repeat that, just to make sure I have it in the edit'. Believe me, you know he's there all right. In fact, after a while, rather than get easier, it feels like he's the only thing that *is* there, and every movement, every word you say, every (hopefully discreet) look or attempted communication with your wife and family becomes either an attempt at secrecy or the worst kind of silent-movie overacting. The first few hours were very hard indeed.

To be fair, Norman, a handsome, slight Black man from south London, who was cameraman and researcher for this initial 'test' filming, was charm itself. He bought all three boys a present, which won them over immediately, though they were hardly suffering camera shyness anyway. I'm not sure they quite got the hang of the whole 'hidden' camera idea, though, and would come running into a room shouting, 'Norman, look at this! I've drawn you a picture!' or something that showed quite obviously that the camera was very much there. He dealt with these regular intrusions with skill and patience, but that in itself presented a problem. Norman was the perfect guest: polite, helpful, great with the kids, but one who also had a whacking great camera permanently attached to his face which, at the very least, is unusual among house guests.

He interviewed us as a family over that first dinner and I can only imagine that it was a bit like interviewing a Stepford family. We all seemed to be sitting bolt upright, the boys wore their napkins without argument and refrained from bickering for the entire meal – seriously parents, if you ever want to control your children at mealtimes, hire a camera crew – *'s'il te plaît'* and *'mercis'* were even used when condiments were requested.

It was a quite surreal experience and rather different from the 'French' meal we would normally have. When I grew up, talking at the meal table, in fact showing almost any enjoyment of the experience at all was, if not exactly frowned upon, then discouraged. If you were talking then you weren't eating and eating was a utility and not necessarily an experience to be enjoyed. This meal took me right back to those times, which though anthropologically may have been interesting, was doing nothing for Norman's efforts. Early days, we thought though, early days.

I think Norman, having done his research carefully, was looking forward to seeing the interaction with the animals the following day. As it was a Wednesday, the boys and Natalie would be off school, so the whole family dealing with (or not dealing with, preferably, for television purposes) the smallholding equivalent of a very angry Disney film would kick-start the thing and give it some focus.

And the early signs were good. Norman interviewed Natalie shortly after breakfast about what her morning might entail, to which, for the first time forgetting that cameras were involved, she launched into an almost scientific lecture about sunny frosty mornings and just why they were so conducive to the collection of animal waste. She did it with the kind of enthusiasm, knowledge and experience that makes the best wildlife documentaries so popular and educational, but poor Norman, though obviously relieved at finally having some meat on the bones of the project, looked like he might throw up as Natalie graphically explained temperature effects on the texture and handling ability of dog poo in your allotment, the best kind of carrier bags to use and basically the full works on what is without doubt her specialist subject.

Later, a vague acquaintance who we'd met briefly at the school gates turned up, a slightly odd individual, who had just heard that we had horses and wondered if he could collect a couple of wheelbarrow-loads of manure from us. No problem, said Natalie, who despite her expertise is always willing to hand over the reins of amorphous deposit removal. The man set about his work with gusto and explained to Natalie exactly why he needed the stuff, while Norman interviewed me back on the *terrasse*, the idea being that me collecting poo in my early-morning mod finery would appear too posed.

After an hour, the man left, offering his gratitude and Natalie brought over his half of this countryside-bartering episode, an out-of-date tub of pool chemicals. The poor trade didn't bother us at all – we need people to come and remove our excess animal evacuations or we're going to drown under the stuff – though his reasons were somewhat bizarre. Fleas, he had told Natalie, fleas; which left all of us – the word flea has that effect I find – literally scratching our heads.

The man's house had become infested with fleas, and rather than pay for the place to be deloused he had done a bit of investigating and found a cheaper solution. I don't know where he got this solution to his flea problem from, perhaps it's an old local wives' tale or someone was having him on, but 'I'm going to line the floor of my attic with horse manure to cure my flea infestation' is a bizarre and potentially disastrous non-answer to the problem and would have, I suspected, the very opposite result to the one he wanted. If the problem, however, was, 'I would like my house to be infested by fleas' then lining your attic with flea egg-ridden horse dung sounds like just the job, or maybe he just wanted shot of his old pool chemicals. We all sat there stunned, trying to digest this information and then Norman asked quietly, 'Does that kind of thing happen a lot?' His eyes betrayed what he was thinking, that there was obviously a rich documentary seam to be mined here somewhere but that we kept hiding him from it and making his job harder.

Nothing of any note whatsoever seemed to happen at all over the next few days, though Norman, endlessly upbeat, kept repeating the importance of 'the edit', 'story arc' and the like. The poor man was floundering. Even Junior, normally a reliable source of antagonistic anti-me behaviour, and who one would have thought a shoo-in for an equine take on those ubiquitous 'how violent modern society has become' type programmes, seemed shy, and strangely lethargic in front of the cameras. To the extent that when I was shoved unceremoniously into his paddock with the express intention of causing the beast alarm, he just wandered up to me slowly and actually nuzzled me. It was a very foreign experience; he would normally try and bite me at least, but he just looked at me with his big, brown eyes, a picture of loyalty and obedience – like the wife of an adulterous politician forced to forgive her husband solely for the sake of the watching press. It only made me more nervous frankly, and though our cross-species communication is normally me swearing at him while he snorts in my face, I swear that under his breath I heard a 'You just wait until this kid with the camera has gone, sonny.'

CAMERA SHY

Norman tried to film at Maurice's football training and at school the next day, but I wasn't comfortable with that at all. If I'm a local celebrity it's because of the way I dress, or my social muteness, not for any other reason, and I simply couldn't allow a cameraman to follow me around in these activities. This is not for any of the 'you can't video your own kid's nativity play these days' concerns, just that I felt it was wrong to do so without their express permission. I told Norman this and I could see that he thought this whole thing was flatlining.

'Look,' I said trying to be positive, 'if we do the whole thing properly then we'll get the permission of the schools and the clubs...'

He wasn't convinced, and a visit to the hairdresser, never a more po-faced moment in a mod's day, and following that an entirely incident-free visit to a *boulangerie* did nothing for his flagging belief in the project. I even saw him, by way of the mirror in the *boulangerie*, shake his head in woe.

'*Une baguette, s'il vous plaît.*'
'OK.'
'*Merci.*'
'*Merci.*'
'*Au revoir.*'
'*Au revoir.*'

That pointless, unglamorous interaction may have been the final straw.

Even the journey back to England to work a few days later was the most stress-free, non-delayed journey I had had in the time I'd been commuting from France and poor Norman, by now beyond the 'tearing-out-hair phase' and well into just abject resignation, finally put his camera away with a dejected,

'Yeah. I think we've got enough.' And we went our separate ways at Manchester Airport.

I was called in for a meeting with Ed the producer a few weeks later, but we didn't bother to look at the 'rushes'. He began by blaming Norman for not being focused enough and not knowing in advance what he had to come back with, but Norman was with us and not taking this personally, so I suspected this to be a ruse to negate my potential disappointment.

'Thing is...' Ed began, 'there's just no jeopardy. We need jeopardy. It's not your fault.'

I wasn't entirely sure what he meant by 'jeopardy' in this context, but basically it meant conflict, friction, not getting on, potential disaster. The idea that I would engineer this kind of clash or high emotion with my family just for television was never going to happen, to my mind it happened enough without engineering it but, sadly for Ed, not when cameras were there. I agreed with him, 'Yes,' I said, 'I can see that. Jeopardy. Right.'

He looked at me and we both knew that I wasn't going to play *that* game.

He wasn't sheepish about his requirements, and why should he be? Reality TV is a big success and he wasn't there to defend an entire genre, but some people are suited to it and some aren't. It turns out that my family and I aren't and that, to be perfectly honest, was something of a relief.

NEEDING ASSURANCE

One of the consequences of watching the brief snippets of footage Norman had shown us was quite brutal. I've never been the kind of comedian who can easily watch myself on-screen anyway. Some comedians do and swear that it helps them hone and improve their act, which they constantly record, but personally I think most do it just to make it look like they're making the effort. I'm always too embarrassed to watch myself, frankly, and avoid it as much as possible.

Having been forced to watch a few frames, though, there was an inevitable conclusion to be drawn and that was that the 'local produce' was having an effect on my waistline. And once seen I couldn't avoid it. Old photos were particularly harsh too, one especially; it was of me, stood with my back to the drinks cabinet (an unusual position in itself) cradling a two-day-old Maurice nervously in my arms, just a few months after we had moved in. It only flashed by briefly at first on the office computer screensaver, but it left its mark, and then seemed to reappear cruelly every other photo. Nearly eight years had passed since that picture had been taken and looking back I barely recognised myself: there was no grey hair, only the one standard chin and I was actually skinny. France, it seems, had taken its toll.

I'd been half-heartedly toying with the idea of exercising for a while, but that picture showed just how necessary it had now become. Over seven years of industrial wine, cheese and bread consumption had left its not inconsiderable mark, as had the constant travel and eating at all hours of the night after work. I had become a chubby mod and that's simply not allowed.

There are no gyms near us, the nearest is in Tours which is 80 kilometres away, and if you see anyone jogging they're generally foreigners and are given short shrift by passing motorists. Cycling, however, is almost a religion here and there's obviously plenty of space to enjoy it. The Tour de France is probably the world's only regular sporting event which also acts as an advert for French tourism. For a couple of weeks the cameras swoop around the picturesque countryside, following the riders on a different route every year, and the French are quite rightly proud of it. But cycling is taken *very* seriously indeed, and especially by old men. I don't know why it should be more popular among old men than other groups of society, but every Sunday you'll see groups of them cycling around the countryside shouting at pedestrians and motorists to get out of the way and generally taking themselves far too seriously.

From a distance it looks like a professional race: they are all wearing brightly coloured cycling shirts – generally the symbolic yellow to add to their personal sense of delusion – and seemingly moving at a pace. But on closer inspection some of them are barely moving at all, a light breeze away from toppling sideways and older than the countryside itself. Their tanned, wrinkled faces scream a pain that is totally at odds with their lurid, professional-looking Lycra costumes, which are surely the only thing holding their ancient bodies together in the first place and when removed will render the wearer a mass of boneless skin on the floor, like human flubber.

Nevertheless, ancient as most of these riders are, they were now putting me to shame.

I quite like cycling, well I like the clothes, anyway. A lot of traditional mod clothing is magpied from all over the shop: military parkas from the US Army, pork-pie hats from Jamaican rude boys, and to add to the sporting theme of Fred Perry, original 1960s cycling tops are very much a part of the mod summer wardrobe. That's as close as I'd come to exercising in years and so the initial forays, in the corn and sunflower fields that surround us, had ended in disaster. Samuel doesn't like exercise and had been a reluctant cyclist from the start. It took him ages to learn how to cycle without stabilisers and I was a demanding and impatient teacher, which didn't help. So when he finally learned, I was keen to take him out, but also insisted that he didn't need a helmet and that we 'never wore them in my day'. I was wrong, of course, and as I spent the rest of that first day of the father–son cycling adventure in the local casualty department waiting for Samuel's face to be patched up I had time to reflect on my stupidity.

It was a few months before I got back on my bike again too, Samuel quite rightly refused to come with me, and so it was just Volcan and I who went careering around the local fields. My relationship with Volcan, our short-lived mod-hating Brittany spaniel, was a strained one at the best of times, so it occurred to me that we might actually be able to bond if we went out together: me on the bike and him running beside me. It didn't work.

I lost him for about ten minutes and I couldn't see how. The fields had all been harvested so they were flat and you could see for miles, but then I saw him emerge from one of the deep ditches that border the fields, the ditches are there to stop the Romanies from putting their caravans on agricultural land, and he was limping. Typical, I thought, he's got a thorn in his paw or something, twisted his leg spinning around trying to catch a rabbit. If only.

He eventually reached the point where I was waiting for him and he was covered head to toe in blood. He looked like he'd taken an enthusiastic role in some frenzied butchery somewhere but was feeling very sorry for himself. Initially I just stared at him in disbelief because it was such a gory sight. A car slowed down as if to ask me directions, but as the driver wound down his window he saw Volcan, took a frightened look at me and sped off. Volcan had unluckily stumbled upon an old boar trap, brutal things that I think are actually now illegal, but which had been raked up by a plough. It looked worse than it actually was, but as I sat in the vet's that afternoon waiting for Volcan's body to be stitched up, I decided to give up the whole cycling thing for a bit as every two-wheeled foray seemed to end in a bloodbath.

Needs must, however, and as I blew two months' worth of cobwebs off my bike and, for the first time in my life, successfully mended a puncture (from my previous ill-fated attempt to pick Maurice up from the bus stop and the very limit of my mechanical capabilities), I set off with renewed enthusiasm. Maurice insisted on joining me and, like the good parent I am, I insisted on him wearing an oversized helmet.

NEEDING ASSURANCE

'Do I have to? he asked.

'Look at your brother's face,' I said, pointing at Samuel, who was ironically playing a cycling race on the Wii.

It would be good to have Maurice with me, I thought, as we set off. It means I can take it easy to start with, not overdo it on the first day by setting off too fast. As it was I had trouble keeping up with him as he and Toby – Volcan's much more genial successor – set off at a pace I just couldn't match, as my gears seemed to be rusted in low, hill-climbing mode. My legs were whirring around, almost a blur to my mind but I didn't seem to be going anywhere, so it was a while before I caught up with them – and did so just in time to hear Toby let out an excited yelp and go chasing after a deer.

'Toby!' I shouted, Volcan's bloody image in my head. *'Viens ici!'*

My front tyre hit a dry, tractor-tyre rut and knocked me slightly off balance, just as a startled heron emerged from the reeds next to me and took off, narrowly missing me as I ducked. I lost my balance completely, failed to brake in time and fell off. I lay there and, not for the first time since we'd moved to France, just asked myself what the bloody hell did I think I was doing?

A soaking, muddied Toby returned and slobbered all over me as I lay prone under my bike, one of the wheels still turning. Maurice, though concerned, couldn't keep a straight face and went roaring off to save my embarrassment with an excited Toby yelping after him.

I bow to no-one in my admiration for Bradley Wiggins and his achievements, but some mods, it seems, just don't belong on bikes. I stayed there for about ten minutes idling on the irony that there was no film crew to see this Chaplinesque calamity, but also knowing that I had to clean myself up for the afternoon appointment with the insurance man, otherwise the premiums would go up again.

There are fewer things more certain in life than the knowledge that if the phone rings in France during lunch or dinner, it's definitely a sales call. No self-respecting French man or woman would ruin these sacred times of the day with anything so crass as modern telecommunications, and the poor saps who do have to do these things for a living have a weariness about them, an *ennui*, totally unsuited to the pushing of conservatories or broadband packages.

It seems that France doesn't really do underhand selling, or customer service either, but there is generally an honesty about it rather than a slickness and it's actually quite refreshing.

We had decided to change insurer, as our current company seemed to regard us as something of a cash-cow and would ring up constantly offering whatever kind of insurance someone in the 'whim department' had come up with that week, or even just turn up out of the blue to introduce a 'new member of the team'. This new man, however, after a spectacularly truculent sales call, was different – he was a stocky, middle-aged man wearing a leather jacket and looking more like low-level mafia than an insurance go-getter, but for an hour he provided wonderful entertainment.

Natalie had decided that the school idea wasn't dead after all and so, on top of her new job, was planning to advertise herself locally as a private tutor giving English lessons to adults and children; she opened the door to her 'classroom', a monument to Laura Ashley, Kate Forman and those kind of pastel-coloured flowery prints that to me just scream *The Little House on the Prairie*.

'This room is forty-one metres square,' the insurance man declared dispassionately, after roping me into helping him measure the place.

'Yes,' Natalie said, waiting for an explanation.

'That means it's more than forty metres square,' he said, unblinking, as if we were idiots. 'For insurance purposes it counts as two rooms. You've done a lovely job on them, though.'

Natalie and I looked about at the one room and actually thought he was a bit of a lunatic: 'Does he want our business at all?' I whispered. In truth I was a little sore at the man. Here he was praising Natalie's Kate Forman, distressed furniture and duck-egg blue interior design skills, and yet he'd taken one look at my beautifully authentic, 'swinging sixties man-pad' upstairs and had looked at me like a disappointed father who'd caught his teenage son painting his bedroom black. I swear he'd tutted.

We left the classroom and he asked about the animals. 'For insurance purposes' apparently dogs, cats and hens count as pets; horses and goats are classified as beasts. He counted the horses, two he said, looking at us for confirmation. He counted the goats, again in exaggerated pencil-pointing fashion, 'Two,' he said again. 'So. You have three beasts.' And with that he strode off.

Natalie and I again looked at each other in total confusion.

'Er, Monsieur...' Natalie began, going after him.

'For insurance purposes,' he explained, 'two goats count as one beast.'

'Is that because they're pygmy?' I asked, though he ignored me. 'What if we only had one goat?' I persisted, beginning to enjoy myself. 'Would we have to hide it in one of the summer rooms?' The thing about salespeople is that if you can't poke one of them with a stick occasionally then really what is the point? But he just looked at me with an expression that showed his distaste for my office still stuck in his craw.

I'll admit here that I am a terrible salesperson myself. I once had a part-time job as a cold caller on behalf of charities. I was ringing up people who had already given to the charity and asking them to give more, yet after a week I was 'released' as the majority of people I called actually cancelled their regular donation rather than increased the amount. Apparently, my surly approach to winning over hearts and minds was as 'anti-sales' as it gets, though in my defence I did once star in an ITV documentary about just how gullible people are and managed to sell pigeons to some tourists in Trafalgar Square. One man from Devizes actually got quite angry when it was explained to him that it was just a TV stunt, 'But what am I going to get my daughter for her birthday now?!' he pleaded as security stopped him from attacking me.

The mafia insurance man wasn't for poking, though, and pointedly ignored all my questions. 'You wear glasses,' he said, which could have been taken as a threat. 'There's a limit to how many new pairs you can claim for in any one year.' He turned away slowly and went into the workshop/fruit store/*cave*.

'I don't think he likes me,' I said to Natalie as we followed him in.

His face had brightened as he pointed out the jars of homemade chutney and piccalilli that filled the shelves. I

NEEDING *ASSURANCE*

was about to make some quip about whether 'for insurance purposes' chutney would count as two jams or vice versa, but unfortunately my French wasn't quick enough for the job. He was beaming at Natalie though and praising her for her culinary skills, he himself, he said, greatly enjoyed this old-fashioned pastime. Natalie pointed out that they were all my doing; that it was my hobby, how I relaxed. He looked at me and kind of squinted his eyes as I waited for a newfound respect from him. I smiled broadly, which I'm not good at, and so the respect never materialised.

In truth though, stocks were down. Through a combination of violent horse attacks on the trees themselves, terrible spring weather and bees being in such short supply globally these days, we had had precious little fruit at all from the orchard. Oh, we'd had a few medlar fruit, but they are an unappetising prospect at the best of times. The official name for medlar in French is *néflier*, but the unofficial one is far more evocative, they call it 'the cat's arse'. Accurate, descriptively, though it doesn't necessarily induce confidence in the product – but then, everything about medlar seems to be a bit low rent. They are the last fruit of the year to blossom, and are generally harvested after the first heavy frosts, then left to rot, or *blet*, before they can be used to their best potential. As with quince, which can't be eaten raw, I don't know how these fruit 'rules' were arrived at, but looking at a sad crate of rotting feline backsides in late November is hardly the stuff of haute cuisine, though they do make a lovely 'jelly' which is just gorgeous with cold turkey at Christmas, or stirred into a gravy with a roast dinner (see full recipe at the back).

I'd normally compensate for a lack of home fruit produce with a bumper crop of autumn/winter squashes, pumpkins and the like, but even they had failed me this time. This had had nothing to do with climate or horse shenanigans, though, and everything to do with the fact that my squash plants were the wrong gender. I realise I have many things to learn about country living, but I wasn't even aware that squash plants had a gender. All my plants it seemed, or at least all the flowers on them are male and while they are thriving, one could even say it's a gay squash Mardi Gras out there, they can't 'produce' together. I presume there are rules about the male squash plants adopting smaller squash fruit and we'll look into it, but why on earth was I sold a full tray of male plants in the first place? Why are they kept apart from their female counterparts? I went to an all boys comprehensive and believe me this kind of forced separation doesn't help development in any way, emotional or otherwise.

I'm quite inordinately proud of my chutney–relish–jelly skills, and seeing as this insurance man was also something of a connoisseur it seemed we'd found some common ground; it may even get us a better deal, I thought, and as I had everything set up in the kitchen ready for a bout of mid-afternoon jelly production it seemed like a good opportunity to show off a bit while he and Natalie discussed things in greater detail at the table in front of me.

What I hadn't considered was just how hot my sterilising jars still were and as I blithely picked one up to fill it I scalded my hand, dropped the jar and squealed loudly in front of the astonished man, dropping to my knees behind the breakfast bar, like Basil Fawlty disappearing behind Fawlty Towers

NEEDING ASSURANCE

reception. He didn't even mention it. He just looked at me like I was a fruitcake, rolled up his sleeves and produced an enormous file of thick 'advertising products'.

'I take it your husband has life assurance?' he asked Natalie over his glasses. Bloody cheek.

He left with a sizeable chunk of our insurance needs fulfilled and we felt that we had got a good deal on the whole thing too. In hindsight, his timing was poor, because if he'd visited us just a week later he could have easily doubled his health and life assurance premiums and we would probably have bitten his hand off. Because a week later, it felt like we were living in a war zone.

LA DÉLIVERANCE

There are many reasons why we moved to France: financial, health, educational... They all, put together, made it a fairly simple decision when we made it. But also pretty high up on the list was a sense of personal safety and an escape from what we perceived to be, rightly or wrongly, and possibly media-fuelled, an increasingly antisocial society back home. So we hadn't bargained on local hunting parties blasting a hole through that woolly-headed thinking and turning the calm of the Loire Valley into what sounded like a war zone.

Monsieur Girresse, fast becoming the bad cop in our good-cop, bad-cop neighbouring farmers relationship (and the spreader of seditious anti-Romany eating habits rumours), had decided that there was a great deal of money to be made post-harvest, pre-sowing winter time by hiring his land out to shooting parties, and these groups were now descending on us, sometimes twice a week, like sinister stag parties at a paintball course. Girresse owns all the land surrounding ours; our property is boxed in on all sides by his fields, and his family used to own all the land as far as the eye could see. Used to,

LA DÉLIVRANCE

and the fact that they now don't is a grudge against the world he carries daily.

These shooting parties, to my mind, are an absurd-looking bunch and you can tell the locals from the out-of-town 'tourists' by what they're wearing. The 'guests' wear obviously expensive and pristine 'greens' right out of a catalogue – one can imagine how they stand for hours in front of the mirror fingering their weapons. Some of them, in a nod to health and safety, also wear luminous orange baseball caps, which gives the whole outfit the look of an 'Employee of the Month' in a fast-food restaurant specialising in game. It is, however, a sensible option, as grey, dark, misty days coupled with fellow novice hunters and a wine-heavy lunch could quite easily lead to a mishap.

The locals dress differently: their worn, lived-in hunting gear sitting more comfortably on them as they direct the newcomers and try to maintain some kind of order. I don't have a problem with hunting per se and I understand the argument, put forward by a very good friend of ours, that essentially because most of the animals are swift and canny all the hunters are doing really is hoovering up the weak and the sick. I can see his point, but it's also similar to that of an alcoholic justifying a dependence on vodka because 'some of the bottles are nearing their best before date.' There is, though, no justification for mass shooting parties; they are not picking off the weak and the sick, they are being spoon-fed young game, surreptitiously released that morning by shifty individuals out of the back of a van. I know because I saw it happen. That's not hunting, that's shooting fish in a barrel.

The novices were having a bad day and you could hear them being shouted at to 'stay in line', 'raise the gun', 'take it out of your mouth' (I may have made that one up). It was more like an Afghani wedding where the males shoot their rifles skywards in celebration than an organised hunt; as crazed, excitable zealots fired pointlessly and relentlessly into the air. But they were close, too, just yards from the end of the garden and it was increasingly uncomfortable being outside, even Thérence was moved to shout 'bloody gits' at them from the relative safety of the *terrasse*.

I returned from some errand or other to find the hunters gathered in my driveway, looking more like a Barbour-clad lynch mob than the hunter–gatherers their delusion led them to believe they were. I was approached by the farmer's son, François. In his get up and with his greying beard he looked like a hirsute Elmer Fudd and it was difficult to stop myself laughing at him, but he had a nervous, matey look about him.

'*Bonjour!*' he began, warmly, although we had barely spoken previously since we'd moved here. '*Ça va?*' I knew something was wrong not just by his chumminess, but by the nervous shuffling about in the background of his colleagues. 'Anyway,' François continued, 'er, we shot down a partridge and it landed in your garden but hey, you can keep it.'

It was a clumsy attempt at a bribe. They had been firing too close to the house, illegally so, and had obviously even shot over the garden while Natalie and the boys were outside and so one of their victims had landed on our property. By offering me the partridge he was tacitly admitting that there had been a serious breach of the rules. I picked up the pathetic bird from the paddock, narrowly avoiding being run over by Ultime who was clearly in distress with all the gunfire. The bird was tiny, one of the new, specially-bred-for-hunting partridges that I'd seen being released that morning.

'I've phoned the police,' Natalie said, 'I've had enough of this.'

According to the *gendarmes*, the hunters are not allowed to shoot within 150 metres of a property, making this and almost every other hunt here illegal. They certainly are not allowed to shoot in the direction of a house. The *gendarmes* promised to come by, though the hunters were already, and rather hurriedly, clambering into the back of a van and leaving the scene. The advice of the police was to talk to Girresse and sort this out amicably.

'Do you get on with your neighbours?' the policeman asked Natalie over the phone. 'If so, go round and have a chat.'

Now this is either a very sensible suggestion, and the kind of community-based policing that should be lauded, or it's the logic of a lunatic, asking an unarmed woman to go around to confront a man whose gun is still warm. I reckoned on the latter and insisted that Natalie cool down a bit before she went round and offered to show our neighbour how to use a partridge as a suppository.

The next day Natalie bumped into Monsieur Girresse. Now, French farmers have an international reputation for truculence and a fiery temper when confronted by... well, by anything really, but a diminutive woman and a foreign one to boot was never going to be greeted warmly by this Wild West-style patriarch.

Natalie gave him the partridge; the poor animal, as if its life wasn't pointless enough was now being bandied about roughly like an unfavoured old hat. The fact that he took the partridge says much about him, but then he exploded.

'None of what you say happened,' he said. 'I was there.' He wasn't, so this was quite some opening gambit. 'I know all the laws and legislation pertaining to hunting,' he continued. 'I can shoot as close as ten metres from your house as long as I am firing *away* from it and standing on *my* land.'

'You couldn't have been firing away from my house,' Natalie said. 'I was standing in my garden underneath the bird when it was shot at!' To which she received a heavily scientific explanation about wind, trajectory and angles, all 'justifying' the fact that the bird, apparently defying all known laws of physics, had landed where it had.

'And anyway, you are saying all of this just to piss me off!' he railed. 'I have tolerated your intrusion for years.' 'Intrusion' seemed a bit of a harsh way to describe the use of the public footpaths, whose existence he resented as they were adjacent to his land, and a failed wild goat chase. 'Well, I've had enough. From now on, if you encroach on my land I will regard it as trespassing,' he said implying a more sinister use of guns. 'Your children especially,' he added menacingly. And with that, he drove off in his aggressive 4x4.

Natalie relayed all this to me later that evening, a sense of disbelief and fear in her voice. We talked about it, argued about it, but whichever way we looked at it, it was about as unveiled a threat as it's possible to make. And about our children, the boys! Was he really threatening to shoot the boys?

Half an hour later, and in the pitch black of a cold autumn night, I was hot-headedly storming down the road to the farmer's house...

LA DÉLIVRANCE

Now, admittedly, I can be fairly volatile. I have a very short fuse these days and often completely overreact to things, though ironically not when I'm on stage, where over the years I have taught myself to stay calm. That was out of necessity, though; very early on in my career a big agency came to see me perform with a view to taking me up to the Edinburgh Festival. They didn't take me in the end, clearly feeling that my assaulting a front-row heckler by smashing the microphone over his head showed a certain 'inexperience' and I was told to go away and work on my 'anger issues'.

Over the previous hour and a half Natalie and I had talked about the apparent 'threat' made to our children by Girresse. It really did seem quite explicit, that should any of the boys stray on to his land they would be in danger and, seeing as our property is hemmed in on all sides by his land, this was a very frightening turn of events. I had initially tried to calm Natalie down, tried to play it with a cooler head but that didn't last and it wasn't long before we were turning on each other. We felt numb and also a bit impotent; what exactly could we do about this? That's when I decided to confront the man, walk the hundred metres or so in the dark to his property and find out exactly what the hell he meant.

'Take one of the boys with you,' Natalie shouted from the top of the stairs and I assumed she meant to act as translator rather than as a human shield, but that didn't feel right at all.

'No,' I said giving it the full John Wayne, 'I'm going alone.' The image of the doomed hero was given greater emphasis by Maurice who, as I put my jacket on, started to cry uncontrollably.

'He might shoot you!' he shouted through his sobs.

'No he won't, son,' I said with a confidence I didn't actually feel.

So I left with a level of anger even I rarely have, determined to sort this business out one way or another or, and this wasn't to doubt Natalie in any way, to have the threat repeated to *my* face and deal with it then. But as I stomped along something changed, my pace slowed and it dawned on me that I didn't know what the hell I was going to say! I've performed material on stage about how inadequate language textbooks, listening tapes and role-playing courses actually are for real-life situations, but really there is nothing in a *Tricolore* school textbook for this, no vocabulary table for 'Threats against children by local farmer', so I began to dawdle as I started to translate everything in my head and look for pointers in the dubbed films that I was now trying to learn from. For language purposes the English of what I was going to say changed to suit my more limited French and as it did so, as I went through the mechanics of translation, I started to calm down. The red mist began to evaporate and I regained my 'cool'. I knew what I wanted to say now and it wouldn't be inflammatory, nor would it be obsequious; it would be what my French language skills would allow me – that is curt, to the point, polite definitely, but not cowed.

The farm was pitch black when I arrived, but as I approached the house itself a security light came on revealing two guard dogs chained up by the garage. They stood up together, in total synchronicity, but didn't bark. Perhaps they recognised my smell, although the only smell I could possibly have been giving off at that point was a strong whiff of *eau de bricking it*, but either way they remained silent yet watchful. I rang the doorbell and Madame Girresse answered.

I asked politely if I could speak to her husband and she looked at me in some surprise – this was possibly the third or fourth time I had spoken to her since we had moved here seven years ago. Obviously they see and speak to Natalie far more, but I've found it easier to pretend to be a mute with occasional lapses of sound, though this has nothing to do with language, I was the same with neighbours when we lived in England. Monsieur wasn't in, she said, and she didn't know when he would be back. I'll admit that my disappointment was mixed with a fair amount of relief, but I'd come this far...

Had she heard what had happened earlier? I asked, to which she unconvincingly said that she had not. I redundantly explained to her what had happened and that I felt this was a shame. We are neighbours, I said, and therefore should avoid 'bad blood'. She looked at me strangely at this point, obviously not being as *au fait* as I was with the dubbed French version of *The Godfather*, where I had gleaned an awful lot of my hastily arranged vocabulary. I left the confused woman with vague promises of needing a 'sit-down' with her husband at some point soon and walked calmly home.

Of course, I had achieved nothing. I felt, quite rightly, that I had to show my face and her husband, who may or may not have been there, will know that I went round to see him, and I felt that was important, but the atmosphere was obviously still flat when I got home. We fed the boys, though we'd all lost our appetites, put them to bed and then started to talk earnestly about what all of this actually meant.

'It's a game-changer,' I said. 'If we don't feel safe here...'

And the evening carried on that way, both of us essentially repeating ourselves, still in utter disbelief. Ridiculously, but as a necessary distraction, we began to look at *immobilier* (estate agent) websites and found a few properties not too far away, which, you know… if we had to.

I didn't want to leave for work in England the following day. I still wanted to see the farmer and have a talk with him; for obvious reasons I didn't feel at all comfortable leaving Natalie and the boys behind, but I had no choice. I looked out of my beloved 12-foot-high lounge windows that morning and it didn't feel the same, the whole place had changed. Suddenly it wasn't the paradise I thought it was; it was oddly claustrophobic and the distant mist threatening, and I knew Natalie felt the same.

Later that day I got an email from Natalie. The farmer's son, François, had called round and apologised profusely for the shooting incident and the later words that were said. We had every right, he said, to stop them from hunting so close to our property, but that if we kindly allowed them to continue he would make sure more respect was shown. His father, he continued, had felt 'aggressed' by Natalie, but that of course we and our children could use their paths and land whenever we liked. He had then left, Natalie said, still apologising. It goes without saying that it was a welcome and unexpected twist. Financially they need their winter hunting to continue and obviously realised that they also needed our co-operation for it to do so and, for the following few weeks, there were no hunting parties, at least not close by, but even the distant shooting sounded threatening.

On the face of it, following the Girresse son's welcome intervention, things were how they had been before. I'd return home from work and the boys would be charging about the garden, followed by the dogs. The hens would cluck fussily at me as I checked my barren winter orchard and the cats would be searching for a shelter somewhere to lie languidly and judgementally before attacking some poor rodent or late-season lizard. And the horses... well, they'd regard me with their customary disdain while the goats bleated quietly at their feet. It would be just how I like it.

Only it wasn't like that anymore, not at all. The place had been corrupted and we, perhaps more so me, needed to find a way to deal with that or... or what?

HARSH TREATMENTS

It was hard not to feel besieged. There really seemed to be no imminent threat from the old lunatic, but nonetheless dog walking stopped for a while, the boys didn't go out unaccompanied to play in the fields anymore, not that they ever did anyway and, finally some good news: all thoughts of my cycling-in-the-fields exercise regime were ended with immediate effect. The Tour de France is hard enough for mods, but even Bradley Wiggins didn't have to deal with people shooting at him.

Then, when we were joined at Christmas by twenty or so members of Natalie's extended French family, it felt like the cavalry had arrived and our confidence was able to re-establish itself. Surrounded by bickering and drinking indigenous gourmands reminded us exactly why we'd come out here in the first place: family gatherings like this one, the fun, the warmth and, let's be honest, the safety in numbers. It was a refreshing break for us.

Also, although appalled by the implied violence, Natalie's family didn't take Girresse's threats as seriously as we did. The feeling was that people like Girresse were just anachronistic blowhards clinging to their symbols of power and influence, their posturing wasn't uncommon, but these threats 'rarely' led to anything. Monique, one of Natalie's aunts, told us how she'd found a group of hunters wandering across her own fields recently, where they obviously had no right to be, and who when confronted, seemed utterly bewildered that anyone would even think of restricting their movement, but were moved on unceremoniously anyway. Which is all very well and indeed a welcome piece of information, but which ignores the fact that Monique in full flow would stop most large-scale military invasions, let alone a group of *chasseurs* pootling about after lunch.

The general consensus was that it would all blow over; we were making a mountain out of a molehill and should take a break for a while, get away. Natalie and I didn't need to be told twice.

It has become something of a between-Christmas-and-New-Year tradition for us to try and get a couple of days away together somewhere anyway. It's not just an opportunity to have some time away from the children and the animals, but also Christmas itself – not just the big family gathering, which although a welcome annual fixture can be overwhelming, but sometimes Christmas traditions themselves. For instance, and I'll admit this may be a minor grouch, the relentless attempts by people to flog you a new calendar.

The postmen and binmen I get, it's a reward for a job well done, they'll keep up the good work next year and, because you purchased one of their calendars, they'll make sure your letterbox remains junk-mail-free and that your rubbish won't be strewn all over the drive. It's extortion, obviously, but you expect to give a tip to the postmen and binmen at Christmas, but the firemen? What would happen if we didn't buy a calendar from them? Would they not stretch out their ladder far enough for a tree-stuck cat? Throw less water on a fire? And before some of you get excited at the prospect of firemen selling their calendars, it's not that kind of calendar at all. Largely the pictures are of them slightly out of focus and taking it in turns to sit behind the one desk that their station has. It is a quite poor affair. By the time the new year rolls around we have at least a dozen calendars, none of which are particularly attractive.

Aside from hunters and my pedantic arguments over calendar collections, there were other reasons to try and get away. Natalie was becoming increasingly concerned for Junior and needed a few days respite from his apparent failing health and spirit, and her own subsequent fears for his welfare. Happily, we took advantage of Natalie's parents' offer to look after the place and sought refuge in a health spa a couple of hours south. Bless the French; only they would build a health spa and detox centre around a high-quality gourmet restaurant and a well-stocked wine cellar.

Just about the only experience I have of a health spa or gym is the opening 20 minutes from *Thunderball*, but we were both in need of a good break and looking forward to seeing what our 'treatments' – which were included in the price – would turn out to be. There was an 'algae body wrap', which sounded more like a detox lunch from a fancy deli than a treatment, a massage and chemotherapy. Well, I heard it as chemotherapy anyway and immediately began suggesting to the receptionist that maybe they rethink our treatments, when Natalie pointed out that the now-flustered woman had actually said 'chromotherapy', something entirely different altogether, apparently.

The treatments weren't to start until the following day, however, so for the first afternoon we could lazily enjoy the pool, the sauna, the jacuzzi and the saltwater jet-stream thing. I had a problem, though. I don't own any gym or leisurewear and the thin robes that we had been given at reception to wear around the hotel were frankly an affront to mankind: a shapeless, almost doily-thin affair that was completely see-through and just screamed 'No dignity here.' I refused to wear mine and insisted that Natalie do likewise, so we hired a couple of towelling robes that were much more the part and enabled us, me really, to look down on those that hadn't done the same. To be perfectly honest, I was still prickly from having to buy a pair of trunks. I had assumed that swim shorts would be banned, for rather spurious hygiene reasons, as they are certainly in most municipal pools in France, and so on Christmas Eve I had flown around the shops looking for a pair of 'legal' trunks. Twenty-nine euros I had paid for a pair of budgie smugglers, twenty-nine bloody euros, and yet I seemed to be the only one in the place not wearing shorts! I felt robbed, semi-naked and self-conscious, and for a time also reluctant to let go of my towelling robe.

Natalie had no such qualms and was immediately in the pool and relaxing while I smarted at the poolside. Relaxation really isn't my thing – what looks like a calm environment to you, or Natalie, is just another opportunity to get worked up for me and I felt aggrieved that there were no free loungers.

Eventually I had no choice but to get in the pool as well, as my brooding poolside presence with my robe done up tightly to my neck was actually beginning to look a bit menacing, and I was getting some worried looks, clearly upsetting the relaxation vibe.

I'd only been in the water a few minutes when Natalie insisted that we try the sauna. I quite like saunas, though I'm not at all sure what they're supposed to do. They always seem to descend into some kind of unspoken competition to see how long you can stay in. Frankly, I'd had enough after a couple of minutes, but seeing as no-one else was budging I stayed in until, through the tiny window in the door, I spotted that one of the jacuzzis was completely empty and I made a dash for it.

It was wonderful. The warm bubbles massaged my perennially sore 'traveller's back' and for five minutes I allowed myself to relax completely, eyes closed and head back, just soaking it all up. It was sheer bliss.

'*Monsieur? Excusez-moi?*' I was woken from my reverie as an elderly woman tried to step over me to get in and was signalling for me to move around. I did so and inadvertently let in a further four people. My solo jacuzzi paradise was immediately gone and I was now squashed in between the others, with all our feet touching each other's in the well in the middle! I refuse to get on cramped trains sometimes, so this was absolute hell. I also hate feet, yet someone else's toes – SOMEONE ELSE'S TOES – were on top of mine, leaving me paralysed and unable to move. I was in there nearly forty minutes, ramrod tense, until the others got out and I could finally get myself out too, by this time a wrinkled wreck and looking a very long way from the picture of health and happiness I'd seen in the brochure.

HARSH TREATMENTS

The dinner that night was magnificent. I don't know how many detox diets contain *déclinaison de foie gras aux poireaux et rhubarbe,* followed by *pomme de ris de veau aux pois gourmands et fondue de carottes de Créance,* but I'm all for it, and if detox also revolves around the hearty consumption of the sort of red wine that makes a grown man purr with delight then again, count me in. I mean it's entirely possible that I was ordering from the wrong menu, but people go on about the barren, cheerless austerity of dieting and detoxification, and the strict discipline involved – well they're clearly not doing it right and I expanded loquaciously on this theory to Natalie over the immaculate table. She quite rightly wasn't listening, her mind was elsewhere and I knew exactly where too. It was going to take more than a swim, sauna and a *baba poires au vin à la cannelle* to distract her from thoughts of Junior.

According to the vet, he'd developed something called equine exertional rhabdomyolysis or – wait for it – 'Monday morning disease'. Apparently, it's common not only with every human who has a proper job, but also working horses – or horses who have too much carbohydrate in their diet, or horses with a thyroid or reproductive hormonal imbalance, but which must be fairly rare in workshy geldings who stand around all day eating grass and hay, and whose only previous known activities were angry sex and a bellicose spirit.

He'd become a shadow of his former self and even (and this shows how unwell he was) seeking my company when I was in the paddock, nudging me and apparently looking for support. I'm no Doctor Doolittle, but the temptation to lean in close and tell him that this was penance for being an utter shit for most of his adult life was a strong one, but I was actually feeling quite sorry for him. He had been put on a course of medication, which hopefully would bring him physically back to his prime, but the mental scars from his usurpation by Ultime were going to take longer to heal. She had become almost wild in defending the goats, which meant that it had actually become unsafe to enter the paddock at times as she would come charging towards you, snorting her anger like some grudge-bearing rugby player.

The farrier had paid his regular visit and had said that this behaviour isn't uncommon among fillies at all, far from it. 'They turn,' he said wistfully, looking into the distance. 'You give them everything you have, and then bang! They want more...' Clearly no longer talking about female horses, we just left him to get on with things.

'We'll just have to see what happens,' Natalie had said when we were out of earshot of the farrier, 'but we can always send her back if she gets out of hand.'

'Really?' I asked, incredulous. 'But I thought we'd rescued her from an abattoir?' Natalie looked at me like I was insane.

'No! Do you ever listen? We're like a foster home for her, we don't own her. She can go back at any time if she gets too much for us.'

'Right. So who did we get from an abattoir then?'

She'd already gone, which was probably just as well as I'm pretty sure that 'abattoir' has been used as an excuse for taking on at least one other stray.

We talked about Junior and everything else over the meal, the chance to get away giving us the opportunity and the distance to do so, and then had an early night in preparation for our

HARSH TREATMENTS

'treatments' the next day, and also to sleep off my 'detox' indigestion.

Natalie had rather nervously ventured the question of whether I'd actually be able to 'control myself' during the massage, which will give you some idea of how little she thinks of me, but really, there was never any problem on that score.

It seemed to be a house rule that whether you were having a 'blissful full-body massage', 'a full cleansing facial' or just bobbing about in a flotation tank you would be subjected to Enya's *Greatest Hits* whether you liked it or not. I say 'hits', but surely she's only ever done one song and just managed to cleverly rename it ever since? As a result, although physically relaxed inside I was ready to punch walls as 'Sail away, sail away...' kept reverberating around my head for the next two days like a metal ball banging around in a pinball machine.

But the overall rest was magnificent. I don't de-stress well, if at all, but just two days in that detox–retox paradise was the tonic we both needed, giving us renewed energy to tackle home life again.

We woke on the Saturday morning, our last day, to a beautifully bright and clear view that went on for miles across the valley of La Creuse and the Limousin beyond that.

'You know what?' said Natalie wistfully, taking in the breathtaking sight. 'It's nice to see beautiful countryside and not feel I have to go and clear the poo up.'

Well, quite.

Unfortunately, Junior's condition hadn't improved any in our brief absence. The vet had recommended a course of treatment that, while initially giving him some sort of fillip, was now having no effect whatsoever, and in fact seemed to be making him worse.

I found him in the field one morning later that week, lying down on his haunches almost like he was crouching, surrounded by the seemingly worried goats, and he didn't look good. The whole tableau, especially with his long mane, actually made him look like the defeated Aslan surrounded by a host of Mr Tumnusses (Tumni?). I approached him gingerly and he bowed his head almost in supplication, his heavy breathing making great clouds in the frosty air. Despite his illness you could still sense his enormous power, but it seemed to be fading.

Strangely enough, Ultime was also lying down not too far away, but then she immediately shot up, whinnied and started prancing around like a dressage diva, clearly pleased with herself. Was she mocking him? Surely not? Yet it definitely seemed like that and Junior watched her coldly, but with resignation.

'We need to get the vet out again, I think,' I said to Natalie, though obviously she had already been on the case. Our usual vet unfortunately was taking a holiday for the new year in her native Belgium and, not only that, she was planning to sell up her practice and move back there for good! She had moved here at about the same time as us and, though very likeable, she was, I think, slightly mistrusted by a number of the locals, certainly the men who possibly didn't think a woman should be prodding about at livestock. She also had a very sinister monobrowed boyfriend who we hadn't actually seen for a few years, but who you knew was lurking in the surgery because of the pungent smell of his odious brand of cigarettes.

HARSH TREATMENTS

So, after eight years she was going back to Belgium. Obviously the almost full-time job of being personal physician to our fluctuating menagerie was paying so well she was planning to leave this rural backwater and head back to Brussels, where the only patients would be pampered, hand-bagged toy dogs carried by EU gravy-trainers. I felt slightly let down by this, I admit, but these things happen. I used to work quite regularly in Mumbai, where my presence practically built the empire of a local off-licence owner, probably putting his children through college, but then I stopped going to India and the man may be back now to knocking out homemade hooch for a couple of rupees. These things happen.

With our vet not being around it enabled us to get a guilt-free second opinion on Junior's plight, though Natalie was once again convinced that she had found the problem and that he was actually suffering from sand colic. In short, a horse chews down the grass so far that he takes in a mouth full of dirt each time, and with our soil being so sandy Natalie reasoned he was probably full of the stuff.

'Can't we just tip him up then?' I asked, hoping to save money on yet another vet house call. 'You know, like an egg timer?'

The new vet arrived after lunch and confidently beeped to drive her van through the gates and towards me, where I was tentatively holding the lead rope of a thankfully upright Junior. She stopped the van a few yards away, turned off the engine and this colossus emerged from the vehicle. I didn't honestly see how she would be able to fit back in; she towered over me and was far, far broader too. For a moment I thought it was Hagrid. I stole a quick glance at Junior and I swear I saw, for the first time, fear in his eyes.

'Daddy?' Maurice whispered at my side. 'Is she American?'

'Why?' I whispered back, unable to take my eyes off the giant.

'She's huge.'

I handed her the lead rope and she inspected Junior gently. It wasn't just her size, there was something about her manner as well; she instilled total confidence. She produced quite possibly the biggest pair of rubber gloves I have ever seen – seriously, I could have worn them as a gimp suit – and snapped them on with a sense of purpose that frankly terrified the lot of us.

Junior is a surly and, I think, ungrateful animal. I have shown him kindness in the past; I have fed and watered him only to be attacked, bitten and spat at for doing so, so how this woman got her huge fist and not inconsiderable forearm up the beast's backside is quite staggering. I mean, there was an initial recoiling obviously – he looked like Kenneth Williams being given a bed bath in *Carry On Again Doctor*, all teeth and flared nostrils – but largely, he just took it as she had a right good rummage about and a delve inside. She was in there for what seemed like a good five minutes and from a distance it must have looked like she was advertising an enormous oven glove, but Junior remained calm. Considering he once spat at me for giving him an apple, this was decidedly out of sorts.

She eventually brought her arm back out holding a massive lump of excrement and then proceeded to take off the glove, turning it inside out as she did so, so that the poo remained in the glove. Maurice and I were ready to vomit to be honest, but Natalie was making encouraging remarks as one poo-recovery expert to another is wont to do I guess. The vet then filled the glove with water and explained that as the mixture settled you'd see a base of sand form confirming indeed that it is sand colic. It was all very impressive I have to say but hanging the said glove on to the crossbar of Maurice's football goal was a bit much, though Maurice eyed it gleefully.

'Don't you dare!' I shouted at him as he prepared to take a potshot at the thing.

'But it's like having a goalkeeper...' he moaned, setting off all manner of Robert Green jokes in my head, though feel free to insert the rubbish goalkeeper of your choice into this simile.

'No!' I shouted again.

The vet carried on her work, taking blood samples and such, with Junior being as compliant as I've ever seen him and Ultime giving off from her paddock, no doubt jealous of all the attention. The vet said she'd get the samples analysed and be back in a couple of days with some medicine for the colic too, and with that she got back into her improbable vehicle and was off.

It was a brighter prognosis than we had dared hope for, so maybe the new year wasn't going to be as bleak as we had feared. We felt refreshed and energised, ready to tackle anything that was thrown at us. Nobody could get that rubber glove off the goal though; none of us had the stomach or indeed strength for that.

BULLIED GOAT GRUMP

I'm not naive enough to expect a fanfare, but after driving all night from Manchester to the Loire Valley in wintry conditions and after a few days away, I did expect one of them to at least stand up and go through the motions of a greeting. Granted, Natalie was clearly shattered and lying on the sofa, but the others might have made an effort.

'Hello Daddy!' said Samuel, cheerfully, though without taking his eyes from the recording of the previous night's generic emotionally blackmailing TV talent show, which they were all watching.

'Have you got a toy for me?' asked Thérence, hopefully, but again without looking up.

It was nearly midday, they were all still in their pyjamas. The fire wasn't built and the breakfast dishes were still on the dining table, with the cats hovering menacingly close for scraps. Clearly I'd been away too long and standards had slipped in my absence; slipped too far.

'Right,' I said decisively and putting my case down for emphasis. 'You lot get dressed while I go and get some kindling and logs.' Nobody moved, 'Come on! Chop, chop!'

BULLIED GOAT GRUMP

I went outside to gather the firewood; it was a beautiful, crisp winter's morning and, above all, it was peaceful. After the brouhaha with the local hunters we had briefly looked into moving. We'd even visited a house which from a distance looked perfect for us, but which turned out to be a former doctor's surgery and still contained some macabre-looking medical equipment, making the place feel more like a serial killer's lair. In truth, we had already come to the conclusion that we were staying put. The upheaval was just too daunting for a start; in the eight years we'd been here we had successfully managed to fill two huge buildings and all the outbuildings with, well, crap. But crap that will, I am reliably informed, be useful one day. Add to that all the animals as well and even moving house just 10 kilometres down the road would be like a cross between relocating an entire village and the circus coming to town.

But there was something else too; like a truce in a battle, the guns had stopped.

Not only had the hunters sensibly moved further away from us, which made a huge difference, but old Girresse was apparently being kept away from public view as well, clearly now regarded as something of a liability.

Neither of us had ever really had the stomach for a move, anyway. We love where we live and it would take more than a cranky old man of the soil to push us out of here now. I stopped and sucked in the clean, fresh – silent – air, an incongruous sight, still in my stage suit, shirt, tie and pocket handkerchief, and wandered good humouredly over to the goat pen.

'Morning, kids!' I hailed heartily, as I approached the pen searching for the still-nervous Popcorn and Chewbacca in the shadows of the stable. 'How's things with... what the bloody hell?'

For a moment I stood there, in shock, and then turned sharply and stormed back towards the house, giving it the full Yosemite Sam 'rassum frassum' under my breath. Natalie and the boys had barely moved in the intervening few minutes, though their television programme had been put on pause, my swift return clearly anticipated. None of them would catch my eye.

'I may be tired,' I began as calmly as I could, 'but I swear that when I left here just a couple of days ago, we only had the two goats.'

Silence.

'Goats. We had two. I just counted three.'

It took a few seconds and then the boys all began at once. It was the kind of thing you see in a 'family' film; the sweet, butter-wouldn't-melt-in-their-mouths Hollywood kids, all high-pitched self-justification trying to melt the heart of their cold, unfeeling work-away parent and all ending with a harmonised 'Can we keep him?' 'Can we keep him?' 'Can we keep him?' And which might very well work the first time, maybe even the second, but by my calculations this was now the fifteenth and it was wearing thin. I looked at Natalie who, as usual in these situations, had a 'I really had no choice' look on her face.

She also had a slight look of guilt too, though, like this addition was going to be harder to justify than most of the others. Natalie's teaching job meant two hours' driving a day and preparing English lessons for primary school children; it also meant that with me being away a lot she had a job, a zoo and three young boys to take care of. She was already tired and our recent conversations had been about her not having any time to herself, no chance to rest, too much on her plate, to which my response had been and I'm paraphrasing here, 'No! You don't say!' It also meant that Sundays were the only chance of a morning's rest; hence the rather louche setting when I'd arrived.

It hadn't been the easiest of starts to the new year anyway, as my right foot had stopped working. Well, it didn't actually stop working but I couldn't use the thing, the pain in the joints had suddenly, overnight, become unbearable and it swelled up to a non-loafer-fitting size, making walking virtually impossible and going out at all a complete no-no. None of which would have been too bad as I was at home when it flared up, Natalie was at work and the boys were all at school, so I'd just built a fire, put my elephantine foot on a cushion and settled down in front of the cricket, glad of the rest to be honest, even if it was medically induced.

As I'd settled down the phone rang but it was far enough away for me to not bother trying to get to it, yet close enough for me to hear the message. It was Samuel's *collège*, he had had another fall – this now being about the fifth since he'd started in September – and could I pick him up and take him to the doctor's? Not easily, I thought, but I'm nothing if not a trouper, and gamely hobbled to the car and drove to the *collège*. I was greeted at the school by Monsieur Pitou, who acts as a kind of office manager cum security guard for the school. French secondary schools and above employ a *conseiller principal d'éducation* and their role is a kind of logistical secretary, though as far as I can tell their main duty is to take the 'shout loudly at kids' burden off the teachers, presumably to protect their throats. Pitou in particular is like an army sergeant major, constantly barking at some poor victim, telling them either to hurry up or slow down. He's also a sceptical individual and he shook his head as he saw me hop through the car park and then continually hop back for my loafer as it kept falling off the foot I'd vainly stuck it on the end of.

'He falls over a lot your son,' he said as he shook my hand without warmth. By now I was sweating with the effort and pain and unable to form an articulate reply, but was able to wince when I saw Samuel, who had a ping-pong-ball-sized lump above his right eye.

'What's up with *you*?' he asked me, as I clung on to the furniture in the sick room trying to get my breath back and control the pain.

'You'll have to sign this form, Monsieur,' said Pitou, 'to show you are…' he looked me up and down contemptuously, 'to show you are… responsible.' He spat the word responsible out as if to say, 'Yeah, who are we kidding here?', but by now the pain was so bad I really felt he had a point, especially as I leant on Samuel to get back to the car.

As we sat in the packed doctor's waiting room, the other would-be patients eyed us suspiciously. Samuel's hair was covering his bruised lump so initially the old ladies were cooing at him and singing his praises as the kind of youth who'd accompany his old dad to the doctor's. Then he brushed back his hair to reveal his injury and they just assumed that we'd spent the morning kicking lumps out of each other and were, with our strange language and clothing, a new band of Roma, so they gave us a wide berth.

BULLIED GOAT GRUMP

The doctor examined Samuel thoroughly and in the end concluded that it was indeed just a bruise and that he needed to rest up. I, on the other hand, had weightier issues. 'Firstly,' he said, 'you have high blood pressure. Why do you think that is?'

'Erm, because I'm in agony, hopping around town wearing one shoe and have a son who looks like he's been in a car crash?' I ventured sarcastically.

'And,' he continued, ignoring me basically or not understanding my poor French accent, 'you have gout.'

Gout. Wow. Gout is one of those things that everyone thinks they know about – it conjures up images of dissolute aristocracy off their heads on port and servant-baiting. It's too much red wine, red meat and rich living. It's a payback illness. You've earned it and you deserve it.

'I think you've overindulged on white wine and chocolate,' said the doctor, who ever since my vasectomy request has decided that I'm not a real man anyway, and if I had gout then it was definitely of the 'lady' variety. 'White wine and chocolate,' he repeated, clearly convinced that I was just a rom-com boxset away from full sisterhood.

The truth is, tragically, that I had been drinking a lot of white wine and I'd also been going at the chocolate like rationing had just been stopped, so either he was spot on or this was denial on a national level and that in France a festive season of red wine, game meat and *foie gras* couldn't possibly be bad for you, certainly not gout-inducing.

This was all something of a blow frankly, not least because I simply don't have the footwear for gout. This may sound prissy but I'm deadly serious when I say that if I can't fit on a pair of shiny loafers I'm half the man I should be. There's a precedent for this. I broke my toe a few years back while away working. I call it a sporting injury if asked, but actually I slipped on the stairs at Natalie's parents' house celebrating England taking a wicket against India on the radio and ended up with my toes wrapped the wrong way around a balustrade. The wait in Crawley casualty was surprisingly short but I wish it hadn't been. The nurse, I could tell, didn't like me and delighted in showing me the X-ray of what looked like a completely severed toe.

'It needs righting,' she said, fingering it gently, 'putting back in place,' she added, making it sound like a threat. Her eyes then went cold and she looked at me like Kathy Bates looked at James Caan towards the end of *Misery* and yanked the toe roughly back into position.

It was a full five minutes before I stopped screaming, by which time she was writing up her notes.

'My ex was a mod,' she said bitterly, and then turned to look at me again. 'You won't be wearing winkle-pickers for a while, will you, sunbeam?'

The French doctor was more forgiving and gave me a pile of medicine to get me through the worst, but there was obviously going to have to be some lifestyle changes and a need to control my blood pressure. An extra goat, therefore, wasn't going to help. And it wasn't as if the multitude of animals we had were a work-free bed of roses – it wasn't just Junior that needed constant attention anymore but Tallulah too. In fact, she seemed to have flipped completely.

In *Blackadder* terms Tallulah had put some underpants on her head and was repeatedly squawking 'WIBBLE!' The hens had barely laid any eggs for a couple of months anyway and, frankly, were lucky to be with such a soft, non-French family, or they'd have been squashed into a large Le Creuset by this point.

Tallulah had taken to hiding in the bushes and then jumping out at unsuspecting passers-by. I was wheeling a barrowload of firewood and kindling back to the house one morning and all of a sudden she jumped out of a hedge, squawked at me in what appeared to be rather salty language and with her wings flapping aggressively, before suddenly stopping, folding back her wings, pausing briefly with embarrassment like she'd hassled the wrong person and disappearing back under the hedge again.

I wasn't the only one being singled out for this behaviour either, nor was it restricted to unsuspecting humans. Poor Toby got the fright of his life as he took what he thought would be a quiet, back-of-the-hedge morning dump, only to be scared witless as the mad old bird gave him exactly the same performance. He nearly jumped out of his skin and was practically constipated by nerves for a good couple of days afterwards.

As if this wasn't madness enough corpses had begun to mount up too, specifically pigeon corpses. I didn't realise just how many pigeons there were around here until their cadavers started piling up everywhere, but clearly they're as numerous as wildebeests on the Serengeti. One afternoon Natalie counted 12 dead pigeons, which had all appeared in the past 48 hours, all on the face of it the victims of different deaths. Some were decapitated, some were totally butchered and some had no discernible marks on them at all. We were investigating a particularly gruesome victim that Gigi had found by the well;

she seemed very proud to have found it and sat by us as we prodded the thing in lieu of a proper investigation. Suddenly Tallulah came charging out from behind a tree and practically knocked Gigi over before running off into the distance still screeching at the top of her voice. Maybe her insanity was more sinister than we had thought? Far from being some comically demented park flasher, she was actually capturing, torturing and murdering the local pigeon population, like some avian Jack the Ripper.

The point – and I was trying to make this as forcefully and lucidly as possible to my family, who obviously just wanted to get on and watch their programme – was that this was hardly the time to be adding to our burden. This new poor goat would probably have been better off where he was, was my thinking, before checking that he indeed was a 'he'. (I was willing to let the thing pass if it was a 'she' and I could have a go at making my own cheese.) It is a 'he', they confirmed.

How on earth had this happened? I launched into a plea and I could feel my blood pressure rising and my foot – all psychosomatic obviously – begin its Incredible Hulk transformation.

The story was simple. They were driving to the *boulangerie* when a local man had flagged them down and said he had a little goat that was being bullied by the other goats and 'COULD THEY HELP?' There you go. It happens all the time. You're driving along with bread on your mind and then some ornery old man of the soil pops up, shows a bit of leg on the roadside and the next thing you know, bang! You have a runt of a goat with esteem issues in the car boot. It goes relatively unreported this kind of thing – some people are unfortunate enough to live in areas where you can't walk down the street without your phone being stolen by some hooded youth, here it's elderly strangers foisting damaged livestock on you. It wasn't as if our record with goats was entirely blemish-free anyway, what with Toffee's disappearance still leaving its emotional mark. Maybe that's why they'd agreed to take it on.

'So, let me get this straight,' I said, my frustration mounting as I once again found myself fighting this losing battle. 'You've taken on a bullied goat, to place him with two bigger goats who are already being bullied by a horse that is itself being bullied.'

They all looked at me.

'What are we doing here, running some sort of bullying finishing school? I mean, is that it? Do we need fresh meat? What is this, Goat Gladiator?'

Again, silence.

'We really have…' I never reached the end of the sentence, as the boys started up again, the charade that I ever have a choice in these matters being played out to the end for the sake of form. So Bambi (I suspected they were really after a deer) stayed; another addition, another mouth to feed, another maladjusted animal to add to the list of needy cases that we've already rescued.

I picked up my case and hobbled towards the door. 'Where are you going, Daddy?' Maurice asked as they all settled down again.

'I'm going to stand by the roadside for a bit, maybe flag a car down, tell them *I'm* being bullied, hopefully find a new home.'

'Silly Daddy,' he said cheerfully, and un-paused the television.

It was beyond mayhem in my opinion. A few weeks earlier we had seriously considered, albeit under duress, moving house

C'EST LA VIE

and now we were building up the squad again. I just shook my head in disbelief, genuinely at a loss for words, utterly helpless and completely frustrated, thinking about turning straight round and getting back on the road again. A couple of weeks later, though, and I'd have given anything to be back there.

THE HOME GUARD

'Excuse me, do you have any Christmas puddings left?'

The rather startled woman working in the Sainsbury's bakery department looked me up and down, trying to gauge if I was winding her up.

'Christmas puddings? It's February, love. Are you late or early?'

It was a reasonable response to a question I didn't really want to ask frankly, and for two reasons: firstly, I pride myself on my supermarket shopping capabilities; my lists are in the same order as the shop layout (if it's a supermarket you've never been to before, do a recce first), I eschew offers of packing help, because nobody does it as well as me and I never ask an assistant for assistance because I have my shopping pride. Secondly, I'd been backed into a late-Christmas pudding corner and I was still confused as to how.

A few weeks before Christmas I was at home alone during the day, preparing for the onslaught of Christmas party gigs, when the doorbell rang, or at least the bell connected to the front gate.

That's actually quite a rarity, one of the many beauties of living in the middle of nowhere is that very few people come to your door at all, though of course it usually means that when the doorbell does actually ring it'll likely be an unwelcome call. Sometimes, it's a roaming gang of salesmen offering to scrape the moss off your roof or some such niche occupation or, on two occasions, a very attractive Swiss Jehovah's Witness, wandering around on her own through the Loire Valley, spreading a message that frankly nobody wanted to hear. So when the doorbell rings now, I run upstairs and peek through the window first to see if it's worth going to the gate at all or just to release the dogs.

As it was coming into the festive season, I thought that it was probably the postman with a parcel and I bounded out to the gate. It wasn't the postman.

Now, I am particular and fussy about clothing, I know that. There are rules I live by and, while I don't expect everybody else to reach those standards, I do expect certain basics to be adhered to. The very tall, grinning man standing at the gate talking to the dogs was wearing a turquoise shell suit, huge black slip-on shoes and, sitting improbably on his head, was a tiny purple bobble hat. Our paths wouldn't, in a just world, normally cross.

'You're the Englishman!' he said, somehow making his grin even wider revealing big gaps where there were once teeth, and holding out a huge hand.

I'll be honest, much as I was put off by the look of the man, and because of a lisp I was having difficulty following what he was saying, I am also at the lower end of show business and therefore needy enough to have felt flattered that I had apparently gained some local level of celebrity.

'I am the Englishman!' I said warmly, calling off the dogs in French with what I hoped also had a hint of landed gentry English 'poshness' about it.

We chatted for about ten minutes, well I say 'we' – he talked for about ten minutes and I occasionally offered a nod and a *'oui'*, *'non'* or *'c'est vrai?'*. Standard responses for someone who is not entirely sure of what is being said to him. His conversation was erratic, to say the least. My French has improved and I can, if I concentrate properly and if I don't daydream (which I do no matter what language is being spoken to me), hold a half-decent conversation. But throw in a few detailed non sequiturs and I'm constantly playing catch up.

He would begin with one topic, switch topic mid-sentence and then return to the original opening gambit. For example:

'I see Kate's pregnant, that's good news,' he began.

'Well...' I am no great royalist, but I try not to be a churl about it.

'And Depardieu!'

Eh? He's pregnant too? Forgetting the Kate pregnancy briefly, he then launched into the news that Depardieu, a local boy by the way, was leaving the country, 'with Bardot!' he added, though I must stress for rumour fans that they were apparently leaving separately.

It was difficult to keep up, but he also had immense charm and was obviously a genuinely nice man and an anglophone too, which while neither here nor there for me, was something he wanted to share and something which I warmed to. The perception is that the French have the same antipathy towards us as we have towards them, and they just don't. The Parisians do, but they're not proper French.

He kept saying it was a pleasure to meet me, shaking my hand and walking away towards his van, then he'd remember something else and the largely one-way conversation would start up again. Insurance companies, tax, caravans, a seemingly endless list of conversational subjects and then finally it seemed, he was spent, but no.

'I had completely forgotten why I came!' he said, slapping his forehead in standard slapstick style. 'I've never had an English Christmas pudding.'

He was obviously angling for me to get him one when I was next back in England, and the preamble about emigrating actors and royal pregnancies may have been a nervous ruse, but I doubt it. He was just a charming, but scatty individual. He began to stutter slightly and then he asked directly.

'Could you get me a Christmas pudding, please?' he made the request sound almost Uriah Heep-like.

'Of course!' I said. 'My pleasure.'

I was actually, before he'd called, writing out an immense shopping list for my two weeks in the UK. I was driving back in an empty car, but I would return with the kind of Christmas vittles that they just don't do in France: crackers, a box of Roses, water biscuits, Stilton, Celebrations, the usual crisps, brown rolls and, of course, Christmas puddings.

He was so grateful when I said yes, that somehow his grin got even bigger, and he pulled off his bobble hat and shook my hand again.

The first pudding transaction took place just before Christmas, again accompanied by a scatterbrained conversation, this time shifting from the weather to cherry brandy and that, I thought, would be it, but I was wrong. He returned after Christmas

THE HOME GUARD

with a bottle of expensive sweet white wine and effusive praise for the quality of the puddings (I hadn't skimped on quality).

'My father loved it!' he said, with a surprising intensity. 'Really loved it.' He obviously took his father's praise and happiness very seriously indeed, 'Really, really loved it.'

'That's good; I'm pleased,' I said, his passion somehow making his father's happiness my concern as well.

'It's his birthday in February...' he said, almost guiltily, catching my eye.

I looked at him, still not quite able to work him out and then I twigged. 'I'll see what I can do,' I said.

The Sainsbury's lady was still unconvinced about my motives.

'So, you haven't got any Christmas puddings then?' I asked, and for the first time noticed the shiny new rows of Easter eggs.

'No, love. Sorry. I've still got one at home from two years ago, you know!' She laughed at the thought.

'Really?' I said. 'How much do you want for it?'

She stopped laughing and walked away.

Oh well, I tried.

In truth, I was glad of the daytime conversation and an errand to occupy my time. I think, after three full and busy weeks away, I was beginning to go a little crazy. Any descent into madness would hardly involve a massive plummet for me, but by the end of this trip I was spending my days unshaven, shuffling around my in-laws' large, empty house in Crawley, in my pyjamas and refusing solids.

There's a reason why solitary confinement is a punishment, but normally being alone doesn't bother me – in fact, I'm quite good at it. Stand-up comedy is a lonely business; you write alone, you travel alone and you perform alone, therefore, if you do it for long enough you either become happy at being on your own or you were pretty much a loner to start with. When the media rakes over the aftermath of a serial killer or lunatic running amok with a gun, the phrases 'he kept himself to himself' and 'he was a loner' are always trotted out as character traits. Well, comedians have those traits too, so just be thankful we write jokes instead – and hecklers really should bear this knowledge in mind before they casually open their mouths in future.

But being good at being on your own is one thing; three weeks is a whole other proposition, especially when you have a family. It gets into your head that this is it, this is your future and those people you occasionally call or email are actually a mirage, not real at all. Professionally speaking, it was a great three weeks. What began unpromisingly with snow and the ensuing travel chaos turned out to be three weeks that included a number of corporate events and a sold-out weekend at the best comedy club in the world, The Comedy Store in London. There had also been a week in Cyprus doing the armed forces decompression gigs, including a high-profile one to members of a helicopter regiment as they returned home.

The decompression gigs in Cyprus, though, I found emotionally draining. The idea of decompression is that for all troops returning from 'theatre', Afghanistan and initially Iraq, there would be a 24-hour stop-off in Cyprus, a chance for the soldiers to let their hair down and get things out of their system before they go home. They spend a day at the beach, or play golf, or go horse riding and so on; they have a

THE HOME GUARD

barbecue and in the evening they have a show: two comedians and a band and their first alcohol – a limit of four cans – for six months or the duration of their tour. They are also briefed about what to expect when they get back home, such as the potential difficulties in adjusting to civilian life, and about how to deal with the very different change in their daily routine. Though not everyone wants to be there, they'd much rather go straight home, obviously, I have done a lot of these tours and the response is nearly always positive and makes a difference to the returning soldier.

They are humbling gigs and we, as 'entertainers', are looked after and paid for our work, but I personally find the gigs themselves very hard. I am not a rabble-rousing comedian, I don't do one-liners or filth, and though these armed forces gigs very rarely actually demand those skills, I find it hard not to go in with the mindset that I am out of my depth, way out of my comfort zone. I had always been nervous of these shows from when I first did them; there's a responsibility in these shows that a lot of gigs don't have and then, a few years ago an incident occurred which, while putting everything else into perspective, has affected my confidence ever since.

We had finished the show, performing at a packed-out event for 200 or more returning personnel happy to be on their way home. It was raucous, full of banter, nerve-wracking and hugely enjoyable. A young soldier came up to me after the show, behind the marquee where I was standing alone.

'I really enjoyed that,' he said, though he never took his eyes off the ground.

'I'm glad, thanks,' I replied. There was silence and he continued staring at the floor. 'You must be looking forward to getting back?' I'm not good at small talk, but this seemed like the obvious opener.

'Not really,' he said, and burst into tears, great big sobbing tears. I won't go into why or what had happened – there's a great need for privacy regarding each individual who goes through the decompression system, and sometimes emotion in these situations can just be all about relief, a very necessary comedown after months on high alert. He stopped crying before long and went to rejoin his mates, I think perhaps relieved to have got something off his chest.

I stayed there behind the marquee and then I burst into tears too. In many ways, what had just happened is exactly what decompression is all about, but I couldn't handle it; I'm not cut out for things like that. Heckle me and I'll deal with it, but I'm too soft off stage to cope with such things. I'm never a million miles from an emotional collapse anyway, but suddenly – and selfishly – *I* felt a long way from home, I thought about *my* children and I needed to see them, and Natalie too.

I didn't go out with the others after the show that night, I couldn't. In fact, every time I go back to Cyprus for decompression I think back to that incident. I am very grateful for the work and, like I say the gigs are humbling, but I find it difficult to relax there anymore; it's a week of draining high tension and emotional turmoil and always seems to be at a time when I'm away from home for a long period, which doesn't help. I rang Natalie from Cyprus after the show, relieved it was all over and needing the palate cleanser of home-life news. I got it in spades.

Natalie was in full-on Miss Marple mode and determined to solve the dead pigeon mystery. OK, it wasn't as if you had to wear a hard hat outdoors for fear of suddenly deceased falling birds, but the sinister appearance of dozens of pigeon corpses was nonetheless macabre and too disturbing to be ignored. As always, the internet is the first port of call for investigations of this kind and once you've managed to filter out the crackpot conspiracy theories – really, I don't think the CIA are all that fussed about the Loire Valley pigeon population – there were a number of potential explanations which we'd considered before I'd left.

Trichomoniasis, common in pigeons apparently, is related to the human STD of the same name, which suggests that pigeons, particularly the racing kind I suspect, are putting it about with wild abandon. There's a line in the Blur song 'Parklife' which implies that pigeons are highly sexed creatures, which is scant evidence on which to base what appeared to be some kind of epidemic granted, but, no pun intended, we were fumbling around in the dark here. Whatever it is it's fatal, but because most of the victims we had found were pretty mangled we couldn't gather the proof.

Natalie reported over the phone that the crows were attacking sluggish pigeons in mid-air, like a fighter plane skirmish, but again it couldn't account for the sheer volume of deaths. In the end though, it's not the internet that solves these mysteries, it's local knowledge, for which there is no substitute. If our two farmer neighbours play a good-cop, bad-cop routine, then Monsieur Rousseau is definitely the good cop. Natalie told me that he'd delivered the monthly hay and walked around the property with her, as intrigued and baffled by the avian carnage as we were. He even took a carcass away with him for further investigation. The next day Natalie phoned him again, there'd been another killing she said portentously. Rousseau didn't hesitate and brought round a local expert who, he said, would hopefully find an explanation.

He did too. According to this expert the fault lay with bad-cop Monsieur Girresse. It seems he had been lazy in preparing his fields and had left the corn stalks and some of the corn husks unploughed. We suspected this to have been deliberate, to provide 'sport' for his shooting parties, something for the specially bred pheasant cannon fodder to hide behind before being blasted apart. The problem, though, is that corn left in this state is poisonous to the pigeon; it expands in their gullet, leaves them unable to breathe and is therefore fatal.

'Ah,' said Monsieur Rousseau nervously, 'I'll have a word with Girresse, tell him to get it sorted out.'

Natalie and I talked about the likelihood of Girresse actually doing something about it and we reckoned the chances were between zero and 'you must be joking'. It was good to be in a position where we could finally laugh about that mad old man, a ridiculous brooding individual, whereas not so long ago we had felt genuinely threatened by him.

It was just good to talk to Natalie and the boys really; something we normally shy away from on these long trips, as it rarely actually helps and only makes the longing harder. But we seemed to be back on an even keel again after a tense couple of months, and it was lovely to hear all the chatter in the background. I couldn't wait to get home, and I kept telling myself – again something I don't do often enough – that I was very lucky to be doing so, because some don't have the choice.

SEUL MAN

Going home this time, however, wouldn't be the morale boost it normally was. Yes, I wanted to be home more than anything, but I also knew that when I got there Natalie and the boys would be on their way to England for a half-term break. We would literally be passing each other as I arrived home and they left for the dubious delights of Crawley. Once again, I was ruing what we had as a life as, in practical terms, in terms of actually spending time as a family, it didn't seem much of a life at all at present.

Obviously I was always going to miss Natalie and the boys while they were away, there's nothing new there, but it is very different when I'm at home and they're abroad. Yes, I miss them enormously, but it gives me the opportunity to get on with stuff other than winding up hotel receptionists or browsing TK Maxx for hours on end. And anyway, it was only really for three days, so like any good fusspot left to their own devices I'd written a list and was rather looking forward to it all – especially the meals. I could cook what *I* wanted to eat for a change, and not be subject to the confines of childish palates.

C'EST LA VIE

The drive back from Limoges airport was without incident; a lovely sunny evening, the cold wintry sun lighting up the beautiful Limousin countryside. I gently pootled along knowing, from expensive and painful experience, exactly where the speed cameras are located. I knew something was up, though, as soon as I got out of the car at the gate of the house, the amount of noise coming from the animals was like they were all being attacked at once.

First I noticed that Chewbacca, the most troublesome of the goats, had broken into the orchard where the hens also live. This meant the hens were making that low 'I don't like this' long clucking sound, exactly like the slow-motion parts of a Bruce Lee fight scene, but Chewbacca wasn't bothered in the slightest and was happily raiding their coop for any leftovers. Popcorn, a friendly but skittish goat, was attempting to mount Bambi, the small goat newcomer, in a highly forceful manner. I've no issue with goat gayness in the slightest, live and let live and all that, but no is no and Bambi didn't look like he had acquiesced at all. On seeing me, Popcorn dismounted and started running around bleating at the top of his voice the goat equivalent of 'Run, it's the Rozzers', which also disturbed Chewbacca who started doing the same.

It was not the gentle start to my few days alone that I had envisaged. I eventually managed to lure Chewbacca out of the orchard and back into his paddock, all the while trying not to snag my suit on a tree or tread in anything untoward.

That evening, despite everything, I dined heartily on pancetta-wrapped chicken breast with tarragon cream sauce and lemon couscous.

SEUL MAN

I woke early the next morning and began goat-proofing, or should I say, re-goat-proofing, the orchard fence. I hammered in dozens of tent pegs so that Chewbacca couldn't force his way under the wire meshing. It took hours in the freezing cold wind, and by lunchtime I could hardly move my fingers, but I stood for a while thawing out in front of a roaring log fire and felt relatively pleased with my work. I sat down to lunch and, almost as soon as I had, the doorbell rang. I sneaked a look out of the upstairs window to see who this heretic might be and recognised him immediately, the Christmas Pudding Man. He'd been badgering me almost constantly since the turn of the year about getting him a Christmas pudding from England for a party. I had told him that I would try and I had too, but with no success. Natalie had told him this already, but clearly he wasn't taking no for an answer. 'Sod him,' I thought. 'It's lunchtime; he can bloody wait!' He got back into his car and drove off and I went back to my lunch.

Then the phone rang. Again, for the same reason as you don't knock on anyone's door during repast, you don't ring them up either. I ignored it and allowed the answering machine to kick in.

'*Monsieur? Monsieur?*' said a voice, either unsure of answering machines or aware that I was there and just hiding. It was the Pudding Man again! He could only have driven about a hundred metres down the road before ringing! Again, I just ignored it.

Part of the routine I'd now set myself at home was an afternoon nap, which on the face of it might have been another sign of an early descent into age-related infirmity, but which was actually for the good of everyone. If I can rest at some point after lunch I will be less cantankerous by the evening;

I might also be able to stay up later and enjoy some quality time with Natalie after the boys had gone to bed and not, as had become increasingly the case, get tucked into bed by my youngest son. I think it's a good idea and I was determined to try the routine before the others returned and ruined it.

Fat chance.

I had maybe 20 minutes' sleep before the doorbell rang again and this time in my sleepy fog I went to answer it. It was the Christmas Pudding Man – again! Anyone would think I was supplying him with a necessary heroin fix.

I looked at him and didn't bother to hide my displeasure. I admonished him for disturbing me during my lunch and now my nap, but the irony of an Englishman telling off a Frenchman for not being French enough was lost on him and all he could say was, 'Do you like my car?' It was a Mini Cooper with a Union Jack roof. 'Very English!' he added smiling.

I didn't smile back. I wasn't having any of it. I explained that I couldn't get a Christmas pudding and his face fell. I don't think he actually believed me and he looked a little hurt, 'Come back in November,' I added tersely.

'OK,' he muttered and kicked at the ground like a little boy. Then he raised his head and beaming said, 'I've got scars!' and unzipped his tracksuit top to reveal a scar almost the length of my forearm. 'Heart bypass!' he said with real excitement, though I don't know how he expected me to respond.

'Maybe try the end of October?' I said, pathetically, but he wasn't finished yet.

'And I found your cat!' He ran over to his car and picked out Vespa from the backseat. A decidedly bemused-looking Vespa too who, if she had been lost, certainly wasn't aware of it.

SEUL MAN

'Late autumn, anyway,' I continued, wondering what else he would pluck from the air for this ridiculous haggle. He seemed happy with that though and left, leaving a bored Vespa in my arms. I don't think she had been lost at all, but if there was even the slightest chance that she had been, the Pudding Man had just saved my life.

That night I dined heartily on sautéed chorizo and noix de Saint-Jacques with a lamb's lettuce salad and raised a few glasses of local Vouvray to the Pudding Man.

I hadn't planned to get up as early as I did the next morning, Vouvray can do that to you, but something told me things weren't quite right. I went downstairs, almost collapsing at the stench coming from the cat litter tray, and saw that once again the Steve McQueen of the goat world was in the orchard and harassing fowl.

It was freezing and blowing a gale outside, and I was in my dressing gown, pyjamas and initially my oxblood tasselled loafers as I couldn't grab anything else. I ventured into the orchard and immediately slipped on a pile of chicken poo, so went back to the house and put on my wellington boots, my first pair since childhood and not exactly a well-received Christmas present, but a necessary one. This time Chewbacca seemed to anticipate my every move and would not, would not, go back under the fence. It took ages, my swearing volume going up at the same rate as my body temperature fell. At one point I even stopped and looked around for a lasso and then tutted at the lack of lasso-type equipment on offer. I mean, what was I thinking? I've never lassoed anything in my life! Like I would know where to start? I eventually cornered Chewbacca as he slid back beneath the fence he had crawled under and, as he did so, all in one move he took one last bite at the longer orchard grass, it was the goat equivalent of Indiana Jones just rescuing his hat in time.

Finally, I thought, and turned around just in time to see Gigi, who seemed to be regressing obedience-wise, scurrying across the terrace with one of my discarded loafers in her mouth.

'Nooooooo!' I wailed. 'You little shiiiiiiiiiiiit!' And went chasing after her.

I was seriously thinking that next time the animals could go to England instead, and we would all stay here and have a rest in their place, and I began to plan that evening's meal of orchard stuffed curried goat in a puppy jus, but first, again, I had to deal with the goat-proof, or rather non-goat-proof, fence. It was a long three days.

The second week of the February half-term, which is much longer in France so that people have time to ski as a family, was marked in our diaries in bright, red ink. In management speak we had a 'window' and it was 'ring fenced'. The boys would be away with Natalie's parents, and various other assorted aunts and cousins, holed up in a ski chalet somewhere in the Massif Central, while we, just Natalie and I, would have a week – a whole week – on our own. We were, to put it mildly, looking forward to it.

Plans had been made for doing bugger all. The odd long walk with the dogs here, an intimate candlelit dinner in a local restaurant there, making wild plans for the future and generally just relaxing in each other's company for a change. Cold days spent browsing antiques markets, long evenings just relaxing in front of a log fire…

In time-honoured cinematic cliché fashion this is now where you hear the soft, stirring strings of a romantic lullaby crudely interrupted by the violent scratch of a vinyl record.

It didn't happen.

We had planned to spend our week largely talking about what we were going to do with ourselves. We really were now in a position where we rarely saw each other at all. January and February had now become my busiest time of the year, but even when I was at home Natalie either had her teaching job in Châteauroux or was successfully building up her private lessons locally and also now running an English language club for adults in the area, putting our classroom, finally, to good use.

Their brief trip to England had put paid to such marital navel-gazing, however. Having gone to England ostensibly to see family, the trip had actually resulted in them piling themselves up with more germs than a dirty protest in a Beechams laboratory. First Samuel got sick, then Natalie and finally Thérence. Maurice doesn't get sick as such, that would get in the way of his constant need for physical exercise. It was obvious, therefore, when I met Natalie et al at the airport that 'our week' would be compromised somewhat. Samuel and Maurice were fine to still go away, but little Thérence definitely could not, though even as a three-year-old he was aware how much Natalie and I had been looking forward to some time alone together and was convinced that he would be packed off anyway. When we told him that no, he was definitely coming home with us he beamed a sickly smile of relief, like a Dickensian waif told that he'd been sprung from the workhouse. That may have been the week's high point.

C'EST LA VIE

I have to confess that one of the reasons for wanting Natalie home was that I could relinquish my farm duties. By the end of my time alone with the beasts a kind of uneasy truce had set in, but they were obviously missing her even more than I was. Chewbacca, while not actually managing to escape further, had taken to walking the entire length of the paddock fence and actually leaning into it hoping to find a weak spot, like a furtive thief trying car doors. Junior, now apparently recovered and back to his simmering, poisonous best was jostling me aggressively when I tried to feed him. The cats had decided that litter trays were obviously too bourgeois and now preferred rugs instead.

Natalie, though, was too ill on her return to deal with the animal upkeep, so the look of resentment that Junior gave me when I carried on feeding him, even though he knew Natalie was about, was positively evil. Then the snow fell. Three or four inches isn't much snow, obviously, but when one of your (forced) daily animal chores is horse poo collection, it's a definite hindrance. There's an art to horse-poo-picking-up and Natalie had given very clear instructions: which tools to use and which pile this week's collection needed to go on.

And so, with as much dignity as I could muster, every afternoon I was in the field digging out horse excrement from the snowdrifts and, croupier style, raking the stuff on to a shovel. The whole task is ignominious enough as it is but when the horses, working as a team, are literally dive-bombing you as you do it, it's also quite dangerous. Junior was definitely trying to tip me over, while Ultime would go charging around and then run straight at me, daring me to stand still instead of diving through the fence like a rodeo flunky. All the while

Natalie watched from the warmth of the lounge, grateful for my stepping into the breach no doubt, but also bewildered by my incompetence.

Even Toby, normally an oasis of good humour, was joining in the revolt. An evening glass of wine, thoroughly deserved I might add, had now become a target for his new party trick. I'd sit on the sofa, glass in hand and he'd creep up and 'nuzzle' my drinking arm therefore tipping the wine all over me. It was an act of pointless, wanton mischief, like coarse graffiti, and our relationship became somewhat strained.

The cats, while continuing to find increasingly more obvious places to defecate, had decided that the supermarket own-brand food that I bought in haste was beneath them and were permanently camped out in the kitchen demanding an upgrade. They were positively mutinous. Also, Flame appeared to have had a run-in with a barbed-wire fence and torn one of his ears in half down the middle from the top to the bottom; making it look like he had three ears and he seemed determined to live up to his new found ex-con looks by strutting about the place looking for trouble like a football hooligan. Vespa, normally placid, started whining at me whenever I turned the television off. She'd become addicted to the snooker and didn't take kindly to not seeing the end of the Judd Trump–Dominic Dale match in the Welsh Open. Gigi, seeing that the cats were on some kind of go-slow, was killing mice on their behalf and bringing the cadavers in with her of an evening.

In footballing terms I had, it seemed, 'lost the dressing room'. I had no authority whatsoever. I had a three-year-old who was obviously quite unwell and therefore stroppy with it and Natalie, equally unwell, had decided the only medicine that could possibly improve her health was to repeatedly watch a Take That live video, adding further to my woes.

I felt particularly betrayed by Junior, though. A few weeks earlier he'd been craving my support as his health deteriorated, now as his recovery gathered pace, it was like he was embarrassed by his weakness and was determined to make up for lost time. A month ago I had to help him up from the floor and felt, naively it seems, some warmth; this week I'd given him a wheelbarrow load of hay and he had tried to bite my arm off in response.

The talk in England was all about the 'horse meat' scandal, as it was, surprisingly, in France too, though with a subtle difference. Actually eating horse isn't the problem (though it very much is for Natalie) – far from it – it's all about the labelling. Horse is eaten with gusto in France, but they like it to be called horse, not beef; whereas in the UK there is some kind of taboo about eating horse – whatever it's called – and yet this from a nation that will happily eat 'saveloy', a meat product of indeterminable if not totally dubious origin. From my own point of view I have no idea how I would ever control Junior and Ultime, two of the most cantankerous equines ever to belligerently stomp the earth, if I couldn't occasionally threaten them with a visit from 'the Findus people'.

But it was by now becoming seriously unwise for anyone except Natalie to venture into their paddock, which made feeding them hay a tad difficult because of the electric fence. It was a necessary installation when we first got Junior, as he kept turning up on the doorstep in the middle of the night demanding food with menaces; in the intervening time however the voltage had to be increased, as subsequently the goats took over the mantel of Farmyard Escape Committee, until it stood at just under 'Texan State Penitentiary' wattage and crackled away in the background like Frankenstein's laboratory. It nearly killed me.

For some unknown reason I decided I had no need for the warmth of my parka, and so in an act of dress-down folly, one which won't be repeated, I had put on my denim jacket instead and gone outside to feed the angry throng. Natalie's instructions for feeding the horses were clear, before placing their feed buckets over the fence, TURN THE ELECTRIC FENCE OFF; I hadn't done so up to now, being taller than Natalie, and though I'd brushed the fence a few times the military outerwear Parka had obviously protected me against any shock. The denim jacket didn't, however, and the metal buttons on the breast pockets didn't help…

The pain was intense and in the brief throes of the violence I could almost picture myself, cartoon-style, as a glowing, throbbing skeleton. I was thrown about three metres across the ground, screaming. My chest felt like it might explode and my mouth had a taste of burnt coal, in fact everything seemed like it was just smouldering. The horses looked up from their buckets, then looked at each other as if to tut and then carried on eating.

I sat up, everything ached. I stood up, and immediately fell down again. I stayed sitting down for a good 20 minutes, trying to gather myself. I'd had a genuine escape, not only that but supposing the worst had happened? Natalie would have eventually dragged herself outside possibly when one of the animals looked a bit peckish and found me, insubstantially dressed in the thawing snow… Here lies Ian Moore, born in hope, died by nipple-button-pocket electrocution.

C'EST LA VIE

I felt peculiar for a good few days afterwards, my tooth fillings especially seemed to throb with pain. In cartoons or comics, of course, when such things happen to a fellow he's rewarded with some kind of superpower and goes on to fight crime and the like – not me. I sat on a train a few days later trundling through North Wales, convinced I could smell burning. I was surrounded by a large hen party, slurping vodka jellies through willy-shaped straws and planning their weekend around various levels of alcoholic oblivion.

In truth, it was just about the most peace I'd had all week. So much for my supposed bucolic idyll, some would say deathtrap – soon I'd be back working the late-night clubs again and standing up to random acts of travel bureaucracy unpleasantness, doing what I do best. In all the madness we hadn't had a chance to sit down and talk about our future, more specifically my future and how I was going to travel less and be at home more. But just for now, as I cocooned myself into music heaven, drowning out the banshee hen party, I was just happy to be away from electric fences and shoe-chewing puppies, it was good to get a bit of peace and quiet for a change.

FINDING YOUR VOICE

'Daddy, *please*, when can we go home?' Samuel pleaded, holding his hands across his stomach in time-honoured 'starving-waif' style, his grey hospital gown adding to the put-upon nineteenth-century orphan look he was trying to cultivate.

'We're seeing this thing through, son,' I responded strongly, though wilting myself. 'We've been here seven hours; I'm not going until you get the all-clear.'

It's not often I get a Saturday at home, and aside from the sheer unadulterated horror of Saturday evening television, it is a wondrous thing. A 'weekend' at home feels like a holiday, in some ways it is, but its rarity makes you appreciate that weekend even more. I hadn't banked on this, though.

The previous week Samuel had been rushed to the hospital with acute stomach pains, which turned out to be nothing more than severe constipation from a lack of fruit eating, something he gets from me, and a lack of fluid intake, which he certainly doesn't get from me. A week later the pains were back and it wasn't a blockage, something else was happening and he was in agony.

Now, I use the term 'agony' advisedly. Samuel has two main interests, his '*théâtre*' (acting lessons) and watching football on television, both of which mean he has a tendency, and the skill, to 'exaggerate' any physical complaint, but surely this was more than play acting.

Maurice is different. It's only when he stops moving that you know something is wrong. He'd had stomach aches too the previous week and in order to rule out appendicitis we'd taken him to see the doctor.

'It's nothing serious,' the doctor said, 'but he obviously has very fragile intestines, prone to acid build-up... exactly like you Monsieur,' he said to me over his glasses. I had my first stomach ulcer at the age of 15. I looked at Natalie who *again* had her 'he's taking after you' look on her face.

There's an ongoing inquest going on at home and has been almost since our first child was born. Firstly we are trying to determine exactly what my good points are and see if any of those, should they exist, have been passed on to any of my offspring. The signs aren't good. It's not just intestinal, lack of a rounded diet or mood swings, Thérence went through a stage of over-indulging in his favourite tipple and belligerently urinating on the floor, which also – and unfairly in my opinion – got chalked up as a Moore trait.

'So, are you in much pain?' I had asked redundantly, as Samuel flapped about on the lounge rug like a fish on dry land. His returning tears were enough confirmation. As our doctor was now on holiday one of us had to take him to casualty in the nearest local 'big' town, about half an hour away, and as the other option was lawn-mowing, horse and goat husbandry, and moving the un-ironed ironing from one room to another, it seemed like the easiest option.

I remember the casualty departments in the UK from my time as a weekend footballer and these overstretched, barely financed, rundown, half-forgotten hospital appendages tended just to be full of 'blokes', either suffering from some cut or sprain from ill-planned Saturday sport or just sobering up from the night before and realising they had a cut or sprain from an ill-planned Friday night. The common theme tended to be the discussion of car-parking charges, which united the room and is a clever, modern NHS tactic for distracting the patient. It helps save on anaesthetic.

There are no car-parking charges at French hospitals, and nor were there any queues, so Samuel, still doing his 'I've been shot in the stomach at close range' thing, was ushered straight through once I'd gone through the bureaucratic necessities. 'Are you his father?' 'How old is he?' 'Where was he born?' The answers to these questions were all on the *carte vitale* (health card) that I'd handed over to begin with, except the parental one which had to be asked a few times as, for one thing, I couldn't hear the woman because Samuel was by now giving it the full *Carmen* death scene, and, for another, she mumbled.

Everybody in the hospital seemed to mumble. Everyone. My French has improved, I've worked hard on it, but some people seem determined *not* to be understood, the French medical fraternity especially. Is this the result of a more litigious public? I don't know. But it's like there may be hidden cameras around and they don't want any legally qualified lip-readers literally putting words in their mouths, but it's hugely frustrating, especially as I was, rarely for me, feeling confident about my French.

I had been working in Antibes, in the south of France, all week and though the gigs themselves were in English we, my colleague and I, stayed with the French wife of a friend and their son, and

C'EST LA VIE

I got plenty of opportunity to show off my French skills which were, much to my surprise, complimented, boosting my fragile confidence no end to the extent that I even did a couple of well-received jokes in French during one of the shows.

I hadn't been to Antibes since I was 21. At that time I was an unhappy person, troubled and lacking any self-belief. I'd just graduated, and I mean just, the last six months of my degree course a blur as I failed to make any lectures that coincided with pub opening hours. I had no idea what to do with myself. I wanted to work in film and television, starting off as a runner, but no-one would give me the chance because I didn't have 'experience'. 'Really?' I asked, increasingly frustrated at job interviews with what I saw as a closed world. 'But I've made tea before.'

We were staying in La Turbie at the time, which is in the hills just behind Monte Carlo and which I've been told is now Monaco's premier dogging site, but we went to Antibes ostensibly so that my stepmother, one of thousands ripped off by the late Robert Maxwell's laissez-faire attitude to other people's pensions, could hurl abuse at his huge yacht which was still moored there. I've said before that I love a port. The sense of possibility, of another world, anonymity, of even running away always gets me, but on that holiday especially it seemed to offer a solution, a way out of my then depressing world and into a newer, more exciting one. I trawled the yachting job centres, answered adverts pinned on café walls, even walked gang planks brazenly asking for a job. Nothing. Again, I 'didn't have the experience.'

All of this came flooding back to me in Antibes. The audiences were largely made up of exactly the young, yachting type that

I'd so desperately wanted to be, and whereas I think once I may have resented their bronzed, smiling faces, I didn't have a sense of that at all. Maybe I'm mellowing, but I felt almost paternalistic towards them, envying their lifestyle yes but genuinely hoping that they were enjoying it too and inevitably wondering what kind of life I'd be leading now if I had had that opportunity. Of course, there's always the possibility that I wouldn't have lasted five minutes, that the first time someone had tried to insist on me wearing a 'fleece' I'd have been off, back to the world of sartorial enlightenment. I don't know, though.

Anyway, mumbling is one of the issues I have with languages, the other is concentration and I realised that while this nurse in front of me was saying something incoherent I'd been away daydreaming again about Antibean port ramparts! The mumbling nurse gave way to a mumbling doctor and, I'll be honest, Samuel had to help me out at times not just because his French is *parfait* but his hearing is better. Poor Samuel. The ignominy of the arse-bearing hospital gown was bad enough, but he was prodded and poked and pulled about. Early on we went for a *radiographie* which revealed he had a lot of *gaz*.

'On a scale of one to ten Samuel, how bad is the pain?' asked the doctor.

'Nine and a half,' croaked Samuel, gripping his deathbed.

'Really?!' said the doctor, for once not mumbling. 'Then we need blood tests,' he added.

Samuel looked at me, his bottom lip wobbling, 'He says we need blood tests, Daddy! Please no!' I knew that's what the doctor had ordered, secretly I was very happy with my ability to cope linguistically thus far, what I wasn't prepared for was being told that we'd have to wait in the hospital for another three hours for the results to come back.

'Really?' I asked. 'We wait here?'

'Of course,' said the nurse like I was an idiot for asking, 'we don't know what the problem is yet.'

You hear horror stories of people waiting in casualty, particularly from the British press: MADE TO WAIT ON A BED IN THE CORRIDOR! is the most often stated hyperbole. At least you're on a bed and in the right place! It's not like you've been stuck in a skip outside the library for crying out loud, and as the *urgences* department began to fill up it was clear that more room was needed for more urgent cases. This was lunchtime in France, one can only imagine the kitchen-based accidents taking place up and down the country as people tried to live up to their culinary heritage.

'I've been here since five a.m.!' shouted the woman in the corridor on the trolley next to Samuel's.

'She says she's been here since…' began Samuel.

'I know,' I said, 'five a.m.'

I really was beginning to feel on top of the whole thing, but boredom was setting in for both of us.

Lunchtime passed and Samuel was refused food until they could determine his ailment, and I was refused too out of some parental solidarity, something which I was perfectly willing to forego frankly. It became clear that the old woman's conversation was limited solely to the 5 a.m. diatribe, and thankfully we were moved back into our room where boredom once again took root.

'Let's play hangman!' I said, trying to change the mood.

It became clear after ten minutes of pretty much a one-subject game – the answers were 'BLOOD/TESTS', 'BORING', 'STARVATION', 'SANDWICH' and 'CUTE/NURSE' – this wasn't the distraction I'd hoped it would be. Then, four hours after the blood tests the doctor and a consultant came in. This looked serious.

'Yes, hello!' thundered the consultant, for once a non-mumbler.

'Wrong room,' said the doctor, and off they went.

'Daddy,' said Samuel, 'please go and find out what's going on.'

He was right, it was time to be proactive and by now my confidence in my French was such that I felt able to do it. I found CUTE/NURSE and was told that the results had arrived and the doctor would be with us shortly.

'Mmm...' said the disappointed doctor into his shirt collar, 'these show nothing.'

'Great!' said Samuel, hopping off his bed. 'We'll go then.'

The doctor, for all his mumbling and laid-back attitude was having none of it.

'Echographie!' he declared.

It was now 5 p.m. and we'd been there since 10.30 a.m., we were both starving and had seen numerous shift changes.

'I'll book you an appointment!' the doctor announced triumphantly.

We waited another hour before Samuel was finally wheeled in for his *échographie*, by now his stomach pain had changed he said, it was now acute malnutrition. The *échographiste* was an elegant lady from somewhere in Eastern Europe (seriously why people moan about an 'influx' of Eastern European immigrants is beyond me, they keep us soppy Westerners from completely falling apart). Her French was impeccable and, as a 'foreigner' she enunciated every word clearly and perfectly. I understood everything, she guided us through the whole of Samuel's stomach and intestine area, and it was a pleasure not just to listen to her but to understand her. Initially I had felt like I was the wrong parent for this hospital vigil but I didn't feel like that anymore.

'And the problem,' she continued eloquently, 'is these *ganglions* here. You see these *ganglions*. They're *ganglions*.'

'*Ganglions*,' I said to Samuel knowingly. 'You know what *ganglions* are?'

'No,' he said, mesmerised by the screen like an expectant mother.

And that's the thing – neither did I. We'd been there nearly eight hours and the whole crux, the entire *raison d'être* boiled down to this one piece of vocabulary.

Ganglions.

'Ah,' said the doctor, the length of his shift and certainty of diagnosis bringing him out of himself. '*Ganglions*.'

Armed with a prescription that was now useless until Monday morning, Samuel and I made our way home via the *boulangerie*.

'Well...' Natalie said on our return, desperate for news as I'd accidently left my phone at home and Samuel's had run out of battery. 'Is it serious? How is he?'

'*Ganglions*,' we both said in unison.

'*Ganglions*?' she asked. 'What's that?' Frankly we were rather banking on her knowing the answer to that.

I was trying my best with French, I was 'making the effort' as they say, but when an entire day is reduced to one bloody word

FINDING YOUR VOICE

that even someone fluent in the language hasn't heard before, what sweet chance in the name of buggery do I have? I thought I had the situation licked, I thought I was in control, but in the end it was just one missed word and I felt deflated.

Ganglions, it turns out, are lymph glands, and Samuel's were infected and swollen in his stomach, like an internal glandular fever. It's not terribly serious, though, it may flare up at any time. But I took the whole thing as a bit of a blow. Just the one word I kept repeating to myself needlessly, 'I'll never be fluent in French.' It was a self-pitying whine really and Samuel was having none of it, 'You don't know all the words in English, doesn't mean you're not fluent.' He was right of course, and self-assured enough to say so too; and it did help, especially when I found out *ganglions* means pretty much the same in English!

Samuel, now 12, seemed to have pretty strong ideas about most things already, and he wasn't afraid to express them. People who know me may be surprised to learn that actually I don't like confrontation all that much, unless it's a battle I actually want to fight; most of the time I'm just nodding at what people say to me, not through tacit agreement but because I'm probably not actually listening. Maybe it's an age thing, but I just don't have the energy to jump all over every statement that I disagree with – and I disagree with a lot – but then, I'm not 12.

'He needs to find his voice' is one of those comedian sayings that old hands come out with in the dressing room when confronted by the threat of a talented open spot, or newcomer. In short, it means you have to work out your 'stage persona' so that your performance is consistent. It sounds like utter nonsense, but there is a ring of truth to it even though it only really crops up when old hacks, like me, are asked for advice by newcomers – which we hate.

'You've got some nice stuff,' we'll say sagely, 'but you need to find your voice.' It's our way of saying 'Please leave me alone.'

I always found that the best comedians were those who knew who they were off stage, they'd 'found their voice' in life and so the performance was just an extension of that, and it showed in how natural their stand-up was. Some people have a natural confidence, most comedians certainly do not.

Samuel's confidence was causing problems though, not at home where open discussion is actively encouraged (unless I'm tired), but at school, where articulate and enthusiastic debate apparently needs to be quashed before it can turn into dangerous intellectualism. I know, in France of all places!

Samuel had just had his second-term school reports and, while the marks were very good, his *comportement* (behaviour) had been called into question. The teachers, and it seemed to be pretty much all of them, were full of praise for his willingness to help others but he also had, they choroused, a cocky streak; he doesn't suffer fools gladly, he has a sharp tongue and can be quite moody. Natalie read all this out and peered at me over the damning document, again the 'Moore' traits being held responsible.

'I wonder where he gets *that* from?!' she snorted.

The teachers' main gripe though wasn't this side to his behaviour at all but his enthusiasm, which he certainly didn't get from me. He's always putting his hand up, one said. He's always got the answer, said another. The maths teacher was apparently so exasperated that he'd threatened to ban Samuel from his class unless he stopped calling out the answers. Yeah, it must be really hard having pupils take an interest in class, what you really want as a teacher is a bunch of violent crayon-chewers at the back who'll just let you get on with your job and not worry too much about being educated. What an absurd complaint! What am I supposed to do, tell him off?

'What's all this, Samuel? Good marks, intelligence, taking an active interest in the learning process – I'm really disappointed in you, son.'

He has opinions and he's not afraid to share them, but by far his biggest bugbear is languages and he's become something of a purist.

We were watching the lunchtime news and in a report on something or other, I can't remember what exactly, it's French lunchtime news though so it would have been food related, the correspondent used terms like *'le packaging'* and *'le marketing'*. Samuel went apoplectic, a full-on meltdown railing against the laziness and stupidity of using Franglais. I've pointed out to him on numerous occasions just how many French words there are in English, 'nuance', 'gaffe', 'suave' and so on, but no, the lad insists on very clear linguistic demarcation lines and is prepared to throw a right old wobbly to argue his case. It was magnificent stuff and I felt quite proud of him, actually. Passion for language in one so young is a good thing in my opinion, a full-on hissy fit is even better, but as the tantrum went on Natalie just peered at me again with her 'he's taking after you again' look on her face.

I seemed to be copping an awful lot of flak here, it struck me that if there is anything that goes wrong anywhere in the Loire

Valley then the fault will lie somewhere between my character flaws and the local Romany, we get the blame for everything.

Saturday evenings at home follow a pattern at this time of year; firstly watch *The Voice* (UK version) and then switch over and watch *The Voice*, pronounced *Ze Voice* (French version). *Ze Voice* just sends Samuel off on one again. What has him jumping up and down at *Ze Voice* though is the use of English by the judges. It's constant and it winds him up magnificently. At the sing-off stage of the show the contestants go into battle with each other singing the same song, so you would expect to hear French expressions like *se battre* and *la bataille*. No. In this episode I was forced to watch one of the judges (Florent Pagny, a French musician and actor who looks like an ageing Musketeer) tells one of his duelling pairs that he felt they were ready to '*bien vous* fighter *pendant la* battle'. The presenter of the show then introduces each sing-off with the same expression: '*Que la* battle *commence!*'

And this has Samuel screaming at the television, 'Why can't they get their own bloody language?'

It doesn't annoy me quite so much obviously, I like to think the French are trying to be so accommodating with me and my own struggle to speak their language that they are, as a nation, all learning English to make it easier for me to get by. In England, if you drop French into a sentence, for example, 'Do what you want, I give you *carte blanche*' you are deemed somewhat pretentious. In France, if you drop English into your sentence, simple words like 'yes' and 'news' are now becoming commonplace, you are either cool or guilty of dumbing the nation down, depending on which generation you are talking to.

FINDING YOUR VOICE

Thankfully I'm not at home much on a Saturday as I just can't contain my own *comportement* while this dross is on, but basically the differences in the two versions are these. *The Voice* is certainly of a higher singing standard than *Ze Voice* and has an interplay between the judges which is playful and tongue in cheek. *Ze Voice* is utterly po-faced and takes itself oh-so seriously. That is essentially the difference between the French and the English though, why is there no historical culture of stand-up in France? Because they don't know how to laugh at themselves.

I was expounding on this theory after Samuel's weekly meltdown, giving full vent to my theories on stand up and the difference between the two nations and how they regard themselves, and no doubt I was doing so with typical, post-dinner pomposity and certainly not expecting anybody to actually listen.

'Why don't you do it here, Daddy?' asked Maurice innocently.

'Well, because I...' I spluttered, suddenly flustered.

'It means that you'd be here more, closer to us,' Samuel added.

From the mouths of babes, they say, and for some reason they went running off. Natalie looked at me, 'It would help your French,' she said, trying to make it sound like my French didn't actually need help, although we both knew the reality.

'It's not that simple,' I began. And the room waited for me to explain why it wasn't that simple.

'It could make a huge difference to the amount you travel.'

'Daddy! Daddy!' Maurice and Samuel came running back down the stairs. 'There's a comedy show in London in June IN

C'EST LA VIE

FRENCH!' They screamed in unison having just googled me into a corner, 'You could do that!'

Suddenly my stomach hurt, I was sure I could feel a *ganglion* coming on.

NO PAIN, NO GAIN

I made it very clear when we got the goats that I was dead against the idea; they would be trouble, I said. Mark my words, I said, no good will come of it, I said. They are, it hasn't and Samuel's 'Please, Daddy' promises about looking after 'his' goats on a daily basis turned out to be only so much goat poop. They seemed to be taking up far too much time for starters, and I didn't actually think they were very nice animals. One of them had headbutted Vespa one morning leaving her visibly dazed, and this was following the traumatic removal of a tick so large it looked like she was wearing a hearing aid. Chewbacca especially, the least sociable of the goats, was an increasing problem.

Monday is my weekend. I rarely sleep on a Saturday night because of travel, so I go to bed early on a Sunday night when I get home, lie in on the Monday and laze about while Natalie is at work and the boys are all at school. I don't answer the phone or the door. It's 'me time' and I guard it preciously, even if it rarely actually goes to plan. Thérence, though, his cold having lasted almost as long as winter itself, was unwell again

C'EST LA VIE

so he stayed at home with me. Then I got a call from Samuel's *collège* late morning, saying that once again he had fallen over on his head, and on an old scar too (as if there are now any scar-free areas) and was complaining of dizziness. He needed to come home they said.

It felt like a conspiracy, especially after the previous Monday's efforts...

'Come on! Get up! You're going to be late!'

At first, as Natalie sadistically opened the shutters I thought it was a dream. Get up? Monday morning? Are you sure? 'Come on!' she repeated urgently. Far from being allowed to gently recover from yet more sleep deprivation I had, it turned out, been 'volunteered'. I was due at Thérence's school for 8.30 a.m. to 'help out'.

'Help out with what?' I asked still half asleep. 'Surely they can eat their own plasticine? What do they need me for?'

Apparently it was the annual *défilé*, a procession around town featuring the youngest pupils from the primary school, all in various fancy-dress costumes and Natalie had, in a fit of guilt that she couldn't actually be there herself, volunteered my services as a general fancy-dress dresser, walker, holder of hands and traffic cop; forgetting of course that I have almost as much patience with four- and five-year-old children as I do with escaping goats.

It looked like a riot in the wardrobe department of a heavily dwarf-based pantomime. Of about a hundred children there were probably thirty Spider-Men, including a couple of girls, which is either progressive or the direct result of lazy parenting and an older brother; there were also about fifty princesses, some who'd been really dolled up as if for one of those sinister beauty pageants for little girls in the United States. There were also a lot of tears being shed and much crying at an alarming pitch. Thérence, I noticed, was keeping his own counsel in the corner, his Yoda costume lending him a gravitas that the proceedings desperately needed.

I entered the room nervously and stood out like a... well like a Yoda in a Spider-Man/princess mash up to be honest. In a sop to what I hoped was finally spring, I had on a light, 'Michael Caine in *The Ipcress File* mac', grey dogstooth trousers and a pair of Loake Chelsea boots. 'Glad you've made the effort,' said Thérence's teacher, looking me up and down. 'Now, put this on.' It was a bright yellow high-vis jacket that made me look like I was off to fight the Cold War, but only within the allowable parameters of health and safety. It all added to my discomfiture as I was not only separated from Thérence but had a Spider-Man on one side and a princess with a serious mucus problem on the other.

The first stop in the procession was the next school up, Maurice's school. Unfortunately he wasn't there as he was away on a school trip, some of his footballing friends were though.

'Look at Maurice's dad!' they said pointing; clearly my costume was getting more attention than any of the kids'. 'What's he supposed to be?'

The next school on the route was a good five-minute walk away and as we wound our way around the streets we were accompanied by the only other male who'd 'volunteered' and he got to carry the music. Once, of course, someone would have played an instrument on one of these jaunts, but this was an enormous, 1980s-style ghetto blaster and was being used to pollute the quiet morning with some appallingly inappropriate instrumental music: 'Ride of the Valkyries' to start us off and, at one point, incongruously, 'The Stripper'.

The bigger school was waiting for us and the children were already lined up in the playground opposite as we entered. It looked like the start of a battle, a *Raggedy Rawney*-style army of nine-year-olds about to unleash hell on the midget Spider–princess people from the other valley; Thérence, ever sensitive to these things, stepped forward from our group and administered some pretty aggressive lightsaber manoeuvres in their direction, which seemed to break the ice a little.

It was getting colder and the children were feeling it. Fortunately, Natalie had insisted that Thérence wear his coat under his Jedi Master garb, but some of the princesses in particular were suffering and, as princesses do, weren't keeping it to themselves. Even the Spider-Men were feeling the chill. One, even smaller than Thérence and incongruously wearing a cast and an arm sling, ran into the *boulangerie* and refused to come out, the warmth of the place offering succour to the poor, shivering crime-fighting mite.

On we went, a bizarre sight, wending our way through the town stopping startled passers-by and getting them to dance. This wasn't my job, I hasten to add, this was the role of people who'd helpfully brought along a large dollop of brio and had seemingly left their dignity in a jar by the door, 'Eleanor Rigby'-style. My job was to stand at the back, frown a bit and give the whole thing a bit of a moody presence, which otherwise it would have lacked. I watched the teachers and some of the mums frolicking about to the music, obviously enjoying it far more than the freezing kids, and wondered what on earth this whole thing was in aid of. Was it a charity thing? I had no idea, and this was my third tour of duty. I had been roped into something, surrounded by whooping, swirling apparently drug-free adults all dressed as tits, frankly, and nobody seemed to be collecting any money at all. Utter madness.

Then we stopped at the *mairie* so that the 'press' could take pictures. Just as I was about to sneak off to a camera-shy corner, Thérence's teacher once again collared me and gave me a huge bag of confetti. For the past 20 minutes the kids had been docile, rendered inactive by plummeting temperatures and skimpy costumes, but blimey, you show a bag of confetti to a French kid and all hell breaks loose. I stood there for a second with the bag and there was a brief pause. Then all of a sudden it was like holding a bag of chips on Brighton beach and they swooped like hungry seagulls. I got covered in the stuff, which of course only added to my overall merriment and only fuelled their spirit, as what seemed like a Lilliputian Mardi Gras kicked off.

Finally, warmed up and spent, we moved off to our final stop, *la maison de retraite*. The old folk, and I mean old, had been wheeled out in their beds and wheelchairs to view this vivid, bizarre procession as it snaked slowly around their TV room. Some of the people were barely conscious, some clearly resentful of any whiff of youth and all as befuddled by the exercise as I was. The children recognised the change in mood; for some it must have been utterly terrifying, as they would suddenly be grabbed by bony, yellow hands and cuddled against their will. In order to keep the children's spirits up in this heavy atmosphere, they had been promised sweets, but it didn't help.

This final visit did appear to be the sole purpose of the event, though, and for that I suppose it can't be knocked. The local schools are very much a part of the community here, teachers and education respected as they should be. What might seem a little old fashioned in the UK is everyday life in France; children are to be seen and to be seen enjoying themselves too, and even an old cynic like me thinks that's a good thing. Having said that, as we finally made it back to school there was a lot of tiredness, frozen hands, hunger and quite a few tears. The kids seemed fine, however.

A week later and it looked like this Monday was going to be hijacked too, by child illnesses. Samuel was gingerly lying down on the sofa and groaning, Thérence was streaming with a cold, but not groaning, and then the doorbell rang.

'What now?!' I yelled as the dogs went berserk at the front gate. Maybe the new suit I'd ordered from Italy had arrived, so I allowed myself a brief moment of optimism and went to answer the bell. It was a young man with very definite Parisian looks.

'*Bonjour*,' he said, a tad warily I thought, 'erm, have you lost a goat?'

I sighed heavily and let my head drop. 'I don't know,' I answered resignedly, 'possibly.'

The man had come from our immediate neighbour, Madame LeBoeuf, an old lady of 90-plus years who values her roses even above her independence and who had instructed one of her visiting grandsons to see if I'd mislaid any livestock. I followed the man next door and there indeed was Chewbacca munching perilously close to the young rose bushes. The young man was joined by his brother, who may even have been his twin, and then they both looked at me. As Parisians they were clearly unsuited to the task of goat recovery and in seeking help next door I think they'd expected to find a man of the soil, a handy goat man, not a dandy in Prince of Wales check trousers, a cravat and tan Church's brogues.

For an hour I tried to trap that goat, an hour. I tried tempting him with food, I tried lassoing him with a dog lead, having practised since the last time, and I tried shouting obscenities at him, but I couldn't get near him. At one point he ran close by and I tried to rugby-tackle him, missed and hit the driveway pretty hard. I lay there for a minute to gather my thoughts.

'Are you OK?' asked one of the brothers.

'No,' I said. 'I think I've torn my trousers.'

It had all begun in standard comic fashion. We had, all three of us, tried trapping Chewbacca or grabbing him as he sped past, but it had got beyond a joke and the Parisians, now chain-smoking, were seriously wondering if it would ever end and whether in fact I had any plans for catching Chewbacca at all beyond waiting for his eventual death from old age. I had no plan – that was obvious.

'Have you got a gun?' I asked, only half jokingly.

'No,' they replied rapidly and in unison, not seeing the humour and seriously worrying for their grandmother's safety with this strangely dressed nut-job living next door. I think by this point even Chewbacca was getting bored. I couldn't contain myself any longer – my shoes were a muddied mess, my trousers were ripped at the knee and in a fit of genuine anger I tore off my cravat, folded it into my pocket and then, as the goat made another flypast, I howled in primeval anger and took a flying leap at him. I landed on him, put my arms around him and rolled a few yards with him in my clutches, finally coming to a stop dangerously near to the precious roses. The two men stared in disbelief, their cigarettes hanging from their open mouths.

I stood up, still hugging a shocked Chewbacca. 'Open the gate!' I demanded, choosing loud orders over genuine composure. I carried a stunned Chewbacca back round to our house and fortunately he didn't struggle in my arms, or I wouldn't have been able to hold him. I even managed to open the stable door with one arm and hold him with the other; from a short distance we must have looked like a really angry ventriloquist and his dummy. I threw him into the stable, swore at him again and locked him in.

Even after dinner that night I hadn't calmed down. Maurice had come home from his school trip feeling sick, making the place look like a children's ward, and I was now limping after damaging my knee, which I had done, I pointed out to Natalie and Samuel, while ripping my trousers, while catching your bloody goat! I was laying it on thick, that's for sure, but I was very annoyed.

'Maybe it will help you get fit?' ventured Samuel, unusually timidly.

'Lose a bit of weight...' added Maurice, pushing it further.

'Fatty boom-boom!' shouted Thérence insultingly and prodding my stomach.

Natalie was silent.

Now, there are many good reasons to my mind why the French word for bread is *pain*. There's the serious chance of gum damage from some of the more fashionable and rustic 'newer' breads like the *croquise*; you could easily batter someone to death with a three-day-old baguette and, because the stuff is so, so tasty, the resulting weight issues from three-times-a-day consumption cause genuine discomfort.

OK, fair enough; it's not just the bread. There's wine and cheese too, lots of the stuff. Every day. And now, even when I'm away from home working, I've started hunting out French restaurants and patisseries to fill the temporary gap. It used to be that when I was away I'd deliberately eat the kind of things I couldn't get in France, like fish and chips, cheap sausages, carveries and the like. Now I ponce around markets looking for decent goat's cheese, choosing my wine not by price and ease of opening, but by grape, region and year.

My 'gout' if indeed that's what it was (though I remained sceptical) had thankfully not reappeared, even though I hadn't really changed my diet, but undeniably, and this is something that occurs about this time every year when the winter jumpers come off and the extra 'bulk' is more visible, I needed to exercise. The other option of course would be to cut down on my bread/cheese/wine axis-of-evil consumption, but firstly what would be the point in living in one of the richest gastronomical areas of the world if I did that, and secondly, I like them too much. Exercise really was the only way forward. Two years ago I had been a 30-inch waist; I was now a 34, which is just about the mod-1960s-Italian-cut-suit limit.

I gave up football when I was 24 and that was the last exercise I did with any regularity at all, and I gave up that because my body, made more for the arts I feel, couldn't take the strain of 90 minutes of running around once a week. I could consider cycling, but since old Monsieur Girresse had threatened to shoot any member of my family who trespassed on his land, it seemed a risky venture. I bought one of those elastic exercise rope things, which came with a huge set of instructions, and set off one weekend optimistically thinking that I would spend my downtime not in a pub for once, but in various positions and stretching various muscles and 'feeling good about myself', which seems to be the exerciser's cliché of choice. I didn't. Even though I was on my own in my hotel room doing all these stretches, pulls and jumps, I got so embarrassed that I couldn't carry on.

My embarrassment may have had something to do with the fact that I didn't own any gym wear. I had a T-shirt on, but I don't own sports shorts, tracksuit bottoms or anything like that; clothing shouldn't have an elasticated waist in my opinion, so I was just in my pants and in the mirror I looked like a sexual deviant trying some new flamboyant onanistic contraption.

What I needed was an exercise regime that didn't threaten either my dignity or my wardrobe, and modern technology was literally at hand. I started playing the Wii. The tennis game on the Wii, according to my brief internet research, is a decent calorie burner, as is the boxing, and so I'd taken to spending an hour a day getting all sweaty playing both. To be honest, I do more tennis than boxing. The boxing game, while clearly more exacting and therefore beneficial, kept randomly choosing women characters as my opponents and it just felt wrong to be trying to knock them out. The tennis on the other hand I seem to be really good at, so it ticked all the right boxes.

What this form of exercise, in fact any form of exercise, offered was a decent excuse not to be doing any real work. By now I really should have been making a proper effort to write a stand-up set in French, or at least book a French-language gig but, I argued, I wasn't gigging anywhere in any language if I couldn't fit into my trousers.

Natalie watched me for a while as I was trying to show off. 'Your opponents don't seem to be very good,' she said.

'Yeah, or…' I hesitated while theatrically gathering my breath, 'maybe I'm great.'

She wasn't falling for that. When we first met I had told Natalie that I'd actually won Junior Wimbledon and she'd believed me. For about five years in those pre-Google days she'd believed me. She's believed nothing I've said ever since.

Samuel was doing his homework on the kitchen table and, without saying anything, wandered over, took the Wii remote from my hand and pressed a few buttons. I started my next match and didn't win a point.

'What have you done?' I whined.

'You were on the easiest setting, it was too easy for you,' he replied.

'But it's no fun anymore.' I stropped and turned the thing off.

I went over to the kitchen and was faced by 'this month's' culinary tradition, France really doesn't let up on these things, the annual *boulangerie* delicacy of *pâté de Pâques*, or Easter pastry. The *pâté de Pâques* is a cross between a Scotch egg and a sausage roll and it's absolutely gorgeous; high-quality meat topped with hard-boiled egg, wrapped in deliciously light pastry and about a metre long sitting on top of the *boulangerie* counter asking you, almost coquettishly, how many slices you want. It's around for about a month and I can't resist the stuff.

I guiltily picked up a not-insignificant slice and bit into it, noticing that everyone was staring at me as I did so.

'You won't be fit enough to catch goats if you keep eating things like that!' said Maurice.

'Every cloud, Maurice...' I said, 'every cloud.'

CROSS WORDS

It could be argued that my expanding girth – and let's keep these things in proportion, I kept reminding people, 'I am still fairly slender' – was the result of contentment. I was busy; Natalie was busy too; her lessons had taken off to the extent that fitting them all in had become an issue, financially we were back in the black following the sinking, hopefully temporarily, of Les Champs Créatifs and though my stand-up debut in French was a constant 'back-of-the-mind niggle', it wasn't until November, so there was plenty of leeway there. And it was spring too – anything seems possible in the spring.

In *The Moon's a Balloon*, David Niven quotes a Chinese proverb, 'When everything in the garden is at its most beautiful, an ill wind blows the seeds of weeds and suddenly, when least expected, all is ugliness.' In other words, my contentment didn't last long and I can pinpoint the exact moment when rural living, once again, rose up, teeth bared and took a whacking great lump out of my backside.

I had reinstalled the well pump after its necessary winter hibernation and, for the first time ever, had managed it in one go and with no recourse to visit, and revisit, Pascal at the local *quincaillerie* (hardware store cum handyman advice centre) for parts, tools, non-shorn piping and a shoulder to cry on. Even Manuel was impressed. This year it had taken 20 minutes.

It lasted two days.

The well pump is vital. For most of the year it feeds water all around the property from the stables to the allotment to the swimming pool; there is a vast, subterranean network of pipes and hoses, so when the pump fails to retain its pressure the fear is always that somewhere underground there is a leak and then we would be in serious trouble.

Getting the pump to work is a matter of rewiring, replumbing, repressurising and, hopefully, rejoicing when the water eventually comes gushing out of the top of the thing like we've struck oil. I get drenched in the process, the children laugh and winter is declared officially over. But after two days it broke down, and though water was still reaching far-flung taps and irrigation systems, the pump was straining to do its job and not holding the pressure. I set about the thing with sweary abandon, isolating this and tweaking that, so that every half an hour or so we had the gushing fountain, the soaking dad and the giggling kids. This is all very well if it happens once or twice, but after about eight times the humour leaves the situation entirely and the kids see their dad in a pitiful cycle of sodden pain, anger and misery that will stay with them always. Like *You've Been Framed* on repeat, it's not funny anymore, just cruel.

On top of this, the goats, en masse this time, had broken into the orchard *again* and my good humour was now completely spent. I was ready to sell up and move into a bedsit on my own somewhere that would at least promise running water and a livestock-free fruit bowl. Natalie was too busy to deal with the goats, as she was at that moment helping the vet file Junior's teeth, and I don't mean alphabetise them and store them away. There was an ominous silence coming from where I thought there should be lots of neighing and admonishing, but when I rounded the corner I could see why. The vet, in truth larger than either of the horses, had attached Junior to what looked like an equine harmonica holder, but which held his lips back and opened his mouth at the same time. It was a fearful contraption, and while she set about Junior's teeth with what looked like a pneumatic drill Natalie was trying her best to hold Junior back and his tongue to one side, even though the livid beast had been sedated. She was, in truth, struggling to do so and Junior, not used to such ignominy, was staring wild-eyed at the vet as though the minute he was released he was going to tear her apart.

When I appeared, soaking wet and apparently covered in sopping rust, his demeanour changed and rather than the maniacal, swivel-eyed look he was giving the vet he stared at me instead in a much calmer, much colder way. I've seen documentaries about how former Heavyweight Boxing World Champion Mike Tyson used to effectively beat his opponents before a punch had been thrown just with the steely-eyed, murderous stare he gave them when they entered the ring; it was like that, and I decided to back away and deal with the goats myself before I was roped in to separate Junior and the vet.

I had to stop the goats from getting into the orchard somehow. Once again this spring I had been looking forward to the start of the chutney season, which traditionally begins with the cherries in May, and eventually finishes with the medlar fruit in late November. I had bought hundreds of mini, hotel-sized 'breakfast' jars, I bought some nice paisley material to use on the jar lids and a new set of labels all ready for this year's La Maison Moore chutney production, and I was desperate to get started. I still, even now, have some in stock from previous years, but when I hand them out to people they read the label and then look at me and say things like, 'Oh, that's lovely, thanks. January 2010 you made this, yes? Erm, is it still edible?'

It's still perfectly OK to eat, the jars are always sterilised and are either completely airtight or have a special paraffin seal. These things will last forever, they'd survive a nuclear attack, but in this day and age where even 'natural bottled water' and yoghurts, yoghurts for Heaven's sake, have best before dates, handing over a jar of chutney that's a few years old is greeted with a suspicious look and the obvious misgiving that you might be trying to poison the recipient. Cherry production, for the first time in a couple of years had gone well, though, and it was good to be back in the fruit business again. In the previous few springs I'd been like the eponymous character Jean de Florette in Marcel Pagnol's novel, stomping confusedly around my produce willing it to grow and unable to understand why it wouldn't, and all the time my family watching me, eager for things to turn around for me, but deep down feeling that I was doomed to failure. Well, this year seemed to be different and I wasn't going to let a load of hairy-arsed goats ruin it for me.

My much-vaunted chutney business had suffered miserably because of the now apparently annually atrocious spring weather. There have been no cherries because early spring was too cold, then it's been too wet for the plums; the quince tree seemed to go on strike last year in protest, the pear and walnut trees didn't look well and Junior, just to cement his place at the top of the Spiteful Horse rankings, like it was ever in doubt and despite him still being obviously some way from full fitness, had eaten my apple trees. Eaten my apple trees. He knows full well it makes him ill, but he does it anyway because severe colic is a small price to pay if it goes some way towards ruining my life.

When the weather is bad in the UK I'm often asked if 'it's as bad where you live?' I say asked – it's never really a question in the proper sense, but more a plea for confirmation; that while the UK's weather did its usual post-apocalyptic thing and clouds continued to gather like angry mobs on a street corner, all violent energy and aggression, there was somewhere – not too far away – where the sun was busy getting its thing on. More often than not I'm honest enough to admit that no, the weather is pretty dreadful at home in France too and this will be met with a sad shake of the head and a doleful look in the eyes as if this is indeed 'the end of days'. Sometimes the pleas for a better weather report are so desperate that I don't have the heart to be honest and just offer an 'oh yes, it's glorious' instead, not wishing to heap misery upon misery. The truth though, is that while the UK was being battered senseless by endless storms and rain, France was too, but it was slightly warmer which was sending the garden into full-on triffid mode.

The result of this climatic- and equine-inspired mayhem was that I had been bereft of fruit. We'd planted a fig tree but it was as yet too small for any decent produce, and in the autumn we planned to plant some more apple and pear trees, which

I will defend viciously. But it's in spring that I need the stuff. Chutney making is not just a hobby, it's my get-out, my escape. Standing vacantly over a boiling pot of fruit, wine vinegar and various spices, churning away absent-mindedly with my wooden spoon, helps the relentless self-absorption of stand-up comedy. If you stand next to me while I'm stirring a pan of nascent chutney, it would be like holding a shell up to your ear, you'd hear a light zephyr and soft rolling waves, there is nothing going on in my head. Nothing at all – and it's joyful.

I wasn't in the mood for goats, anyway. I'd arrived back home early that morning from one night in London where I had been to see the much-vaunted stand-up comedy show in French at The Comedy Store. It's a show they put on twice a year, French comedians are taken over to London and they perform to an audience of French expats and assorted Francophones. It was sold out, about four hundred and fifty people, and was a far more raucous affair than I'd expected, though I don't know why I'd expected anything else. There isn't much of a stand-up circuit as such in France, there's no tradition of it like there is in the UK, but that's all changing. In a similar way to how rap grew from the ghettos to the suburbs in the US, stand-up in France is growing at a pace from the *banlieue* of the bigger French cities and being driven largely by ethnic minorities, particularly those of North African descent, who feel disenfranchised from 'the system' as it is, and who are using stand-up to get their message across; to have their voices heard. To a fan of the simple concept of stand-up comedy, or humour as a tool of expression, it's very exciting and has a raw, edgy quality to it that perhaps has been mainly lost in British stand-up comedy since the 'alternative comedy' of the early 1980s. But exciting, raw and challenging are all very well from the cold-eyed observer; from the point of view of 'man in suit using barely passable second language to get foreigners to laugh' it was seriously daunting and quite, quite worrying. A lot of work would need to be done.

I had gone to London just for the one night and had not slept for nearly thirty hours, and though I can normally manage this in some kind of good-ish humour, Poitiers airport left its mark on my return. The ticket machine for the car park was *en panne* (out of order) as usual, so I had to queue to pay at the electronic barrier where there wasn't an official car park attendant but an opportunistic tramp who was putting the tickets in the machine for each driver while expecting some recompense. I don't actually mind things like this; my car is right-hand drive and the barrier designed for a left-hand drive, so it should help to smooth the process. The tramp though was in an even worse mood than me.

'Why have you got the ticket in your mouth you idiot?' he barked at me. 'It's a magnetic strip! You'll break it!'

'What?!' I started, a bit taken aback.

'Take it out of your mouth! It won't work!'

'Sod off!' I responded and proceeded to stretch myself across the passenger seat in order to cut him out of the entire process.

'Well, it won't work!' he said again. 'Idiot!'

He was wrong, it did work, but as I managed to try and sit back upright without pulling a hernia, stare him down triumphantly and give him the finger at the same time, my foot slipped and the car went careering off on to a verge, narrowly missing a fence post as I grappled with the steering wheel and slammed the horn for some reason. I drove off with as much dignity as I could, as the tramp, disappearing in my rear-view mirror, shook his head like he'd known all along that that would happen.

I knew then it would be a long day, and now with the pump playing up and the goats playing out it was getting longer. In truth, we had tried to re-home Chewbacca. He was the worst of the goats and we suspected him of leading the other two astray, maybe that's what you get when you name an animal after a rebellious, gun-toting Wookiee, but there had been only two responses to our adverts (pleas), both from people we suspected of being possible suppliers to the 'value, frozen beef burger' market. The goat vet in Valençay was unsurprised by this lack of interest; we even asked if *he* knew anyone who needed a goat.

'Ha! You must be joking!' he laughed. 'Goats are monumental pains in the arse – everyone knows that.' And he's a goat vet! He's supposed to be a fan.

It had reached the point where we could not countenance spending any more money on goat security, but if we could just get rid of Chewbacca, the obvious ringleader, then we felt the others would behave. It wasn't looking like a likely prospect, though, and I approached the raided orchard with a weary sense of déjà vu, chuntering loudly about exactly what I'd like to see happen to Chewbacca. Toby had taken himself off somewhere when the vet arrived suspecting that he was in for a good seeing-to no doubt, but he now reappeared and with a prize.

On close inspection it turned out to be the lower leg of a deer, but for one glorious moment I thought Toby, not hitherto known for his intelligence, had taken my angry rants and performed a drunken knight, Thomas Becket 'will no-one rid me of this turbulent priest' scenario and solved the escaping goat problem by simply disabling the creature in the same way that a cyclist might remove his front wheel.

'Good boy,' I said, 'good boy. Well, it's an idea, old son…' Man I was tired.

It just seemed to be one of those days, even a simple shopping trip with Samuel had proved more problematic than usual. The alarm from the checkout till security 'gates' went off the second I went near it. By now I had been up for a full day and a half and the loudly beeping alarm startled me, shaking me awake. It's the kind of gate alarm system that's usually kept by shop doorways, but our local supermarket has them on every till and they're more sensitive than a hormonal teenager with a skin complaint. I made a big show of emptying the bags in front of the checkout assistant who eyed me sceptically. Samuel was with me too and he could see that already, only five seconds into this confrontation, I was losing my temper.

'And your pockets, Monsieur?' said the assistant and I threw down my wallet, some loose change, a tube ticket and, adding to the assistant's suspicion, a sachet of tomato ketchup. 'Try and pass through again please,' she ordered.

I did and the alarm went off again. She stared at me, trying to figure out where I'd hidden whatever it was I was trying to steal.

'Maybe it's your machine?' I said angrily, while Samuel backed away quite obviously thinking that my shaking anger was caused solely by rage and not exhaustion. She asked her colleague for help while the entire shop gathered to stare at me. I had put my arms up and by now was talking loudly, proclaiming my innocence.

'Is that a new shirt?' said the colleague suspiciously and clearly thinking I'd grabbed it off the shelf.

'This?' I said, very close to losing it. It's one thing to be accused of stealing but the idea that I might wear supermarket clothing was frankly beyond the pale. 'This is a limited edition, Paul Weller-designed Fred Perry shirt, that is at least six years old.'

'Your shoes, then? Maybe there is still a tag in there from when you bought them?' Her tone had become more conciliatory, she clearly didn't want a showdown with an angry mod so she was now making a play about 'having to do her job'.

'No,' I said and ostentatiously placed my feet, one after the other and with scant regard for hygiene on to the till packing area.

'Your trousers?' she said nervously.

'You want to check?' I shouted, while beginning to unbuckle my belt.

It looked like the poor woman was about to scream and the manager was called. Though the alarm issue wasn't solved, he obviously just wanted me to go, as did Samuel, who, for the most part, had been hiding behind the photo booth curtain as a lot of his friends' mothers had day jobs in the place. The manager was equally suspicious of me, but without a full-on strip search, something I was perfectly prepared to do as long as it was carried out at the till itself, he had no choice but to let me go, even though he kept looking like he had, Columbo-style, one more question to ask. I have to say, and much to Samuel's surprise, the whole thing cheered me up enormously.

'Why are you smiling?' he asked. 'Do you like arguing that much?'

'No Samuel. Not at all. But I just had that argument *in French!*' Maybe this gig wouldn't be completely beyond my capabilities after all.

BEYOND *REPAS*

I walked past a collection of deserted bikes and scooters towards the house. I knew Natalie and the boys weren't going to be there; Natalie's sister and our two nephews were staying, so they'd gone out for the day. Their plan had been to go to the zoo, but not only was it too cold, they'd also reckoned, probably correctly, that most of the exotic species would refuse to come out and remain indoors in something of a mood. Instead, they'd gone to a big, indoor soft play area about an hour away which, when it's full, is exactly like the zoo anyway. Well, the chimp house at least.

Natalie's sister and her boys were over to celebrate Maurice's birthday (he was turning eight), which is always a momentous occasion because, as Maurice was born shortly after we moved here, it signifies just how long we've been in France. When we'd moved in on a glorious winter's day in January, the place had looked very different indeed. The gravel was pristine, for a start; the vast garden was just two acres of sparse lawn with some young, spindly fruit trees to break it up and there was only our Jack Russell running around the place. Now, eight years on, and in the middle of the worst spring in living memory, it looked like a cross between a pebble-dashed rainforest floor and a city farm.

Junior's initial excitement that someone had returned home and therefore he would be fed quickly subsided into contempt when he saw it was me, and he went back to angrily snorting at the world.

I began to tidy up as soon as I got inside the house, which was a pointless exercise, even more than usual, as the next day would be Maurice's party and an industrial-sized tidying up operation would be necessary after that. Normally I dread his annual birthday party, but I felt quite sanguine about this one, tiredness partly but also I was pretty thoroughly prepared too. I had vittles.

I had been offered a lucrative gig at short notice for the previous Saturday night which everybody, seeing as it was Saturday, was only too happy for me to take as I was a serious barrier to their Saturday evening television enjoyment, but in an act of foolhardy bravado I decided to drive there and back overnight.

In total I drove for about seventeen hours, was 'at work' for about two and a half hours and spent 45 minutes in a mad supermarket sweep around Waitrose in Esher; the main purpose of driving being to fill the car with 'provisions'. Provisions? You may ask incredulously – you live in the Loire Valley, man, you have some of the world's finest cuisine on your doorstep; some of the world's most celebrated wines produced within spitting distance; award-winning goat's cheese made literally next door; what can you possibly need from England that you can't get there? Well look, I love French cuisine, I love its sauces, its textures, its flavours, its importance and its sociability. When I'm away I miss the smell of a *boulangerie* in the morning, the 'saving some room for cheese'-sized main course portions, the acceptability of wine at midday. I love real cassoulet, homemade tarte tatin and even the ethically reprehensible foie gras. But the one thing that the French, with their rich culinary history and Michelin stars, have never got right, the one thing in which they lag woefully behind, is crisps.

As usual I had my timetable worked out down to the last minute: leave home at 8.50 a.m. local time, hopefully get to the Eurotunnel for around 2 p.m. and arrive in the UK at about 1.30 p.m.. I allowed an hour and a half to get to the gig at Sandown Racecourse, where I had a call-time for 4 p.m., giving me an hour somewhere in the Sandown vicinity to track down and raid a supermarket. Everything went like clockwork, there was the odd snarl up on the *périphérique* around Paris, but I'd factored in contingency time so I still had a good forty-five minutes at the supermarket. Only I couldn't find a supermarket, I wanted a big, out-of-town supermarket; the kind that has ripped the heart out of the British town centre, but could I find one? I was badly eating into my 'food'-buying time when I spotted the aforementioned Waitrose on Esher High Street.

I know people who swear by Waitrose – I did when I lived in England; its quality and its freshness they opine, its range. Well that's all very well and obviously a good thing, but if what you're after is the baser elements on the culinary food chain then its smaller stores can be a sad let-down frankly, the Esher branch especially. Nestled in the High Street, the store is neither one thing nor the other: it's too big to be a corner shop and too small to be a modern, behemoth superstore. I'll concede that with the necessary constraints of space, coupled with the demands of the Esher public, knowing what to stock must be a delicate balance, but for my purposes they had got it sadly wrong. It was very busy and I appeared to be upsetting the natural order of things by going the wrong way down certain aisles, swimming against the Esher tide, as it were, and drawing the kind of approbation normally reserved for more serious transgressions. Nobody actually said anything to me, but there was an awful lot of tutting going on.

I just couldn't find what I was looking for: the crisp section was lamentably underwhelming, taking up a tiny portion of the shop – the size of an area normally reserved for the Loyd Grossman cooking sauce range in any sensible establishment. This can't be it? I thought, and went careering around the shop again assuming that I'd missed something. My local French supermarket is very parochial, the range on offer quite narrow – you'd be hard pressed to find non-French wines, say – but I think if the regulars of my local Super U were to be dropped into Waitrose Esher they wouldn't have a clue where they were. If in my trolley dash I'd been looking for antipasti, black linguine, my local goat's cheese (four times the price of home), various naan breads, myriad packets of flavoured couscous, pawpaw, and the world's largest and most pointless collection of aged balsamic vinegars I'd have struck gold, and of course if I lived in Esher I'd be very happy that I had access to such a wide range of world foods. But I wasn't and I don't; I wanted Wotsits and my time was running out.

Eventually I had to ask an assistant if they sold multipacks of Wotsits, he looked down his nose witheringly as if I'd just sneezed all over the dried apricot section, and informed me that 'No, sir, we do not.' I filled my trolley with Skips, Twiglets and Quavers, the latter a poor Wotsits substitute in my book, a few token biscuits of various colours and made my way to the till, defeated. The boys, I thought, would be very disappointed.

It was 4.30 a.m. when I finally got home and, bleary-eyed, dumped the shopping on the table and went to bed, exhausted. Normally the boys leave me until whenever it is I wake up, knowing that I'm a moody so-and-so at the best of times so it's wise to let me get whatever sleep I can, but they woke me quite early on that Sunday morning by jumping on the bed in unison and screaming 'Daddy, Daddy, did you bring all that stuff back? It's like Christmas!'

'It's like Christmas?'

Really? Well this Christmas would be a much cheaper affair then – no more games consoles or iPads for you boys, just biscuits and crisps. English snacks and E-numbers are hugely popular at children's parties here, thanks to our culinary pioneering, and Maurice's party was a huge success. I settled back into a garden chair as the dust settled and the last of the children left, tired yet contented.

'Daddy...' Maurice said, as I closed my eyes to the warm evening sun.

'Yes, birthday boy,' I replied.

'Did you let the goats into the orchard?'

There's always something isn't there?

The goats, Chewbacca *again*, seemed to be able to escape at will and actually, once having done so, then panicked and yearned to be locked up again, more comfortable in familiar surroundings. As such, desperate times called for desperate measures, and it was decided that the electric tape that currently keeps the horses in check should be lowered to protect the goats from themselves and their permanently itchy feet.

The process of actually doing this was fairly straightforward; Natalie and I had become dab hands at the logistics of animal imprisonment, even if the results, in practice, are decidedly patchy. The only potential problem was that Junior, plainly under the weather again with what had now been diagnosed as a muscle-wasting disease, had decided to fight his physical travails with typical belligerence and springtime aggression. So while I was screwing the brackets for the electric tape into the fence posts, Junior was doing something similar to Ultime just a few yards behind me, and deliberately trying to catch my eye while doing so.

I ignored the angry beast and just got on with my work. Having completed the re-electrification it was time to test the thing; the time-honoured standard procedure for this is to get a piece of grass and touch the tape with it, the resulting shock will show whether it's working or not. But you know what? I'd had enough. So often had I had to go through this rigmarole over the years – I have developed a tic to prove it – that I just couldn't face it anymore. I came out in a cold sweat at the prospect, I started stammering with fear. The pain is short-lived but intense, the charge remember is set at a level to deter a horse, a charge far, far higher than most effete English mods can handle, and as Natalie didn't fancy testing it either we decided to just turn the thing on and see what occurred.

What occurred was flying goats. Not literally, of course, but each one of the goats got one blast from the horse-charged fence, was thrown back a few yards and didn't go near the fence again, for a bit anyway. Could it be? Could it really be?

That the great goat–man stand-off was at an end. If so then it was for the benefit of everyone.

Natalie's parents had made it clear that unless the goat problem was solved they would, quite rightly, not be keen to housesit the place for us in the summer when we wanted to go on holiday. These goats had driven a wedge between this family that could be solved only if they'd just stay in their ample bloody field and, though it was early days, the signs were encouraging and that this new system might just work. Occasionally, one would hear a goat that had drifted too close to the electrics but they quickly recovered. Let me make it clear we hadn't suddenly got goats being flung across the place like the weapons of a siege army throwing livestock at a battlement. They seemed genuinely happier, though with their eyes the wrong way up (as all goat eyes are) it was difficult to tell exactly what they're thinking. Inscrutable creatures.

Emboldened by this rare foray into outdoor work, I set about trying to repair the results of the endless spring rain – in short de-weeding 200 square metres of gravel driveway. It used to be that we could put weedkiller down, but as the hens had taken 'free range' to mean 'go where the bloody hell they like' this was no longer an option. Natalie kept trying to convince me that we should allow most of the area to go fallow and therefore provide further grazing ground, but seeing as this seemed to increase the chances of acquiring further semi-domesticated animals or worse, deliberately letting the now re-imprisoned goats out, I wasn't having any of it. I am, I admit, a petty man, but a driveway is a driveway and seeing as we had moved here partly because I'd never had a driveway I wasn't letting it go, and I attacked the place with gusto wielding my hoe like a madman.

I have my standards, as Maurice's schoolteacher would testify. Maurice ruins at least one pair of trousers a week. He can't help himself; there are no half measures with Maurice, so even a playground game of football is treated like it's the most important match of the season and another pair of trousers gets ruined. His teacher suggested to him that perhaps sewing patches over the holes rather than buying a new pair may be the way forward but Maurice, knowing my thoughts on patches, demurred, 'Daddy doesn't allow patches.' Once again my ranking in the local eccentricity league table rocketed. I don't mind that at all, I've got a proud record of being overdressed in all four corners of the globe and if some of that rubs off on my boys then I've done my job.

Maurice loves his football and had been dreading the end of the season, but in the same way looking forward to the big end-of-season tournament in Châteauroux where the best of the teams from the *département* all get together and compete for... well, nothing really. Just for the fun of doing so apparently. There's no 'competition' as such, just another opportunity for the under-eights, still playing four-a-side here, of the area to hone their levels of vision and technique without competitive burden. This may be why continental teams are more technically developed, as the cliché goes, but there's certainly no lack of 'edge' either.

The only problem with these jamborees is that, this being France, nothing starts until after lunch. Nothing. It's a little-known historical fact that the German invasion in 1940 was an early-morning fixture planned in the full knowledge that

France wouldn't be ready until about 3 p.m., and even then might need a nap, post-cheese course, before retaliating. The football tournament wasn't scheduled to finish until about 11 p.m.! That's too late for me when I'm not working, let alone almost every eight-year-old in the area, and though I was keen to support Maurice – as my dad always did me (though at more sensible times) – I went with a certain reluctance. In fact, we all went, as we decided that this would be an ideal family day out and Natalie, Samuel, Thérence and I all went to lend Maurice our support.

The weather wasn't good again. All that week there had been glorious sunshine, and though possibly too hot for football it was certainly better for the spectators than dark, grey permadrizzle. Every other spectator had clearly checked the weather forecast though and as hundreds of us all began to converge on the venue it was clear pretty early on that I was the only one in ironed trouser shorts, beige Clarks Wallabees and a vintage cycling top. I was bloody frozen right from the start. I blame the banks. The whole thing was sponsored by Crédit Agricole, and if you get a bank involved these days there's bound to be trouble. And you couldn't miss them, handing out their little corporate goody bags to the eight-year-olds from their pitched sales caravan and filling the place with loud music, Chumbawamba's 'Tubthumping' – 'I get knocked down...' – seemingly, and ironically, on repeat.

Even then the football didn't get under way until about 5 p.m., which meant nigh-on anarchy as about 300 eight-year-olds went from polite, sedate training exercises to whacking the wet footballs at each other and hitting one another with sticks. It's a wonder there weren't more injuries before the whole thing kicked off as these mini, wannabe footballers proved to be just like their older, professional counterparts, and steadfastly refused to behave and gave way destructively to boredom.

Finally, it began, and we had high hopes.

Maurice is a good player in a good team; nobody could remember when they were last beaten, but they started badly, a dull 0–0 draw, which was played out in the teeming rain and in which they seemed to have forgotten how to pass the ball. They played like they didn't know each other; in the next one they played like they didn't even like each other and were beaten, which left them in shock.

They had a ten-minute break before their next match and time for some soul searching. A couple of them were in tears, unused to defeat, while various parents offered explanations for the poor displays, 'pass the ball', 'look up', 'stretch the play' and 'it's too cold and wet' – the last one was mine. Samuel, however, had become something of a student of the game and was taking each player away in turn and having a chat, clearly more in favour of the 'arm around the shoulder' style of man management than carrot and stick. Plus, being only 12 himself, he could speak their language.

The next game, as the rain improbably got harder, was a much-needed victory, but against the most unathletic-looking bunch of children I think I've ever seen, some of whom would clearly have been much happier eating a football rather than kicking it. It was a victory, nonetheless. A much-needed victory – something to build on. At least it would have been something to build on, if the entire tournament hadn't then been put on hold for dinner! 'Dinner?' I wailed. 'In a football tournament?'

'What?' I asked, by now absolutely soaking with my beautiful Wallabee shoes looking more like possum roadkill. 'We've only just started!'

For the next hour and a half hundreds of us huddled in cars or under umbrellas eating a frankly needless picnic while the kids ran around, wasting their energy for the second half of the tournament and stuffing their faces like the finely honed athletes they were. All except our team who'd been taken off by Samuel, or Samuel Moore-inho as he'd been dubbed, to 'work on some set pieces'.

As we trudged back to the pitches, the music got louder, with Van Halen's 'Jump' being favoured this time, the rain stayed relentlessly on its course and I spotted someone with a *Test Match Special* umbrella. I can't think of a more potent symbol of Englishness than a *Test Match Special* umbrella and mentioned this to Natalie who was attempting to wheel Thérence's buggy through the mud.

'Oh,' she said, 'he's probably English, why don't you go and talk to him?' I mean, really, isn't that the kind of thing a parent says to their child on holiday if they feel said child is too much of a loner or they just want to get rid of them for a bit? I declined, I'm not the sociable type anyway and especially not when I'm shivering and soaking wet.

The football kicked off again but the break had been unkind to Maurice's team. Their manager seemed to wash his hands of them too and it was left to Samuel Moore-inho to read the riot act. I don't know what he said to them, the promise of a better contract, win bonuses, no idea, but it worked and they romped home in the last two matches, played in almost darkness, with Maurice scoring three goals.

'Come on then,' I said. 'Let's get back to the car or we'll be stuck in the car park for hours...'

'But Daddy...' Maurice interrupted and even in the late gloom I could see his lip wobbling, '... fireworks.'

There really was no point in arguing; I couldn't get any wetter and miraculously the rain had relented just in time for the *feux d'artifices*. I have no idea why everything in France has to end with a fireworks display, but it does. Some say it goes back to the French Revolution, but if that's so I'd have preferred a beheading myself; drag out Madame La Guillotine and show this DJ that Van Halen never was, and certainly isn't now, acceptable in polite society. It also irked me that Maurice, along with Natalie, Samuel and Thérence insisted on standing at the very front! It's a firework display! We could stand a mile back (i.e. nearer the car park) and not miss anything.

It was a very French day, the dominance of meal times, the non-competitive competition, the fireworks and, to cap it all, as it took an hour to inch out of the car park, my soaking and squelching shoes worked the pedals and felt less like clutch control and more like treading grapes. Natalie and all three boys were fast asleep before we'd even got out of the car park. I had griped, moaned and whined pretty much all day, and now everyone was asleep as I drove them home. I felt like a proper dad, a dad who had weekends at home, and it felt good.

A TICKING BOMB

It had to happen sooner or later. I'd had this cloud effectively hanging over me since we moved here, so at some point I was going to get caught out. You don't commute between France and the UK for eight and a half years and not, eventually, become the victim of a strike.

Now, I'm a fan of a certain amount of union power, checks and balances and all that, but hitherto all strikes had been planned well in advance; civilised affairs that allowed the traveller to make other arrangements. So either I'd been living under a rock or watching the daytime French news (much the same thing) but this particular air traffic controllers' strike came right out of the blue.

The fact that the airline didn't know that my flight had been cancelled was more of a concern. Maybe they had been watching the lunchtime news as well, but the Air France website, Air France being the partners for the Paris routes, definitely said that the flight was cancelled.

'WE operate this flight and I can tell you it's NOT cancelled,' the rather chipper agent said, on the premium-rate, 'customer service' helpline.

A TICKING BOMB

'I've taken this flight a lot,' I said, trying to remain calm. 'Your partner, Air France, operate the flight and their website says that it's cancelled. As I booked the flight through you, you need to check and then refund me.'

She went away to 'consult her line manager' and returned to the phone five minutes later behaving as if she'd been hypnotised by senior management in the interim.

'Our partner Air France operates this flight,' she began in a monotone voice, 'and it's been cancelled. I can offer you a full refund.'

When you deal with as many different travel companies as I do, small victories like this are all-important in keeping the spirits up, and I allowed myself a few minutes' gloating time, but the fact remained I still needed to get back to England. With Eurostar upping their prices by the minute, because of the sudden rush, driving was the only viable proposition.

I didn't fancy a full seven-hour drive to Calais, so instead went for the Dieppe–Newhaven ferry at 6 p.m.; Dieppe is only four and a half hours away but as it was already 1 p.m. when I booked it, it was going to be tight.

There's something quite old-fashioned about ferry travel, partly because it evokes childhood memories of family holidays and school trips but also because, more often than not, the boats seem to have remained the same despite the operating companies having changed almost biannually. These boats have had so many makeovers they're like old soap actors; they resemble old hospitals or council buildings that have had a 'happy' picture painted on to the wall to distract you from the cracks, the dirt and the overall sense of disappointment.

The *Seven Sisters* ship is just like that. It may have been grand once, but now it has the feel of a neglected school Portakabin which no amount of grandiose names like 'The Agatha Christie Salon' (some tables next to a half empty shop) or 'The Hilaire Belloc Salon' (a cordoned off part of the bar which was occupied by tired-looking scooter mods) is going to change. The fact that the boat was half-empty too all added to a *fin de siècle* feel, a cloudy day leaving Dieppe on a rundown old boat. Almost everything, including me, felt like it had seen better days.

'The Lanes' restaurant was a quiet affair too. Ferry food really could benefit from a Jamie Oliver-type investigation, and I suspect that much of the muck he cleared out of British school canteens has ended up on cross-channel ferries as trucker fodder. The restaurant's spirited attempt at a cosmopolitan menu was divided by nationality, boeuf bourguignon for the French, spaghetti Bolognese for the coachload of Italians that hadn't shown up and chicken tikka masala for the English, obviously. For those whose hackles are now going up, get over yourselves, it's the national dish. I was working in India during the football World Cup and every day the hotel buffet would have a theme depending on who was playing that day – pasta for the Italians, beef for the Argentinians, dog for South Korea (I'm joking!)... When England played they just served extra curry, which I thought was a nice touch. This ferry stuff, though brightly coloured like a good chicken tikka masala should be, was the wrong bright colour and was more reminiscent of the kind of stuff one sees swilling about on the floor on particularly rough crossings; it looked like the kind of curry I used to buy in a tin when I was a student, a real old-fashioned curry from a time before our palates were educated. I really shouldn't have enjoyed it as much as I did.

All the time I was superciliously wandering around this travel throwback, Natalie was having other problems.

'FUCKING GAS GONE N CANT FUCKING OPEN OTHER BOTTLE' is a text that leaves the recipient in very little doubt of the sender's mood. The gas bottles supply the kitchen cooker hob, they weigh a tonne when full and are, frankly, a pain in the backside to attach and get up and running. I thought that I'd left a new one all hooked up just for the, almost inevitable, eventuality of it running out when I wasn't at home. Clearly I had not.

I got a series of texts for the next couple of hours, all slightly escalating in anger and frustration, as Natalie fought gamely with the things – my joke about waiting until morning and asking one of the binmen to help was particularly ill-received. Eventually, though, I got a text saying that there was now a permanent smell of gas and the stuff was going everywhere apart from in the kitchen. These things only ever happen when you're away, thanks to French air traffic control I was stuck on the ghost ship from Normandy when actually I should have been at home enjoying a family, albeit gas-related, evening.

The *pompiers* (firemen) were called and arrived with an equally tooled-up squad from EDF, all apparently looking like that scene from *E.T.* when the 'government' lock down the house. Natalie and the boys had been warned to stay outside and away from the kitchen end of the garden. It was by now after 10 p.m. and obviously quite a traumatic event as Maurice especially wanted to keep rushing inside to 'save his Egypt collection'. The problem, it turned out, was that the second gas bottle was also empty and that Natalie hadn't been able to open the 'new' one as it was already open, her efforts had dislodged the pipes and so the gas had escaped. 'It was nothing really,' said the *pompiers*, 'you were right to call though.' I suspect they'll be wanting a bigger contribution come Christmastime when they're hawking their calendar about from door to door, and they'll deserve it too. It's a small town, so the *pompiers* are largely made up of volunteers who come rushing from their other jobs or their homes to help out, people who you only normally see at the school gates or in the queue at the *boulangerie*. It's old-fashioned-community-heart-warming stuff and they were fantastic Natalie said, as were the EDF people, 'Better to be safe than sorry,' they said, 'you don't want to be blown sky high!'

As if French air traffic control would allow that...

These things really do only seem to happen when I'm away, though, almost to the point where you actually start allowing for it; you build 'potential long-distance disaster aftermath' into your routine and it's like a cloud that hangs over you. I'm not very good at receiving bad news when I'm away anyway. The sense of isolation, helplessness and quite phenomenal levels of drama-queenery kick in so that even the smallest thing gets blown out of all proportion. I down tools and rush home, which to be honest is something I'm generally looking to do anyway. But when Natalie rang to say that she had collapsed the night before and was frightened, I panicked and desperately wanted to get home as soon as possible.

I persuaded her to call the doctor out, something she's always reluctant to do, and to rally friends and family to help with the boys. She did so and promised to call back when she had more news. The news was that it was nothing too serious, a result of exhaustion, her contract with the school in Châteauroux had finished a couple of weeks earlier and her body, after months of stress, travel and for large parts of the time, operating as a single parent who also owns a zoo, had just said 'enough's enough' and shut down. The doctor had been out, medication had been prescribed and the local community, particularly Brigitte, the childminder, and her husband Eric, had indeed rallied and everything would be fine. There was no need to rush home, she said. When I eventually got home four days later it was clear that she was still not right though and we booked another appointment with the doctor who ordered a series of blood tests.

'While we're here...' I said to the doctor hopefully and went on to explain my latest problem. My gout, which had been attributed to excess white wine and chocolate, was back and the medication he'd prescribed was either the wrong kind or was lacking oomph. It had returned with a vengeance, and so he re-examined my foot.

'The main area of pain,' I said, 'is around this toe here which I broke playing sport about six years ago.' There was no need for him to be told the whole stairs-cricket-celebration fiasco. He looked at me and the 'kerching!' of simple diagnosis spun in his eyes like in a slot machine.

He was turning his back on the gout diagnosis and moving elsewhere this time. It seems that a combination of NHS brutality and my desire to be back in 'unhealthy' pointed Chelsea boots had led to this current malaise: I have arthritis in my foot, he told me, and it was also affecting the nerves up my right leg.

Why he couldn't have diagnosed this before is frankly beyond me, but also not all that surprising. His diagnosis history is so poor, Thérence's skin problems, my stomach problems, various issues during Natalie's pregnancies (including getting the sex of the child wrong) that I suspect 'diagnosis' to him is less evidence based and more an internal multiple choice dialogue that, like an enthusiastic but limited child, he consistently gets wrong, always plumping for the wrong answer.

The French are very trusting of their medics. I think there's a rather cynical attitude towards them in the UK, most of it unjustified, maybe it's because for the most part the 'advice' seems to be given for free. The British may love a bargain but we're always sceptical about its 'worth' in the end. The French are more respectful of a doctor's position, as they are with teachers certainly, but also they're more trusting as a society, which is why when something happens that they don't like, it's one out, all out. Our elderly neighbour Madame LeBoeuf certainly put her faith in these people, even if some of these people are frankly dubious.

I had returned home from a trip once in agony from sciatica and as I gingerly inched my way out of the car I noticed Madame LeBoeuf looking at me in some concern. You know your health is in need of a major reassessment when your 90-year-old neighbour offers you help getting out of the car I can tell you, and we stood there on my driveway, both bent over like a pair of those dipping bird executive desk toys. A lovely woman, she asked what the problem was and I told her, 'Ah,' she exclaimed, 'that's a nasty thing. But I know a man who can help you!'

A TICKING BOMB

'Really?' I said, practically in tears with the pain and willing to accept any help going.

'Yes,' she said, 'he did wonders for my back.'

This kind of ringing endorsement is just the sort of thing one wants to hear when seeking third-party medical help; it inspires confidence, but although Madame LeBoeuf was in her nineties and still out gardening and sometimes even driving herself to the shops, she was also completely bent over. She hadn't stood up straight since we'd moved in and in fact was getting more angled by the year; she now stood, if that's the right word, at a perfect 90 degrees. So, while appreciative of the counsel, it was hard to take seriously the recommendation of a back specialist from someone who stood like a bookend and who, in reality, was talking to the gravel below.

Sciatica is sciatica however, and anybody who has ever suffered from it knows that any straw will be weakly clutched at and so I made an appointment with a Sicilian-born faith healer who lived 'three villages away'. Look, I'll admit I'm a cynic – I can't help it, it's my nature – but if you can get past my initial sneer I'm actually quite open-minded; just don't try and dislodge my sneer by spending the first 20 minutes of our meeting telling me my 'chakras are all bent'.

Natalie came with me, ostensibly as translator, but I think mainly for a laugh as she watched me try to contain my volcanic levels of scepticism in the face of born-again ancient mysticism. He was a large, very tanned man with massive hands, I mean really massive hands. I once met Frankie Howerd and I thought he had big hands, but this guy would have given Kenny Everett's Brother Lee Love character a run for his money. We shook hands; mine felt like a child's in his paw-like appendages, and he held it too long.

'Yes,' he said, nodding sagely, his eyes closed for gravitas, still holding on to my hand. 'You are all knotted up inside. Even breathing is difficult, no?'

He was right, breathing was difficult, though I was rather putting this down less to stress and more to the massive collection of joss sticks he had burning away on every available surface.

'Well,' he continued, 'take your trousers off.'

Oh, hello! I thought, here we go.

I've been to enough dubious film and television 'auditions' in my time to know where this was going and if Natalie, who was practically doubled over herself through trying not to burst out laughing, hadn't been there, I'd have just limped out and taken my bent chakras with me. I dropped my trousers and he just stood there looking at me for what seemed like ages. Even I, the victim of some quite horrendous stage deaths in my early days, had never felt more self-conscious. He took my hand again and closed his eyes; he took in a deep nasal breath, held it and let it out slowly.

'You have sciatica,' he said, presumably expecting a round of applause and although there was no doubting the accuracy of his diagnosis it was weakened somewhat by the fact that we'd told him that when we booked the appointment.

He gave me a few different types of massage which, I have to be honest, would probably have been more effective if it weren't for the fact that I was trouserless in a scented, smoke-filled room being watched by a giggling wife and man-handled by what I considered to be a Mediterranean fruitcake. I could tell the frustration was getting to him as I simply could not relax sufficiently for any of his 'powers' to work, and after half an hour or so he gave up while outwardly expressing that his 'work was done'.

'You see!' he exclaimed, 'how quickly you are able to put your clothes on now!'

Ancient mystic or no ancient mystic, this man was patently misreading the reasons for my haste. I can't remember how much I paid for this rather dubious and ineffectual 'medical' intervention, but I'll say this, if your partner is ever stressed and needs to relax, take them with you to watch while you're mauled almost into anger by some shaman, self-deluded charlatan, I swear Natalie's spirits had rarely been higher.

'How did it go?' Madame LeBoeuf asked the ground beneath her the next time we saw her.

'Fine,' I replied, trying to bend down low enough to see if she was smirking or not.

The arthritis, which the doctor was now lecturing me on, was something of a blow. OK, gout is no prize in life's lottery, but at least it gives the appearance of a life well lived. It's known as the 'King's Disease' after Henry VIII and as such gives the impression that the sufferer has over-indulged his passion for wine, women and song, a larger-than-life character with stories to tell. Arthritis has the air of decrepitude and the withering of age. It's the bell just before the final lap in my overly dramatic mind.

Having dealt with us both, the doctor, as is his wont while writing out lengthy prescriptions, expounded on his latest theory of medicine, 'positive thinking'. Seriously, it's getting like a cult around here. 'Think yourself healthy,' he was saying and went off on a lecture about some nineteenth-century chemist who had originally formulated this theory. I should make clear that I'm not against positive thinking per se, but positive thinking is not, nor has it ever been, my forte to the extent that I have made a half decent career out of being a stage miserabilist and have no intention of getting all happy-clappy now, thank you very much. Besides which positivity is an extremely unlikely emotion while a doctor inspects your 'worrying' varicose veins and prescribes 'orthopaedic socks' for you to wear on planes.

The doctor blithely introduced the notion of 'medical legwear' like it was the most natural thing in the world, and not something that a 42-year-old man might find somewhat deflating. 'Yep, there you go, put these tights on – next stop rubber pants.' The ignominy didn't end there either. I thought I'd picked a quiet time at the chemist in which to collect my new undergarments. I was wrong. Not only was the place not quiet it was full of young, attractive, Romany women, all barefoot and outdoorsy but who stopped their chaotic buzzing around the chemist as the strangely dressed 'foreigner' was measured – MEASURED – for his socks. They gathered round as the female chemist rolled up my trousers and put a tape measure to my calves and ankles, and shook their heads as if this decadence was the main reason they decided to drop out of society altogether, what with its rules and too ordered underwear.

'Would you like them in black or beige?' asked the chemist, apparently oblivious to our audience.

'Do you have them in Argyle?' I asked, trying to claw back some dignity.

A TICKING BOMB

You can approach the onset of old age and decay in two ways: you can let it get to you and give up or you can come out fighting, ignore the ravages of time and face it down with haughty scorn. Frankly, I'm all for the first option, but having young children means that you can't let this show, not yet anyway, and following the chemist humiliation I decided to show I still had some physical strength left in me and went off to mend the goats' wooden stable wall. They'd kicked it down the night before, because they can, and it needed putting back together.

I drew the hammer back and attacked the thing with gusto, letting the frustrations of the day, if not life itself, come flying out in DIY violence. The hammer hit the wood mightily, so hard that the iron head parted ways with the wooden handle, flew back and smacked into my forehead, before pirouetting, in slow motion, and bouncing off my watch, smashing the glass face and coming to a noisy rest on the floor.

I stared at the thing for a full two minutes. The wall remained unattached, I had a bruise on my forehead and my watch was in pieces. My chakras had never been more bent.

ACTING UP

If anyone was in need of straightened chakras it was Samuel. The end of the school year would also mean his theatrical debut and his nerves were beginning to show. If full-on melodramatic hissy fits are any gauge of acting talent, or a precursor to success in the trade, then I think he's probably on to a winner. The fact that he was also outstanding at the actual acting part will probably stand him in good stead too. I didn't know whether to be happy or not. His debut was such a resounding personal success that though I was immensely proud, secretly, I'd been hoping that he wouldn't enjoy it quite as much as he did and that the acting bug would become a passing fancy like so many others, and talk of drama school would be quietly dropped.

This wasn't out of jealousy or fear of competition but parental concern. I know actors; I know lots of them and very few are ever in work long enough to make ends meet and, even though he was only 12, that worried me. Maybe it would be a passing fad, like the *tir* (shooting) had been. I'm not sure why Samuel felt compelled to try the rifle range; I know some of his friends were doing it, some on the dubious pretext of mental health too. One of his friends had a slight concentration problem and it was suggested, by the school, that maybe joining the local rifle club would be a good way to get him more focused. I mean, is this new thinking or old thinking? I don't know. In the UK parents are quite rightly worried about childhood diagnoses that lead to early, unjustified labelling and months, sometimes years, on 'helpful' drugs. Here in France they give them guns. Samuel joined the club and immediately became something of a success, by far the best in his age group; the under-tens to be fair not being massively represented at the gun club, but after a few months he got bored, much to the chagrin of the gun club hierarchy who saw him as a future star, and packed it all in.

Then there were the guitar lessons, which I'll admit I badgered him into. I was in one of my more prolonged periods of procrastination and to avoid doing any work entirely I decided to learn the guitar instead; I also decided that Samuel should learn the guitar too, seeing as he'd now given up shooting and therefore needed a hobby. Being in the middle of nowhere, however, meant that guitar teachers were somewhat rare and we had to advertise, and put a card up on the message board of the local *boulangerie*, which like any *boulangerie* is the centre of local gossip and trade. We had a call a few days later which Natalie answered and arranged our first lesson for the following week.

'Well?' Samuel and I asked. 'What's he like?'

'He's very nice, I think,' was Natalie's response. 'Strange French accent though, I think he might be from the south.'

Peter, it turned out, was from South Shields and lived locally. He had been a session guitarist in the 1960s, had worked with loads of bands from that era and was an exceptional player. This was an early foray into teaching, however, and we were exacting pupils. Samuel may have some talent in this regard though he wasn't that interested, but I have absolutely no talent whatsoever musically and so after a few testing months we decided to call it a day, much to the relief of Peter I suspect.

I'm firmly of the W.C. Fields school of thinking, 'If at first you don't succeed, give up… There's no use being a damn fool about it.' And though obviously I would not advocate this attitude to my children I could, even at this early stage, see that it wouldn't be an issue where Samuel's acting was concerned.

He had been attending the local *théâtre* group since the previous September, something which had been noted sarcastically by his teachers, who now had him marked down as something of a drama queen. This debut performance was the culmination of months of rehearsals, tantrum throwing, ego clashing and some quite astonishing flouncing about. The build up to the two shows, one evening and one matinee, had been fraught, as Samuel, holding down two major roles, one the comic centrepiece as a futuristic, intergalactic Charlie Chaplin, struggled with learning his lines and then started getting nervous a few days before.

'How do you learn your lines, Daddy?' he asked when I picked him up from a particularly tense rehearsal. I have a simple rule about learning lines; I've written my own material, so if I can remember it, it means it's worth remembering, if I can't then it isn't. Simple as that. Of course, what I should be doing is rewriting it, so that it is actually worth remembering, but this was no time to be highlighting my own indolence. My history on learning lines for actual plays is patchy. I played the leading role in Alan Ayckbourn's *Gosforth's Fête* in a production that was being 'marked' for our drama O level. The play revolves around Gosforth, there isn't a scene without him, every other character's line is fed by him, but I didn't learn my lines sufficiently and just began improvising. It was chaos as every other participant was left floundering by my lack of team ethic. I told Samuel he had to write his lines out and keep writing them out until he knew them. Once again I was making it up as I went along.

'So how do you cope with nerves before you go on stage then, Daddy?' he asked later that evening at the dinner table.

Natalie gave me a stern look along the lines of 'make something up for God's sake, don't tell the truth' and I gave it some thought. I could be honest and list the early days of chain-smoking, alcohol addiction and little pills, or the latter method of outwardly not giving a toss, while inside my stomach ulcer does a roaring trade in acid production, very much the 'swan' approach. I gave him some management speak about 'visualisation' and preparation which is at least partly true, but which also I don't think was much help to him as the nerves continued to bite.

We had seats reserved right at the front, which if I were Samuel I would have hated – I don't like having anybody I even *know* in the audience let alone on the front row. A couple of years ago a group of old girlfriends came to see me perform in Birmingham, I'd known them since I was a teenager and some of them I'd known very well indeed, and their presence was making me a gibbering wreck backstage.

'What's up with you?' a colleague asked. 'What difference does it make them being here?'

'There's a woman out there who I lost my virginity to...' I said, practically hyperventilating. 'I'm not sure she could handle another bad performance.'

The other problem with me being on the front row was that I was seated right next to the standing video camera operator who, to put it mildly, had something of a flatulence problem and which I hoped wouldn't prove to be a metaphor for the show that was to follow.

The lights went down, the 'sshhing' started and faded away, and the play began.

I'm not sure I understood everything that went on. The play was written by the leader of the *théâtre* group and was an intergalactic *Romeo and Juliet* parody taking in such diverse additions as Rihanna, Snow White, local Berrichon 'peasantry' (Berry being the old word for this area of France) and the aforementioned Charlie Chaplin. It rambled on a bit in truth and wasn't helped by the fact that some of the cast were far too young and simply hadn't learned their lines, or at least were not yet capable of doing so, meaning that there were uncomfortable silences, some almost Pinteresque in length, but without the gravity.

The democracy of the exercise was admirable: every child, ageing from about five years old to 15 or 16, had some role to play in the performance, but it also meant that the limited theatre space which had been created in the local *salle des fêtes* had a rolling 'non-performing cast' issue with those currently not needed sitting in the 'well' in front of the stage. The irony here being that those who couldn't remember what to say on stage a few minutes earlier were now busy chatting away to their friends and disturbing others. The prompter, who by now was becoming a leading figure in the performance, was trying to shush these unemployed cast members, which confused some of the more nervy actors on stage who thought, confusingly, that they were being asked to pipe down.

But the older members of the cast, and in particular those who had learned their lines, were stunning. The knowledge that they knew what they were saying and when they had to say it, meant they had had time to actually learn to do some acting as well and Samuel, and yes I know 'I would say that wouldn't I?', was very good indeed. The truth is, I wouldn't just say that anyway. If he'd stunk the place out like my video operating neighbour I simply wouldn't have written about the event at all, but Samuel, as Charlie Chaplin/the Mad Hatter, had wonderful comic timing and there were whispers of approval all around us whenever he was on stage, making me ridiculously proud and the opening night a triumph.

Matinees are tricky at the best of times, but I'd really hoped that after a good night's sleep and the butterflies of the premier had subsided, things would have tightened up a bit. I think I was expecting a bit too much, and those that hadn't known their lines the night before still didn't know them the next day, but the audience didn't help. There's a reason why I am on stage as a comedian and not in the audience, and that is that I can legitimately and, ahem, forcefully tell people to shut up and bloody well behave themselves. The Sunday afternoon crowd, while still appreciative, were restless and at times downright rude, which meant that I couldn't relax. I've only been to the cinema three times in 20 years and that is because of my rank intolerance of other people's discourtesy and I was glad that, in the interval, I had to dash off and pick up Maurice from a dance spectacular that he'd insisted on seeing, as it meant I didn't have to hang around the *salle des fêtes* and upbraid people about their manners.

I had 15 minutes to pick up Maurice from a different town and bring him back before Samuel opened the second half doing his comic turn. I dashed into the dance spectacular looking for Maurice, only to go crashing clumsily into a line-dancing finale, all a-whoopin' and a-hollerin' and not at all keen on a one-man-mod invasion. A heavily made-up old lady linked arms with me and for an awful moment I thought I might miss the rest of Samuel's performance as I was virtually kidnapped in an endless violin-enthused, shiny-shirted farrago from which I'd never escape. I unhooked arms with the old dear, apologised, grabbed a toe-tapping Maurice and left hastily like they'd run me out of town, making it back just as the lights dimmed and the elderly video man let rip with another cloud of poison gas.

Once again Samuel was excellent and I'm not ashamed to admit it brought tears to my eyes (I lay some of the blame on the video operator for this) as I realised that this was a hobby, pastime, a calling, however you want to put it that he wasn't going to give up on. He has genuine talent and wants to be an actor, and as such a lifetime of showbiz disappointment, frustration, crushing lows and short-lived highs await him, and all Natalie and I can probably do is be there to catch him when we're needed.

It was a very emotional day for everyone. Thérence was so moved that midway through the second half he went to the makeshift bar at the back of the *salles des fêtes* and informed the barman that that was his brother on stage and he, Thérence, would like a beer and a slice of cake please. I fear it's the start of a Redgrave or Baldwin-style acting dynasty and I've given you fair warning.

It wasn't just the day that was emotional, though, it was the end of the school year – *les grandes vacances* – a combination of, 'Thank Christ for that!' and 'le big relief!'.

It's not just the kids and teachers who are knackered, though both are worked pretty hard, and nor is it the drama of school report season that brings an itchy nervousness to the time of year, and Samuel was desperate to see improvement on his report from Christmas. There were no issues academically, but *comportement* wise he had been described variously as 'cheeky', 'moody' and 'melodramatic'. It's difficult for me to lecture or criticise on such obviously appalling traits but Samuel wanted to show that he'd made an effort in this regard so that his end-of-year reward would be more grandiose. His report was better – if sucking the individuality out of someone is an improvement – but seeing as last year's reward was goats his reward was far more mundane, and was a healthy and improving set of books.

Maurice's end of year I deliberately missed. He had built up such an affection for his teacher that even though I was sent to collect him at the end of his last day, I refused to on the grounds that I couldn't deal with the emotional breakdown that would inevitably occur. I know this sounds, at the very least, like remiss parenting, but seriously, every minor setback for all three of them to be honest was being greeted like a collection of widows standing in front of the rubble of their earthquake-flattened village, and though I love the fact that my children aren't buttoned up, that they can, and are willing to, express their emotions, there are limits. Natalie collected him instead, 'How was it?' I asked, genuinely concerned.

'You'd have hated it,' she replied.

Thérence's end of term had the potential to be equally traumatic, as assorted three to six-year-olds were to perform an end of year *spectacle* of their own to parents and guests. Now, I had seen the teachers of this group try and fail to get them to line up in a morning – try watching French passengers board a plane: chaos – I just couldn't see the necessary discipline being instilled with enough success for public performance.

It was to take place in the playground behind the school, but with the stage itself under a concrete pavilion while the audience sat in the open air. I try not to take a professional eye to these things but sometimes the errors are so glaring that you just can't help it and I could see that the sound set-up was doomed to failure.

There were microphones attached to the front of the makeshift stage but the speakers themselves had been placed *behind* the stage, meaning that, at best, the audience would hear a muffled rumble from the deeper recesses of the pavilion and not anything of the *spectacle* at all. As the audience began to take their seats I feared for the clarity of the production. I also feared for my own mood. I know it's a school, I know it's an end of year knees-up, as it were, but keep your bloody kids in check will you? As one child, who Maurice has constant issues with, trod on my toe (i.e. suede Chelsea boot) again playing an inappropriate game of 'it', I nearly lost it.

'I'm going to grab him in a minute,' I said to Natalie loudly, there being no need for whispering when no-one else is likely to be able to understand you.

ACTING UP

'He has to *redouble* next year...' Natalie said, by way of explanation. Meaning that the kid was being held back a year and would have to re-do the previous school year because he was either thick or has behavioural issues. I'm not surprised, frankly, with such blatant disregard for sensitive footwear, if I had my way he'd be held back every year. Most of the kids were well behaved, but too many children in France, far too many in my opinion, are forced to wear the kind of glasses that even a 1980s kids' TV presenter would baulk at. In my day, there were NHS glasses, bottom-of-a-jam-jar thickness and held together with plasters – they were bad enough, but here it seems to be the in thing to have your five-year-old wear luminous, enormous eyewear that an early Elton John would have regarded as a bit outré. Poor kids, they look at you through these optical monstrosities with a kind of pleading look in their magnified eyes that just screams 'Help me!'

The performance began with the muffled strains of the *Mission Impossible* theme tune, surely an irony, as two dozen four-year-olds dressed as pigs were pushed on to the stage. The thing is that these things are compulsory and not everyone wants to be up there, so seeing a number of the porcine troupe in floods of tears was a very long way from joy indeed. Thérence thrives on these things, but he was at the back and as he was also by far the smallest he was lost behind the emotional frailty that was literally breaking up in front of him. I was sitting unhelpfully behind a concrete pillar, being jostled by parents recording the thing on their phones like aggressive paparazzi, unable to hear anything beyond the wails of crying children in brightly coloured fancy dress.... and it was only the first of four acts.

The expected 'sound' problems took their toll early on. The audience, and we are among the older parents at this school, were unable to hear much and were losing attention fast. Some of them, barely out of school themselves, were behaving like they were back in assembly and pretending to be quiet while bothering others, and one young dad was actually pulling the pigtails of a 'mum' he'd obviously known since they were the same age as the kids on stage. It all felt horribly chaotic around me – like I said, I'm not good at being in an audience – and I left my seat to go and stand elsewhere in the playground.

As I did so the final act started and was the work of the eldest class in the nursery school. The barnyard theme had been abandoned for these children, who were improbably dressed in Union Jack ties and singing an English song. It looked like UKIP doing *Bugsy Malone*. Some people turned around to look at me, now standing alone at the back and dressed in what they call around here 'So Briteesh', it was as if they thought I'd influenced the choice of material.

Unfortunately, the kids here had the toughest slot. They were closing the show, the audience had largely lost interest and the sound was as unhelpful as it could be – comedians may fill in the Jongleurs venue of their choice at this point – it all felt slightly harrowing and I started to think about the hen and stag do, city-centre, weekend stand-up gigs I myself was about to leave for back in England. I really did not want this kind of future for my children, I thought moodily and unnecessarily, but then I only had one more weekend to do myself, then it would be *les grandes vacances* for me too.

A VERY CORDIAL *ENTENTE*

On the Paris *metro* I'd recently seen a poster advertising English lessons, and the main picture was of a man with comically black eyes and cuts to his face, the thrust of the message being that if you don't learn English properly you'll get a good kicking. It seems a little strong to me, but in her continuing effort to bring peace and linguistic harmony to the world, Natalie's English lessons were going from strength to strength.

As well as setting up English clubs, offering private tuition and volunteering at local schools, she was also now advertising, despite my curmudgeonly misgivings, intensive 'language holidays', where a student would stay with us for a week, be immersed in the full 'English' experience and have their language skills improved as part of the bargain.

I was a bit dubious at first as I saw it, not without good reason, as a preliminary step on the road from relentless animal adoption to fostering human waifs and strays, which is all very laudable and that, but way beyond my capabilities. Henri, however, a 14-year-old from Paris, duly arrived as our first guinea pig so we set about being as English as possible.

C'EST LA VIE

The language was no problem for us, obviously, but we also had to 'English-up' everything else. I'd planned an English menu (the kitchen being my domain) of sausage and mash, fish and chips, roast beef and yorkshire pudding, chicken tikka masala, belly of pork and the like, also introducing the lad to the delights of specialist *cuisine Anglaise* like Worcester sauce crisps, Wotsits and Twiglets, Dairy Milk, pork scratchings and proper non-fancy, dry as a bone, long-distance sea voyage-type biscuits. The boys also did their bit by playing English games – for example, Henri arrived in the same week that the Ashes cricket began, so they opened a recently purchased cricket set and introduced him to the delights of a sweetly timed cover drive and silly mid-off, while *Test Match Special* crackled contentedly in the background. The cricket didn't last long, as Henri, bigger and older than our boys took to the game with great gusto and kept belting the ball back over the bowler's head and into the fields beyond, probably to a watching Girresse's annoyance. In the evening we watched James Bond films with English subtitles to help with Henri's grammar.

In short, the week we had planned couldn't have been more English, unless we'd taught him how to bottle up his emotions, drive on the left-hand side of the road and get drunk, throw up and then carry on drinking. He kept a diary, in English, every day and also had one-on-one lessons in Natalie's classroom, and the improvement in his language skills and therefore confidence was encouraging to see. He also got a very intensive language lesson from me when, investigating the 'noise' coming from the orchard, he found me swearing like the Norse God of Swear at a peach tree. The offending tree, while not producing fruit for two years had now produced so much that its main branch had become too heavy and snapped off; I was understandably furious and gave full Anglo-Saxon invective to the bloody thing while Henri looked on, his head cocked to one side like a confused puppy.

If this was the most English of weeks, though, we were up against some pretty strong French competition as they were countering our *Rosbifs*-James Bond-cricket mix with two of the most potent symbols of 'Frenchness' going, the Tour de France and Bastille Day. The plan was to go and see *le Tour* pass by a local town, about twenty minutes away, but in order to do that I had to make it back from London in time. I was hosting a corporate awards ceremony in London on the Thursday night but was due to be on a ferry to Dunkerque at 2 a.m. and land in France at 5 a.m.. It would then take seven hours or so to drive home before immediately leaving to get a place by the roadside in time to see the whole thing pass by. The fact that I made it home without stopping and on time, though wild-eyed and buzzing, just goes to show that Lance Armstrong was indeed correct, the Tour de France is simply impossible without the use of drugs. I had so many artificial caffeine stimulants rattling about inside me I think I could have ridden the stage myself.

We found a spot on the roadside just in time to see the *caravane* pass by first. I didn't know what this was, and they don't show it on the television coverage, but it's basically a long procession of sponsored vehicles, newspapers, sportswear companies, estate agents, everything you can think of, which pass by about an hour before the riders themselves. The cars and vans are quite often customised: for example in the shape of a can of drink or with giant, and recognisable, advertising figures on the roof of the vehicles, and they play loud music and shout advertising slogans at you as they pass by at some considerable speed. It's like a carnival with 'floats' all urging you to buy stuff but it also makes it look like the Tour de France warm up is a heavily branded episode of *Wacky Races* as they pass by trying to drum up atmosphere.

Their velocity isn't their most dangerous ruse however, but that they throw 'goodies' from their vehicles, branded goodies obviously, and at you too. It's said that the Isle of Man TT Motorbike Race is one of the most dangerous spectator events in the world, well standing at the side of the road as dozens of vehicles pass by at high speed while launching an assortment of keyrings, pens, hats, *madeleines* and the like in your direction is a pretty hazardous exercise too, I can tell you. It's a health and safety nightmare. A friend of ours got a rolled up copy of *L'Équipe* smack bang in his genitalia, a painful business, but which meant that while he was doubled up in pain an inflatable plastic travel pillow, sponsored by Ibis Budget, went flying over his head and cut open Natalie's wrist! I must admit that at the time I missed the whole wrist-slashing-budget-hotel metaphor as I was frankly astonished to discover that Ibis indeed had a 'budget' branch. I've stayed in Ibis hotels on many occasions, and knowing that they now have a budget chain is like finding out Goebbels had a slightly more right-wing brother.

Following the *caravane* we had a picnic and waited for the riders themselves. I'm not all that fussed by cycling normally, but it was clear Henri thought this was a very big event indeed and was obviously excited – and from our vantage point we had a very good view and could see the lead group approach from a few hundred metres away. To be honest, the actual cyclists-passing bit is a bit of a blur, all a bit brief – though in the searing temperatures that may not have been a bad thing – but it's definitely a thrill. There's something about a live sporting event that can give such a buzz. I've been to Wembley finals, Wimbledon and Ashes tests at Lord's and the thrill as the cyclists went past loudly and at incredible speed, even though they were going uphill as they passed us, was right up there with any sport I've witnessed live. You get carried along by the other spectators and their enthusiasm. Henri, and all the other boys, loved it, especially when we got home and we were all on the highlights on the television; Henri could ring home and literally show his parents that he was perfectly fine.

If the whole Tour de France circus is *très* French, then to have that event followed quickly by Bastille Day is practically a Gallic overload. There is a sense of fun about Bastille Day, a bit like St Patrick's Day, but with less drinking, and without the pernicious overtones of St George's Day. It's huge in France and a public holiday, and it tends to take the same format every year. There's the obligatory *brocante*, obviously, and also the equally obligatory *feux d'artifices*, of which this one must have been about the sixth in as many weeks. It was a poor effort, though. The local town normally excels at this type of thing, but as the music cranked up to herald the start of the show and a hush descended on the hundreds of people on the riverbank, I could sense something was amiss. Normally the stirring strains of 'La Marseillaise' begin and end these things and even if you're not French, it's an emotional rallying cry, a proper national anthem. I still get a lump in my throat when I see Madeleine LeBeau sing it to a bar full of German soldiers in *Casablanca*. However, what we got were the fragile pipes of Édith Piaf telling us that she regretted nothing, French icon to the core no doubt but ill-judged here, and I think this was actually the fireworks director making a point and getting his excuses in early.

Oh, it was poor. A fireworks display should never be lacklustre, but the gap between each firework going off was just slightly too long, making it look like the fireworks themselves weren't really up for it, like moody teenagers forced to visit elderly relatives. The post-fireworks-display entertainment was even worse, as some kind of low-rent accordion orchestra began their set with the improbable, un-French and frankly unwelcome 'Y Viva España!'

Only adult eyes really see these things, though, and all four boys had a high old time, having forged what seemed like a strong friendship, and were joking and giggling away in English. Henri was with us for a full week; a polite, tidy and helpful boy who was staying with strangers and being forced to speak in a foreign language.

We even took him to a concert. Peter our erstwhile guitar teacher was in a band with a local Frenchman, and together they played, largely English it has to be said, rock classics at a local bar. I noticed Henri slope off into the bar during an extended version of Status Quo's 'Rockin' All Over the World', which, let's be honest, isn't for everyone. I found him inside watching the television as the French national football team were in the final of the Under-20 World Cup. I stayed with him and we watched his team win; it really had been quite a week for him. It was obvious at times that he was a little homesick, and a little daunted too, but he never really let on, never moaned or sulked and entered into every crackpot idea

A VERY CORDIAL *ENTENTE*

of 'Englishness' we had with a very un-teenage enthusiasm. As he never really let on about homesickness, by the end of the week not only had his English massively improved but he'd also developed 'le stiff upper lip' too.

It was, actually, in any case far too hot to be showing any excessive emotion. You couldn't move a muscle without getting a sweat on and while the children were happy to be splashing about in the pool or just lounging in the shade, the adults were getting more and more tetchy.

I find weather talk boring at the best of times, but the constant repetition of the phrase, 'Bloody hell, it's hot' is surely one of the most irritating facets of a heatwave. Yes, it's hot, we get it, stop pointing it out. They're the kind of people who make a cup of tea, burn their lips on an over-ambitious first gulp and then exclaim 'Oh, that's hot!' Of course it is, YOU JUST BOILED THE WATER!

Of course, my slightly irritable mood might have been down to the fact that it was *so bloody hot*. The difficulty with being a mod is that the rules are never relaxed: the temperature doesn't hit 90 degrees and we all go out wearing cut-off jeans and sleeveless T-shirts, the rules still apply – as anyone who saw me almost turn into a pool of water while wearing a mohair suit in Bangkok once will testify.

The *canicule* (heatwave) in 2003 was reportedly responsible for 70,000 deaths across Europe, mainly old people and goths, but the effect on France in particular was profound. Nearly 15,000 people died in France alone as temperatures stayed in the forties for days on end. Normally this isn't an issue in most of France, as the nights are colder so the cooling cycle of old-fashioned stone, concrete or brick houses (which hitherto hadn't needed air-conditioning) meant that buildings didn't become too hot during the day. In 2003, however, the nights didn't cool down, so houses became like ovens. In August when most people were on holiday there were a catastrophic number of deaths, which even the Red Cross blamed on 'isolation and insufficient assistance'. Everybody blamed each other, the government blamed people going on holiday (even though the health minister didn't cut short his own) and everybody else blamed the government for not doing more. It has left a legacy of more environmentally sensitive house building but also a national sense of mourning that France, which prides itself on its sense of family, could have left its own to die in such numbers.

Every time temperatures go up, then, and more to the point stay there, there's a disquiet and everybody is reminded through news bulletins and so on of their social responsibilities. Even so, I felt Natalie was taking this too far.

'What do you mean we're having a barbecue for twenty-one people on Saturday evening?!' I asked with genuine exasperation.

We were only a week into *les grandes vacances* and already exhausted, and this just seemed to be the stuff of madness, plus a lot of the invitees would be kids from Samuel's theatre group, so it would be like being on a day course with TGI Friday staff. Also, and I was getting a bit sniffy about this, whenever we invite people round for dinner or whatever, and this happened when we lived in England too, we would very rarely have our invitation reciprocated. Also, if it was too hot for Natalie to be cleaning up poo from the horses' field once a day, as apparently it now was, then surely it was way beyond the reasonable temperature to outdoor cook for twenty-odd French people? And a barbecue too, literally my bête noire.

I went off to sulk somewhere cooler than in the fiercely hot front room, and also to secretly do my 'Barbecue to-do list' and also a 'Barbecue to-do list – Appendix 1 – Shopping list' list as I knew that I'd lose the argument and that the barbecue would go ahead. The beauty of the weather being like this was that at least it was quiet. For most of the day the boys, now that Henri had gone home, were languishing inside, as were Natalie and the dogs, the cats and so on. The horses and goats were trying not to get in each other's way in the stable and even the hens were clucking less. In fact, they were doing everything less. I've no idea if this is the case with all hens but after an initial flurry of eggs they seemed to have become ridiculously sensitive to the weather. It was either too cold or too hot, a bit windy, too damp, it never seemed to be just right and egg production had practically ground to a halt.

It all seemed to be Monica's fault, again showing the curse of all hens named after songs by The Kinks. She was broody yet again and therefore refusing to leave the nest area of the coop. Naturally this was putting the others off laying at all, or at least certainly in the coop, and we suspected that the three others were taking themselves off elsewhere for a bit of egg-laying privacy. We had searched everywhere else but apart from the odd stray egg we couldn't find where they were now laying, if they were laying at all. The chicken man in the market was convinced that they would have found somewhere else but other people, French people at the barbecue I must add, laughed that off and said that as the hens were French hens they were therefore on strike. I separated Monica, put her in solitary confinement if you will, and was hoping that this would make a difference so that I could avoid the last course of action which – and again I quote a chicken farmer here – was to 'dunk her silly arse in cold water' like she was a medieval witch.

I found it all very annoying, to be honest, and it meant that if I heard one of the hens giving off at any point I would go running after them to see if they had added to a secret egg stash somewhere. Something which happened with alarming regularity and much to the delight of our visiting barbecue guests, who frankly thought the heat had got to me. I returned from one of these forays to the nicely cooking barbecue only to find one of the guests, the father of one of Samuel's friends, actually turning the meat himself! Now to my mind there are rules about things like this and you don't, you simply do not, muck about with another man's coals. There were very clear demarcation lines being crossed here, a clear breach of barbecue etiquette and I stomped inside to register my complaint with the salad chef, Natalie.

Just then there was an explosion that came from the freezer as, once again, and I do this with alarming regularity in the summer months, a small green bottle of beer which had been left to chill in the wrong place and for far too long blew up and oozed beer slush inside the freezer drawer. Putting these little bottles in the freezer for a brief spell rather than have dozens of them taking up space in the fridge at any one time is a good idea – on paper. It's just that after about four or five of the moreish little things I completely forget that they're in the freezer at all, until one of them explodes. In the summer it's as regular as a noonday cannon salute, I'll sit down somewhere for a few minutes and then hear a subdued blast as another forgotten beer erupts in frozen frustration.

It's got to the point that if I buy a small crate of 24 bottles I'll actually only drink about fifteen of them, and so it was with good caution that Natalie reminded me I had put a whole crate in the freezer just before the barbecue guests arrived, something I had quite forgotten in between the egg search and the barbecue scandal; so I was told to clear the whole thing up while someone else, my barbecue nemesis probably, looked after the meat. It was a great evening, though: the meat was done well, rather than well done, especially the ribs with a sticky plum and rhubarb chutney coating. The kids all played in the pool, I made strides with dinner-table conversation French, which is like 'speed language' for the uninitiated, and I met some of Natalie's friends who I hadn't had the chance to meet before as I'd always been away working. It was also a chance to say thanks to those who'd rallied around her when she'd been ill several weeks earlier when, again, I had been away.

It was very late by the time everyone had gone and the boys were in bed, and Natalie and I sat on the still-baking terrace in the dark and silence, happy with ourselves and our lot generally.

'I love it when it's like this,' I said, closing my eyes and putting my head back, 'so peaceful and quiet.' And I put my arm around Natalie as she put her head on my shoulder. 'So calm.'

There was a large, muffled explosion as 24 beer bottles exploded in another freezer somewhere, but neither of us moved – it was just too bloody hot.

23

NICE AND QUIET

We hadn't had a family holiday away since the disastrous caravanning break in Biarritz a few years before. Apart from the fact that places like Biarritz aren't supposed to be done on a budget, it's like hiding ticketless in the toilet of the *Orient Express*, the weather had been atrocious too and so, for our first holiday for a while we wanted guaranteed good weather and were going to do it in style.

Part of the preparation for a holiday for me is batting off questions like, 'Your life is a holiday, why do you need a holiday?' and 'You live in paradise, why do you need a holiday?' It's difficult to argue with this really. On paper, yes we *do* live in paradise and people could have paid a fortune to have a holiday at our place (I'm not bitter), but home is now so overrun with maladjusted rescue animals that we (for that read 'I') need to go somewhere without malevolent horses, plotting goats, striking hens, vicious cats and retarded dogs. I was looking forward to it immensely.

'Daddy?' Samuel asked nervously at lunchtime the week before departure, 'did you say we were going to Nice?' He was standing transfixed watching the news.

NICE AND QUIET

'Yes,' I replied, 'Nice. Why?'

'An apartment on the seafront?' he continued.

'Yes, an apartment on the seafront in Nice. Why?' My habitual lack of patience was already being tested.

'It's not that one is it?' And he pointed to the television screen as what looked like Côte d'Azur-based beachfront apartments were not only being 'buffeted' by a ferocious storm, they looked like they were being lifted up and thrown around. This wasn't buffeted, this was filleted.

'Ah,' was all I could say as I was already frantically typing an email to our prospective landlord, Monsieur Filio in Nice. The phrase 'bloody typical', never far from my lips at the best of times, was about to raise its ugly head once more.

Obviously I wanted to know that Filio was OK, but primarily I wanted to know that our beachfront apartment was still actually near the beach and not in bits like abandoned Lego, halfway up the Alps somewhere. The storm, though incredibly violent, was also mercifully short as the camera crew continued to walk about the place and interview assorted *Niçois* under what was now a hot, beating sun. They seemed happy enough but then the camera crew would widen the shot to show 200-year-old-trees that had been tossed aside like used toothpicks. It didn't look good.

I am not a patient man. Partly it's the job I do, with stand-up the responses are immediate, there's no waiting around when you're on stage; everything happens at a pace so it's difficult then not to treat the 'real world' with exasperated impatience when things don't happen as quickly, but even still... 24 hours! Twenty-four hours it took him to answer my email enquiry and that's an awful lot of time to stew in your own paranoid juices.

'Maybe his electricity is down?' Natalie said reasonably.

'Maybe,' I replied, not interested in mundane explanations.

'Maybe he's dead?' Maurice asked, a sense of the macabre winning out over sanity.

I could see how the next few days were going to pan out. Our beachfront apartment would be beyond repair and we would have to frantically make alternative arrangements, which inevitably would mean mending the puncture on the caravan and taking the old girl out for one last hurrah. Only there would be an added trailer off the back of the caravan this time and it would be overflowing with a huge, bloody great 'chip' that I couldn't actually wear on my shoulder while driving. I'd been looking forward to this holiday for months, since we'd booked it in February in fact. It was going to be short enough as it was as, after ten days in Nice, Natalie and the boys were off to a three-day family *fête* somewhere while I had to return home and relieve her livestock-sitting parents.

I was, it has to be said, mildly resentful of this arrangement. Did I say 'mildly'? 'Hugely' might be more appropriate, bloody annoyed would be closer to the mark and though Natalie had made it very clear that I really did need to stop banging on about it, that is not in my DNA and I continued to chunter about injustice as long as I could. It meant though that while the response from the landlord, when it finally came, ('Yeah, cool. See you later.') was very welcome, the relief was also short-lived as Natalie, apropos of nothing and in one of her 'stare out of the kitchen window wistfully' reveries said blithely, 'I think we could adopt something else, you know?' It was obvious she meant of the animal variety but to be honest the first thing that ran through my head, after the sound of nuclear klaxons had died down, was 'how about adopting a "no tolerance policy" towards future adoptions?' She was broody again though and therefore needed to be treated with delicacy, sensitivity and tact.

'Are you actually insane?' I practically screamed. 'I'm having to cut my holiday short…' At which point she rolled her eyes and carried on drying the dishes. The local farmer's advice to cure our broody hen had been solitary confinement and dipping her backside in cold water and the temptation to try the same with Natalie was strong though I was hoping that the holiday and with it two whole weeks of not having to clear up assorted beast excreta would have the desired effect. One could only hope, though she seemed pretty far gone this time.

It was a lovely holiday and I delighted in showing Natalie and the boys one of my favourite places in the world. Nice had been my first ever overseas holiday when I was 11 years old, and that first holiday was memorable for so many reasons: the drive through France, my first trip 'abroad', the beaches, the clear blue water of the Mediterranean and the women. I had my first 'sexual' experience on that holiday so I was always likely to be marked by the place. I was snorkelling off the beach in Nice and dived down to the bottom to investigate some movement, though to be honest there wasn't much movement as there is little to be seen that close to the beach in Nice. Feeling proud that I'd made it to the 'depths' I rested briefly and looked up at the sun filtering through the sea and that's when it happened. A tanned, slender woman front-crawled right above my head and it wasn't just that she was topless – though she was, to my 11-year-old eyes, magnificently topless – or that she wore skimpy, leopard-print briefs; to be honest

I don't know what it was exactly, probably just 'the moment', but I suddenly became aware that I was running out of breath and so made a dart for the surface and got there coughing and spluttering like I had the bends. I felt fantastic.

What I remember most about that first holiday though was the glamour, the sense of another, far richer world that I was too young to resent not being a part of. And even now I still had a sense of that; these gazillionaires with their enormous yachts seem to be caricatures, almost unreal and therefore not worthy of pointless jealousy. I was just enjoying the view. Up to a point.

It started with what I thought was a dead cat and then the evening got progressively worse. To be fair, it wasn't actually dead but ever since someone had thrown a black Labrador at Natalie and me on our honeymoon from a fourth floor window in Havana, we've been sensitive to these things.

The poor thing, the cat this is, was hanging by the neck from one of those pull-down shop security grilles and was motionless. There was a group of 'lads' looking up at it and Natalie, for the only time I can ever remember, had a lower opinion of humanity than I and was convinced it was a complicated cat-based ruse to mug us of our worldly goods at this unfashionable end of Nice's Promenade des Anglais. It wasn't. The 'lads' while clearly a bit drunk seemed genuinely concerned and relieved when we turned up to briefly share their burden but shuffled off pretty sharpish, relieved to pass on the responsibility.

I sighed as I looked at Natalie and the three boys, all looking back at me and obviously expecting me to do something about the situation. 'What on earth am I supposed to do?' I pleaded.

NICE AND QUIET

'It's twelve feet up and I'm wearing brand new linen trousers and expensive Italian knitwear.' I added the clothing detail to let them know what an enormous sacrifice they were expecting me to make, but it made no difference.

'Rescue it, Daddy,' Thérence said simply, adopting the role of spokesperson for the group.

It's at times like these, increasingly often I'm afraid, when my shoulders just drop as the crushing inevitability of my family's needs and animal-orientated whims once again trample all over my good humour. I turned and looked up at the rear end of the cat. It was no stray moggy that was clear, I could see a bejewelled collar shimmering in the seafront lights and this being Nice they could quite possibly be real jewels. The cat had long, silver-white hair, it reminded me of Blofeld's cat in *Diamonds Are Forever*, and rather than struggle with the grille and try to remove its stuck head it remained largely motionless. Typical cat, I thought, left like this it would be dead by morning but no it was giving it the 'I'm a cat and I meant to do this entirely' attitude.

Again I looked back at Natalie and the boys, hoping for a reprieve, not to leave it to die obviously but to maybe call in some experts, the local *pompiers* for instance who would have ladders, a history of successful cat rescue and some protective clothing over their expensively collated new favourite summer outfit. At times like this it's easy to romanticise the scene, Gary Cooper in *High Noon*, the sacrifice of Cyrano de Bergerac, but all that went through my head was the desperate plea of Steve Martin in *Parenthood* and his 'My whole life is "have to"' speech. I knew exactly what he meant. The cat made a noise above me, which may have been the feline equivalent of

C'EST LA VIE

'For Christ's sakes, just get on with it you tart' and I stroppily started to climb the security grille.

Natalie would argue that the grille buckled under my weight but, more accurately, as I climbed it the extra weight pulled down the grille, no more than an inch or so but enough to allow the cat to successfully extract its head. We were now an even more incongruous sight as this obviously pampered puss, rather than run away and get clear of the grille, continued to cling on with its claws and look down at me, now about a metre below, looking like a mod-Spider-Man and not entirely sure what I should do next. Was it too frightened to jump down? Did it want me to climb further and then try to carry it back to the ground? There was a brief interlude, a few seconds maybe, where I looked up at the cat's green eyes and it looked down at me.

He decided to end the stalemate and take the initiative, in short he decided that a *'Merci, bonne nuit'* would be insufficient in the circumstances and that urinating all over me was the more appropriate response. From my (un)vantage point below I could see the large drops of yellow liquid before they actually hit me, and they seemed to fall in slow motion giving me a chance at least to hide my face but each drop that hit my clothes was like a stab in the back from the entire animal kingdom. All the effort – albeit admittedly forced – I've put in and this is how they repay me? I was so angry I couldn't move, but as the waterfall ended I looked back up at the cat and slowly began to scale the fence again with the intention of shoving its bloody head back in the grille. The cat, realising that very real danger was now imminent, leapt over my head and ran off down the road.

NICE AND QUIET

Again my shoulders slumped, but I couldn't move, I was crippled by defeat made worse, it has to be said, by the uncontrollable laughter coming from my 'loving' family down below, practically rolling on the floor in unruly mirth. Another family approached along the pavement, saw the scene and crossed the road, the mother looked up at me and actually 'tutted'; there no longer being any cat in evidence I just looked like another English drunk stinking of cat piss climbing up a shop.

'I think you'd better wash your clothes and have a shower,' Natalie struggled to say through giggles when we eventually got into the apartment. I found it hard to share their humour frankly and stripped off in the kitchen, gibbering to myself, and went to have a shower. I turned the shower on full and the jet was so strong the head shot up and the water powered out horizontally through the door and into my face, the shock of it knocked me over backwards which meant the jet of water was now drenching the entire bathroom. Quickly I shut the door, at least keeping the water in the shower cubicle but swearing loudly.

'What's going on in there?' Natalie shouted through the door.

'Nothing. Nothing at all,' I replied, now staring at an angry jet of water trying to break through the weak cubicle door and wondering how I could turn the shower off without drowning the room again. For five minutes I sat naked in the corner of the bathroom staring at the thing and in the end realised that it was futile and so opened the door, forgot to duck and just stepped in.

Ah, the healing properties of a warm shower. A good quarter of an hour later I emerged and could begin to see the funny side of the evening, my clothes were in the washing machine, I no longer smelt of cat wee and I'd wiped down the bathroom. All seemed good.

I strode into the lounge, a towel around my waist and drying my hair with another towel, in truth I felt a little heroic.

'Well I think I've earned a beer, don't you?' I asked rhetorically.

Natalie and Samuel, rather than agreeing anyway, actually looked at me in horror. 'What towel are you using?' Natalie asked nervously.

'The one that was hanging up outside the shower.' Again my shoulders slumped, 'Why?' I added defeatedly.

Natalie and Samuel again looked at each other, clearly weighing up whether to let this pass or actually let me know what the problem was. 'That's Samuel's hair-lice towel. I thought I'd separated it from the rest.'

Episodes of *Peppa Pig* always end with the family rolling about on their backs laughing uncontrollably. My face at times clearly has the ability to do this with my own family but I really didn't feel like joining in.

'Don't worry about the beer,' I said as I left them to it and trudged up the stairs, 'I'm going to bed.'

'Oh, Daddy,' Samuel said, tears of laughter streaming down his face, 'sometimes it's like we live with Mr Bean.'

Everybody needs their own inner sanctum, their own bolthole of privacy. Modern life is just too hectic and all-consuming to steer through if you haven't got a mental layby signposted on the horizon. France was supposed to be that oasis, and specifically this holiday. That elusive tranquillity is even more necessary now than it ever was but unfortunately, being a petty-minded control freak means that you're always 'on'.

NICE AND QUIET

Conversations that have nothing to do with you are raided for problems, some animal is always making a noise somewhere that you can't not investigate, home life is played out to a soundtrack of bickering, laughter and tears like a Woody Allen Thanksgiving acted out by children. There is no respite from the endless din and clamour of life, and I'd never found a way to silence it or take a step back.

And then I did, thanks to earwax.

I became so itchy and paranoid by the thought of lice that just a few minutes of overzealous cotton-budding led to two weeks of almost serene peacefulness that I will always look back on with great fondness. One moment the world was all 'Daddy, do this' and 'Daddy, can I have that?' and the next, after I'd pushed a load of *cérumen* further in rather than get it out, it was like I was underwater, I still had clarity of vision but the rest was all muffled, like a sedate conversation heard through thick walls. It was bliss.

Of course, I affected some level of trauma. Halfway through a conversation with Natalie or the boys I'd just hold up my hand, contrive some sort of emotion of loss, point to my ear theatrically and then waddle off unsteadily looking for a chair somewhere. After a couple of days people stopped trying to talk to me altogether and I was, shamefully, utterly at peace with the world as a result. I'd bought some de-blocking liquid at a local *pharmacie* in Nice, but it became clear pretty early on that it simply wasn't up to the task. I ostentatiously squirted the stuff in my ear in front of the family so that I could at least claim I was addressing the problem, but in reality all it did was add to the dampening of sound and increase my isolation.

For two weeks I stayed like that, even when I was back home alone and looking after the animals. It was like a holiday in a fancy retreat, but like all holidays it had to end and Natalie, quickly bored on her return with my deaf old man act, began to see through my faux discontent and booked me a doctor's appointment. I could have pretended not to have heard her of course but by now I was only taking written communication and that, as any lawyer will tell you, is binding.

The doctor was not happy. His secretary, also his wife, had booked me in for midday which is odd to say the least as France shuts down at midday for pre-lunch *apéritif*, so when he opened his door to let out what he thought was his last patient for the morning and saw me sitting there, he was not best pleased.

'Have you got an appointment?' he snapped.

'Yes,' I said, 'it was made with your wife this morning.' His shoulders sagged as he looked beyond the room to where his wife could be heard gossiping with the previous patients, 'typical' was the word running through his mind.

'OK, come in, come in,' he said testily while looking at his watch.

I explained the problem to him and he seemed to cheer up obviously thinking that this was easy and wouldn't take long at all. He jauntily wrote out a prescription without even looking in my ear and handed it to me with a flourish.

'Erm,' I stammered, trying to construct the French in my head, 'I've been using this stuff for a week. It hasn't worked.' His demeanour changed again and again he looked at his watch and then at me, a look of 'You're English, what do you know of lunch?' on his face. Again he looked on the verge of some personal defeat and seemed almost crippled with inaction as though he wanted to tell me to just clear off but knew that he couldn't.

'Right!' he said suddenly. 'Come with me!'

He led me into the 'surgery' part of his office and made me sit down by a sink, quite rough as he manhandled me into what he thought was a better position for the operation. He called his wife in to help.

'Blocked ear,' he barked at her. 'And we have to be in Orléans for two.'

'So what?' she replied, clearly used to these pre-food tantrums. 'It only takes an hour to get there.'

'Yes, well… hold this!' And he handed her a kidney-shaped pan. 'Hold it under the ear.'

He then attached something to a tap and then also attached an orange rubber hose. He turned the tap on and the water blasted out into the tiny sink, splashing back at him. He then pinched the end of the hose, like you would a garden hose, to make it a stronger, more concentrated jet of water.

'Ready?' I wasn't sure if he was asking me or his wife.

For the next five minutes, while he practically sat on my shoulder and twisted my head while power jetting my inner ear I was, to all intents and purposes, water boarded. All the while he barked instructions at his wife, 'Don't hold it like that, like this…' which meant he lost his aim with the hose and sprayed my face and clothes instead. 'Honestly,' he berated her, 'you understand nothing!'

That the Sarkozy–Kärcher treatment of my inner ear worked was nothing next to the satisfaction that he'd obviously got from the exercise, a chance to publicly shout at his wife and torture an Englishman seemed to leave him with a sadistic calm, like Laurence Olivier in *Marathon Man* and I could tell he was now going to enjoy his lunch all the more for the experience.

Despite the indignity of the treatment I have to admit that emerging from the surgery to the blast of summer birdsong was actually quite wonderful. I'd enjoyed my detachment, it had felt like a holiday in itself, but the real world suddenly sounded so good.

'Feel better?' Natalie asked when I got back, the boys splashing noisily behind her in the pool.

'Much. Feels good, actually,' I said, and I meant it.

'I've just been speaking to my sister,' Natalie continued almost whimsically, happy to be able to chat again I suppose. 'They've just adopted a Jack Russell puppy... where are you going, I'm talking to you!'

'I'm going to find some cotton buds,' I replied over my shoulder. 'And maybe a couple of bottle corks.'

The holiday was over.

PUSSY WHIPPED

Natalie was still broody, despite the holiday, and I'd enlisted the boys' help in taking precaution against unnecessary yearnings on her part. I was trying to keep a watchful eye – not heavy-handed, hopefully – just concerned, mindful.

When she proposed an urgent visit to the garden centre, then, alarm bells rang. French garden centres have pet stores attached, though in the case of Natalie's favourite garden centre it's not attached at all but right by the tills, potentially leading to the kind of horrible impulse buy which keeps animal charities in business these days.

'Why don't we go to Gamm Vert?' I suggested, knowing full well that Gamm Vert has no 'pet centre' at all. 'It might stock that new horse feed you want to try?' I added. The truth is, this actually killed two birds with one stone, if that's not an inappropriate metaphor, because Junior was obviously still ill, very ill. We appeared to be reaching a critical point as he continued to lose weight, despite our best efforts. He looked to have given up entirely the previous weekend while I was away; he had laid down a lot and had trouble standing. He seemed also, though the vet was pretty vague about this, to be far older than we were led to believe when we first got him and he was obviously struggling now.

'He's like you,' Natalie said at breakfast, watching him out of the window, on the verge of tears and after the increasingly perplexed vet had been again. I had just struggled down the stairs as my gout, or was it arthritis, problem had now spread to my hips. 'It looks like he's got an ulcer, he's permanently grumpy and he's also got some kind of hip-muscle problem.'

'It happens to the best of us,' I said, trying to be cheery, but as usual just managing to sound stoically aggressive, like a resentful war veteran.

'*He's* losing weight, though...' she added, sort of jokingly.

It was so difficult to know what to do. Junior was obviously seriously unwell, but as yet no diagnosis or subsequent medication had made any difference, and unfortunately it might just have been the ravages of age. He was now being bullied not just by Ultime but by the goats as well, like an old man who had married late in life and was in thrall to his younger family.

The sign on the Gamm Vert door was not encouraging, *'DONNONS CHATONS, DEMANDER À UN VENDEUR'* (Literally, 'Kittens to give away, ask a sales person') which, to continue the addiction metaphor is like announcing at an AA meeting 'Free vodka bath, dive in'. I ran ahead, thinking that if I could at least steer Natalie away from wherever the kittens were on show we'd be fine and perhaps even re-emerge kittenless. Who was I kidding, though?

The kittens weren't on show at all. They'd been born wild, *sur place*, and were therefore roaming and liable to pop up anywhere, completely un-policed, which is just typically cat. I don't know if Natalie was looking for them or whether she had seen the door sign, but within two minutes of staring at the wide range of hortensia on offer with Thérence while I kept a watchful eye, we were surrounded. I say surrounded, there was one playful little chap who kept popping out from behind the flowers and surprising Thérence, while his brothers and sisters hid under the pallet.

The *vendeuse* gave us the backstory while this happened. Abandoned blah, no home blah, people on my street kill cats otherwise blah, and all the while Natalie and Thérence played with the thing to the delight of all the staff.

'Ah, they're a great team!' said one. 'He's a little *comédien* your son!' said another.

'Yes. Like his *papa*,' Natalie said, to a dubious response from the staff who had one eye on me as I stood scowling, ten yards away in the dangerous gardening utensils section, angrily fingering the blade of a scythe.

Of course, I never stood a chance. Natalie affected surprise when I agreed to the adoption, as if I was too stupid to see that I was being blatantly emotionally blackmailed in public, and so we took 'Indiana Jones' (Thérence's choice) home with us under the quite absurd pretext of 'one extra mouth to feed is hardly going to make a difference now, is it?' 'A tiny thing like that? What difference could it make?'

He was minute, barely a couple of weeks old and within 24 hours we'd lost him, though he was subsequently found in a cavity behind the chimney. Earlier he had sunk his claws into Thérence's toes, which were dangling down from his chair as we sat eating dinner, and had done so with such viciousness that Thérence's resulting scream made me scream, which made everyone else scream. The other animals also eyed him with suspicion, much like when Oliver Twist was distrusted by his fellow urchins in Fagin's den, and particularly Vespa, strangely enough, who had been rescued in similar fashion but who clearly had no maternal instincts whatsoever.

I went out to see Junior who, despite a new delivery of hay, was sheltering in his stable and letting Ultime and the goats get on with the business of eating and gorging themselves. He looked tired, but calm as well, as though he was enjoying the peace and quiet for a bit, and for one of the few times in our relationship it felt like he didn't actually resent my presence. It felt like we were both hiding to be honest, like two old blokes in an allotment shed, no need to talk at all, just glad of the respite. It was only 30 minutes or so that we spent together, before one of the goats ran in looking flustered and out of place, like a hipster in the saloon bar of an old-fashioned local, but it meant a lot to me and maybe to him too. Finally, we seemed to have bonded in some way even if, as it may turn out, it's just a brief appearance of some kind of 'Cantankerous Anonymous', it will have been worth it.

Junior's deterioration coincided with the advent of autumn, and so it was time to get back to work, real work. Chutney production. I was back in the game.

It had been a good couple of years since I'd been able to actually produce anything, and I'd been bereft of original cooking projects. I'd even tried making my own sausages, nearly causing a serious rift at the local *boucherie*: 'Why are you just buying sausage casings, Monsieur?' the *boucher* had asked angrily, and not unreasonably. 'Is my meat not good enough for you?' Fortunately our relationship was restored when it turned out that my sausage efforts were just plain awful. But now the orchard fruit was back and chutney manufacture could recommence.

The apple trees, after a particularly bad mauling from Junior, had given up on life entirely but the pear tree was back, proudly showing its juicy wares, as was the propped up peach tree. The plum trees had gone absolutely crazy, though – firstly the plump, juicy *Reine Claude* (greengage), followed shortly after by the vibrant purple of the damsons. It all sounds beautifully romantic and bucolic to imagine us getting up for breakfast and foraging for fresh fruit of a morning, and to be fair Natalie and the boys quite often do in the autumn, but I've never really trusted fresh fruit.

Oh, I like the idea of it and I'm hugely protective of my orchard, but just picking a plum or something off a tree with scant regard for what may have laid eggs in the thing is utterly beyond me. Natalie, like her dad and most of her family as far as I can see, thinks nothing of plucking some ripe specimen and munching eagerly around the bad stuff. Madness if you ask me but there's more. Fresh fruit is messy, with its unregulated juice spouting off at every bite, and therefore not to be trusted if, like me, you'd rather not be seen in public at all than with telltale fruit stains all over your Fred Perry.

But the plums just kept on coming. I had already made dozens of jars of chutney; we'd made jam and 'leathers', or 'fruit roll-ups' as they're more commonly known. (See the recipe section at the back of the book.) We had made *clafoutis*, more chutney, extra leathers, another load of jam and litres and litres of damson gin, which all, in total only used up about two branches of the stuff. Now, like I say, I love a spot of chutney making and could quite happily spend all day in the kitchen, but there's a limit and just blindly producing industrial quantities of plum chutney is all very well, but after the fortieth kilo of de-stoning the things the novelty does tend to wear off, besides which I had to go to work at some point and I couldn't just let the things rot.

There's no way we could cope with the year's plum harvest alone – we needed help. Claudine is a friend who lives about a mile away, she has three children of similar ages to ours and we've known her since we moved in. She recently set up her own organic fruit and vegetable business, and was selling her produce at the local markets on Thursdays and Saturdays. Claudine is a very gentle, quietly spoken lady but she knows what she wants and although she was initially keen to sell our plums for us, she had to inspect them too and also confirm that they are in fact *'bio'*, or organic, and that they hadn't been 'treated' in any way.

Of course, my childish nature couldn't let an opportunity like this go past without comment.

'So you've invited a neighbour around to inspect my plums?' I asked Natalie. I know, puerile, and also as is my nature at times, utterly relentless for days on end and so what I perceived to be ribald hilarity, in the best tradition of the *Carry On...* films quickly palled until even Samuel couldn't help himself and just told me to 'give it a rest, Daddy, please?'

Claudine declared herself happy with my plums (you see? I just can't help it!) and took a large basket, possibly around 10 kg and a smaller basket of *pêches de vigne*. She did so the next day too and then two more baskets the following week.

PUSSY WHIPPED

I have to say that part of me, tragically, felt a little sad about giving up my fruit like that, which I know sounds odd but my orchard is important to me and the welfare of its fruit of genuine concern.

'What are you doing?' Natalie hissed at me in the market, spying me skulking about behind a stall opposite Claudine's, which I might add was doing a roaring trade.

'I'm just watching my plums.'

'You're weird,' she said.

I felt some strange kind of parental responsibility as I watched the basket quickly empty and gauged the 'worthiness' of prospective buyers, whether or not they'd treat my plums with the respect they deserved, that they were going to a good home.

'Are you really going to stand there all morning like this?' Natalie asked, after trying and failing to get me to move.

We made about €50 in the first week from Claudine's stall and still I felt some strange guilt about letting them go, a pathetic sense of loss which meant me moping around all through lunch on market day like I'd had to give up a litter of puppies or something. It was a very peculiar feeling. Natalie tried to insinuate that what I was feeling was a delayed shock, that the trauma of my botched vasectomy had come back to haunt me through the metaphor of 'lost plums', which of course brought the house down but which was unhelpful to say the least and a double entendre too far in my opinion.

It was good to be back in production again, though, everything seemed right with the world, like the place was complete again. Natalie had her new addition and I had my preserves, things were just about as normal as they could be. For now at least.

C'EST LA VIE

I remember Michael Caine once telling the story of filming *The Swarm* in the late 1970s; it was a filthy experience, he said. Most people who've seen it would probably agree. 'My new house in Hollywood needed carpets,' was Caine's creative process behind the decision to appear in the film, but that wasn't what he meant by filthy. Despite previous films being made in the uncomfortable jungles of Malaya, the arid plains and harsh mountains of India and even Elephant and Castle in London, Caine's abiding memory of *The Swarm* was when the bees were first released from their hive on the first day of 'bee shooting'. Millions and millions of the things were suddenly free, ready for their big moment in front of the cameras and they all, en masse, defecated on the film crew and assorted Hollywood glitterati.

'Bees, you see,' recounted Caine later on, 'never shit on their own doorstep.'

If only horses had the same level of domestic hygiene and decorum.

Look, I know the score; you have animals and you have to put up with the attendant 'produce'. Believe me, as parents of three growing boys Natalie and I are well aware of hygiene challenges. The constant smell, the incessant low rumbling and muffled farting of young boys followed by the inevitable giggling, and the seeming impossibility of actually urinating *in* the toilet most of the time forms a constant backdrop to our house; as Natalie says often, 'Men really are disgusting creatures.' The dogs defecate, as dogs do, in a free-range, ad-hoc manner, the cats either in their litter tray or next door to the litter tray depending on their mood, the hens generally in and around their coop, the goats whenever I look at them, but the horses...

PUSSY WHIPPED

I didn't realise just how stupid an animal a horse actually is. I've seen *War Horse* and this noble, heroic creature is about as close to the two dolts we have as Katie Price is to Audrey Hepburn, from a distance the same species but entirely different in almost every conceivable way. A certain amount of leeway had to be given to Junior while he was so ill and so when the latest attempt at giving him a boost was to increase his feed drastically, one naturally expected a manure windfall, but there's a time and a place surely.

Two enormous bales of hay arrived and were deposited in the field and they – Junior and Ultime – tucked in. And then they kept tucking in. In fact, they very rarely tucked out, occasionally leaving the 'Eat as much as you like' hay buffet in order to go and get a drink. But that was the only time they left the table, as it were. After a few hours they made the decision that bowel evacuation was simply not a good enough reason to interrupt their extended meal, nor was going for a wee, and so after a few days their pristine bales of hay, which had been neatly placed by the hedge, actually looked like a food fight in a particularly rancid public toilet. Natalie would go out every day for a week to try and sift the horse dung from the food, a futile job as the horses themselves wouldn't budge while she did so and would continue eating and egesting at the same time like some sordid art installation.

It was only a week later when the horses finally realised that what they were now eating was their own matter and they, like pampered royalty at the salad bar in Pizza Hut, lifted their haughty noses and walked away from it, a resentful look on their faces as if to say, 'How do you expect us to eat this muck?'

C'EST LA VIE

I was watching this absurd carry-on from my office where, while the boys were at school at least, I'd been locked in battle with a project that even then, even in its infancy, I was regretting for the sheer lunacy of what I'd taken on. It was mid-September and in early November, less than six weeks away, I would be performing my first stand-up show in French; the fact that, as yet, I hadn't written the set, translated what I had written or even – and this could be the serious fly in the ointment – learned French, was causing something of an earthquake in the confidence department.

There are a number of reasons I had booked the gig in the first place: firstly, I was convinced, 'was' being the operative word, that actually I *am* fluent in the language, but like a stubborn cork on an old bottle of wine my linguistic talents just needed an extra push to become unblocked.

I was wrong – I knew nothing.

I also thought that setting myself a deadline, that is the show itself, would mean I'd knuckle down and do the required work immediately and thoroughly. Fat chance. I had lived with myself for 42 years; I knew myself well and yet was still capable of operating on a quite farcical level of self-delusion.

I also had it in my head, in my head being shorthand for 'wildest dreams' or 'drunken blatherings', that I could become proficient enough to actually do some gigs in France. That by having some foot in the nascent French stand-up circuit I might not have to travel quite so far so often, or be away for quite so long.

I was now finally knuckling down and doing the work: writing, translating – with the help of a clearly worried Natalie – and learning my lines, my put-down lines and my 'improvised riffs'. I was beginning to seriously fret, working on a script I didn't even truly understand in order to bring stand-up, my job, closer to home.

In terms of doorstep, I was definitely more horse than bee.

QUESTION TIME

I had taken steps to improve my French, but they tended to be mainly administrative – a notebook here, a dictionary of rude words or idioms there. I needed conversation and face-to-face practice. The thing is, I am just not a sociable person. Just because I can handle audiences with a degree of confidence and authority doesn't mean that I can deal with social situations in the same way; I get very nervous and constantly have my eye on a potential escape route. I was sitting in the Old Red Lion pub on High Holborn having a nerve-calmer and tonic and already planning my 'leave early' – or even my 'not turn up at all' – strategy when I just thought 'sod it', downed my drink in one gulp and strode across the road and into the pub quiz.

I like a good pub quiz, but preferably with people I know and almost certainly in a language I have some flair for, but this was neither. Because, of my family's continuing and, I might add confidence-sapping, reluctance to speak French with me at home, I was now reduced to joining social language groups in an effort to improve, ironically in London too, and speaking with (rather than at) total strangers, is something I never do.

QUESTION TIME

This particular group was holding a celebratory bilingual pub quiz and it seemed, at least it had when I'd signed up for it a week earlier, a good ice-breaking idea. The pub was heaving.

'I know!' said Chad, apologetically, as he introduced himself as founder and chief organiser of the group; his American accent struggling to be heard above the din. 'It's so busy! There's a rival language group in here tonight…'

I didn't catch the end of what he said, not necessarily because of the noise but I'd drifted away on the idea that there was a 'rival' language group. I imagined them plotting in a dark corner somewhere and that before the night was out there'd be some violent 'conjugation-off' and some pretty salty vocabulary bandied about.

I was one of the first to arrive, and deliberately so; that way I wouldn't feel intimidated walking into a large group and then slink off after a couple of introductions, but the numbers soon swelled to around forty people, which delighted Chad no end. 'I'll bet the other group don't have this many!' he beamed.

The idea of the group was that it was a mix of French and English speakers, so both groups had the chance to improve the language they were learning, the French could meet English people and vice versa. I have no idea if it was roughly half and half English–French or not but the group within the group that I spent the evening with were mostly French, which suited me. Of course, they were there to practise their English, but they seemed equally happy just to be speaking French with other French people, so I got to speak quite a lot of French right from the start.

Part of my social reticence is down to what I do. This isn't false modesty; I'm a naturally shy person anyway, but I'm also aware that I am quite 'exotic'. Stand-up comedy is a fascination for lots of people, it's an unusual job and folk are quite often curious about what kind of people do it and how it works. As such, once I've told people what I do for a living it tends to dominate the conversation, and other people get drawn in on the back of, 'Ooh, have you met Ian? He's a comedian...', until you're surrounded and it's practically a gig; you then start worrying that other people will think that you're just showing off. Which is exactly what happened here, so it was a relief when we were divided up into teams and the quiz began.

There were five in our team, three men and two women, all, and this applied to at least 90 per cent of the group as a whole, as far as I could make out, a lot younger than me. There was Gilles, a Frenchman; Roberto, an Italian who spoke five languages and was just 'brushing the cobwebs from his *Français*', he said, with dispiriting accent-less eloquence, and Margot and Lucie from Paris, who were in London for a year just, equally enviably, 'for fun'.

The trust has gone from the pub quiz – smartphones have taken the innocence of the exercise away – so a couple of 'organisers' patrolled the tables making sure that nothing underhand was going on, but they needn't have worried. The quiz itself was almost secondary to the evening and provided a springboard for enthusiastic bilingual, sometimes pidgin, communication. No-one was taking the quiz that seriously, except for one bloke – me.

Look, I have a competitive streak. I don't like to lose; my granddad always said 'You can only do your best', but my dad also said that there's 'no point in doing anything if you're going to come second' and that's the one that's stuck with me. My

QUESTION TIME

fellow teammates found out pretty early on in the proceedings that this was no jolly, this wasn't something to be taken lightly and that I was, if needs be, prepared to argue my case strongly if I felt we were about to give the wrong answer. Fifteen minutes I spent trying to persuade Margot the folly of her ways and that I did indeed know the correct ingredients for a Mont Blanc, though she got her revenge when I said I'd never heard of 'Durdle Door' in Dorset and doubted that it even existed. We lost the quiz by one point and she subsequently blamed me and my poor Dorset knowledge for the defeat.

Frankly, I think the rest of the team were a bit relieved when the quiz was over and we could just get back to socialising. I was definitely having the better evening in terms of language, in that the vast majority of conversation at our table remained in French so I was learning and practising a great deal. Inevitably the conversation was largely about my job and, with the wine flowing, I began to get more loquacious, even treating it like a gig, shamelessly throwing in jokes and observations. Showing off basically.

'So Gilles,' Lucie asked, probably to cover the silence after one of my failed bilingual jokes, 'what do you do for a living in London?'

A slightly sheepish look came over his face.

'I'm a biologist,' Gilles replied, 'working on a cure for Alzheimer's disease.' Which is proper showing off.

I thoroughly enjoyed the evening and the confidence gained made me think that perhaps performing stand-up in French wasn't as beyond me as I thought, that perhaps it could be a viable option in the future. But linguistic confidence is one thing, personal confidence mixed with exhaustion was the real enemy.

C'EST LA VIE

Through a misreading of my diary I had driven over to London and was due to drive back to France again after work on the Saturday. I had filled the not inconsiderable space in the Land Rover with the usual English 'delicacies' and had gone to fill up the car with diesel in preparation for the long, late-night drive back. While the assistant was waiting for me to make my mind up on whether to buy an original Yorkie or branch out into the more exotic raisin and biscuit variety, her colleague let out an exclamation.

'Ooh Sharon, I think we have a leak on Pump 17!' They both looked at me as a second earlier I'd said 'Pump 17' and then we all three turned to look at Pump 17 and my car sitting next to it spewing out diesel at an alarming rate.

'LOCK DOWN!' said a man suddenly emerging from the back office and Sharon gave me a pitying look as she handed me back my cards and receipt. 'I wouldn't start that up if I were you,' she said, as if having weighed up the evidence in the two minutes that she'd known me she thought that was exactly the sort of stupid thing I'd do. The garage was emptied of other customers and roped off; new customers were denied access, which on a busy Saturday morning at a Sainsbury's petrol station wasn't popular and led to a few catcalls on seeing my car of 'Bloody French! F**K off home!'

The fire brigade arrived within minutes, all massive blokes with a sense of purpose and expertise that just made me look small and inadequate in every way and, an hour later, a cheerily driven low-loader truck was heading off into the distance with my stricken, crisp-laden vehicle on the back of it.

My first thoughts at this point weren't, how much will this cost? Nor, how do I get to work? Or even, which garage is it being taken to? No, my first thought was 'How do I still get home tonight?' During the week Samuel had been in tears again that I was going away so soon after being away the last time. It was heartbreaking knowing that there was still no alternative, he needed me around, and was finding the pressure on him hard when I wasn't. I'd cheered him up by promising that it was 'only for two nights, I'll be back before you know it'. And I was determined to make good that promise, no matter what the cost.

Fortunately, Eurostar cater nicely for the 'no matter what the cost' type travellers and I was back in the Loire Valley by mid-afternoon on the Sunday. I was exhausted, certainly a bit down and quite paranoid too as the mechanic had called the evening before and suggested darkly that my car may have been the victim of foul play and that someone had possibly cut the pipes to drain the fuel.

My mind was racing, to be honest; paranoia fed on a diet of exhaustion and stress is a dangerous mix, and as Natalie drove me home from the station it was with a dull sense of surrealism that I noticed an elephant grazing in a field by the side of the road.

'An elephant!' said Thérence from the back of the car. Why it was there is anybody's guess, but my mind just viewed it and filed it, storing it away in a box marked 'More things to worry about'. It all felt like I was in one of those 1970s conspiracy films, I was being targeted by some shadowy organisation who knew that the best way to bring me down was to deliver regular little blows to my fragile mental state. An elephant on a French farm was just a cherry on the cake from some evil genius in an unofficial government office somewhere.

C'EST LA VIE

Home didn't immediately work to dispel these thoughts either. One of the *dépendances* (outbuildings) was stinking morbidly and covered in flies, proof that there was something rotting in there that needed to be got rid of pronto. Again, the sense of cinematic suspicion was all-prevailing as our 'hero' returns home to find a corpse. It was rats, two of them, and in fairly advanced stages of decomposition, and so we spent two hours clearing everything out of the room, disposing of the maggoty carcasses and disinfecting the place. As homecomings go, it wasn't the best.

The constant travel was by now taking a physical toll as well as a psychological one, and I had been to see one of Natalie's uncles, Pierre, a doctor. He eschewed my previous diagnoses of gout and arthritis, and basically said that my body was 'all out of whack'. A frighteningly fit man himself he referred me to a *podologue* (podiatrist) so that, he added cheerfully, 'we could start at the bottom'. I wasn't keen.

Feet should be a private thing; open-toed footwear allowed only on sandy beaches, and anyone who removes their shoes on public transport subjected to the strongest punishment in the land. Podiatrists, and this goes for their henchmen chiropodists, should operate in gloomy backstreets or do home visits, or preferably not at all. Podiatry is a perversion frankly and those who practise it should be on more than just a medical register.

In any case, the young podiatrist closely examined my right foot, holding it in his hand while I was almost overcome with a feeling of nausea as he twisted it this way and that; he moved his head closer to it, and fiddled with the ball, the heel and the toes. Occasionally he would look up to ask me a question and he seemed confused by the look of permanent

QUESTION TIME

horror on my face, my lip curled as I held his gaze and silently wondered just what kind of deviant he was. I think he took my disdain personally and prescribed surgically moulded inner soles to arrest a chronic foot, back, leg disorder, the fault of which he laid squarely at the foot – no pun intended – at the kind of light, unsupportive dandified loafers I wear often. He'd asked me to bring along a selection of my footwear (Natalie suggested I might need to hire a van for this) and he'd looked at them aghast like they were the very reason he'd decided to fight the good podiatry fight in the first place.

He might be right of course, but after nearly eleven months of various diagnoses for my pain I wasn't going to be doling out any congratulations just yet. I was going to wait and see if the new inner soles actually made a difference and that he wasn't, as I suspected, just keen on collecting casts and drawings of people's feet.

Diagnosis is the hardest part of medicine, I was once told – that's why *House* is so popular, most of the time it's literally a mystery. For example, poor Junior had been ill for a year now and we were no closer to finding out why.

Our new vet, who replaced our previous vet when she'd returned to Belgium, is an unhappy looking man. He has thin, receding hair; almost yellow, unhealthy looking skin; a slight hunchback and a disappointed look in his eyes that betrays his feelings about moving to this rural backwater, which is surely the death knell for the career of an ambitious vet. A few visits from us mind and he seemed to find his swagger, and no wonder.

The kitten, Indiana Jones, needed his first set of jabs and Toby needed some sort of dog booster, and begrudgingly you pay the exorbitant fees for these things, but then he started actively touting for extra business. He made it very clear when he first arrived that he was a domestic animal vet only – horses, hens, goats, etc. he felt were outside of his remit, presumably as a Frenchman regarding them more as foodstuffs than animal companions. He'd changed his mind now though.

Tallulah was a bit peaky again. She was moulting, which is never a good sign, she'd lost her voice and the most obvious sign of poor health, her crest had literally fallen, giving her the look of a late-night reveller whose party hat has gone skew-wiff and had clearly overindulged. Natalie mentioned this to the vet while he was mid-jab and I swear his eyes lit up. I think both of us were just expecting a Gallic shrug but no, he fair bounded over to his medicine cabinet and produced with a flourish a small vial of dark-brown liquid, which he described as a 'tonic'.

He suddenly became like a snake-oil salesman from some old Western film and started listing its magical (or mythical) healing properties, 'five drops of this a day and your hen will be back laying the railroad…' I'll admit scepticism is a default setting of mine, but I was in a mood to believe. Tallulah is my favourite hen, if not animal full-stop. She is like an avian Maggie Smith, bustling about the place, judgementally pecking at the floor, quite often telling me off for being in her way or admonishing the dogs for their apparent immaturity. I'll be honest, I didn't think hens would have a personality, but Tallulah has bags of it and I don't like to see her down.

Still, €137 for two jabs and some chicken tonic was a bit strong. Natalie was taking no chances with any of the animals though and feared any further problems akin to Junior's.

QUESTION TIME

Vespa had gone missing, something which distressed us all, but Natalie more so, so like an old-fashioned matriarch she was defending what was left of her family and at any cost.

Junior's muscle loss and overall demeanour was getting worse, his only daily respite from Ultime's bullying was when Natalie let him out into the garden to 'cut the lawn'. He would suddenly perk up, like he'd won a reprieve, a stereotypical mousy husband escaping his harridan of a wife and hiding in the bookmakers for the afternoon. This annoyed Ultime massively and she would watch from her paddock, occasionally stamping her hooves in anger and frustration as he took long sips from the swimming pool and threw a glance in her direction.

The pool was a relatively safe place to drink from; I had stopped putting chemicals in weeks ago, but the sheer decadence of the gesture was magnificent, like some ageing monarch of a crumbling empire having one last aristocratic hurrah. And in the background Tallulah would be given her sips of hen pick-me-up, while Flame and Indiana Jones tossed small rodents at each other. In animal terms it all had a whiff of the last days of the Roman Empire about it, pampered creatures pushing excess and wantonness to their depraved limits.

And it didn't end there. Having struggled to move the caravan with the punctured tyre out of the field ('It gets in the horses' way'), I took a deserved shower and went looking for my slippers and some 'feet-up' time, only to be told that I couldn't have my new medically enhanced slippers as they were 'occupied'. A toad apparently was asleep in one of them and shouldn't be disturbed.

And apparently *we're* the dominant species…

C'EST LA VIE

Poor Junior, though. Natalie was keen to seek further advice, quite rightly, arguing that she could deal with bad news if it came to it, but not knowing what the problem was was eating her up. The once mighty, albeit cantankerous, beast had by now seen more horse vets than Desert Orchid, but something was terribly amiss. Some had said sand colic, some had said he was older than we thought, others had said worms or an ulcer. Our local vets had been tried and exhausted with no discernible improvement – quite the opposite – so now we were looking further afield for an explanation. Monsieur Corbeau used to be a mechanic in the area until ill health forced his retirement, but he was using his free time now, among other things, to train horses for *attelage*, horse and carriage riding basically, a popular sport over here. Natalie bumped into him in the market and they talked about Junior's plight. Corbeau had been the most conscientious mechanic I had ever met; I remember his look of horror when I turned up at his workshop with a camper van I'd bought on eBay.

'Where have you driven this from?' he asked incredulously and seemingly afraid to touch it.

'Manchester.' I beamed.

'Oh God! You're lucky to be alive!' he said and snatched the keys off me in case I was planning on driving it any further.

He regarded Junior as being in a similar state of disrepair and offered to drive Natalie and Junior in his horsebox to a renowned vet about an hour away.

'This is so kind of you,' Natalie said to him when they returned from the first of two long vet journeys.

He looked at her, slightly confused. 'Not really,' he said. 'It's what we do for them,' he added, slightly embarrassed and handed Natalie Junior's lead rope.

QUESTION TIME

Junior was given a number of blood tests, none of which proved anything, only that the second set were worse than the first in some way. If it was an ulcer, which they couldn't apparently determine without an endoscopy, then the treatment would be €800. An endoscopy could only be done in either Paris or Le Mans, either of which are a six-hour round trip away in Monsieur Corbeau's horsebox and poor Junior would have to be starved for 16 hours prior to the camera exploring his insides. The vet, the most recent one anyway, feared the worst, however, a cancerous tumour, for which there was no treatment.

While in the garden and away from Ultime, Junior had tried to come in through the front door, clearly feeling low and needing Natalie to soothe the savage beast as it were. He briefly gave me a look of contempt when I appeared in the doorway rather than his mistress and when she did appear it was like he was asking her, 'Really, what *do* you see in him?'

She led him gently back to the garden, the bond between them so strong and so trusting, so loving. It was one of his last days.

26

THEY SHIFT HORSES, DON'T THEY?

A number of people kindly pointed out to Natalie that 'at least they're only animals', as if the cloud of frustration and despair would suddenly lift from her and everything would be just immediately hunky dory again. I never really understand this kind of remark: people who go around saying that 'humans are more important and we should take *more* care of *them*' as if you have to make a choice at some point, choose a side, like there's only so much compassion you're allowed to show for living creatures. They seem to be missing the point. It's not one or the other. Frankly, that's just errant nonsense and ignores the fact that animals, especially for us, especially our animals, are *part of the family*. I mean, for Heaven's sake, anyone who really thinks that I'm somewhere in the pecking order above almost any of the livestock we have clearly isn't paying attention. Besides which, both Junior and the still missing Vespa had been integral to so much that had happened to us as a family ever since we'd been here.

The place felt empty. In the days that followed Junior's death Natalie tried to get through, as she always does, by planning big, outdoor things for the spring. The goats had helped her in the garden redesign project by escaping *again*, and eating her precious rose bushes and prized fern, a particularly stupid and wanton act of vandalism when you consider that their only ally around the place was Natalie herself, but it didn't bother her that much. She was dealing with the death of Junior, probable death of Vespa and decidedly unoptimistic future of Tallulah in her usual way.

I also suspected that she had plans in the animal department too. She had tried to convince me a week after Junior's death that what we needed was another puppy, to which even the boys were sceptical and I could tell her heart wasn't really in it, yet. She was just laying down a marker. We had a new neighbour who had moved in in the autumn and who had set up a dog-breeding business, and although they live half a mile away, they could be heard. We're not keen on the whole pedigree dog-breeding industry anyway, and although we had never actually seen them, around feeding time, if the wind was blowing in our direction, you could hear dozens of highland terriers all yapping excitedly for their dinner. Natalie had taken to standing on the *terrasse* listening to the cacophony, her head tilted like she was trying to understand them. I feared that at some point over the next few months she would attempt a night raid or at least a reconnaissance mission to check on their conditions.

Junior was irreplaceable though and, being Junior, was never likely to go quietly, staying in character right to the end, and beyond.

'Darling, the swimming pool engineer refuses to come in until we've put the horse away' is pretty much the apotheosis of middle-class, first-world problems. I found myself shouting this up the stairs to Natalie and immediately needed a sit down, a few moments to take a good long hard look at myself.

The truth was that I had every sympathy for Monsieur DeFrenne, the poor pool engineer. He had arrived, probably in a mood of late-afternoon optimism, no doubt feeling that this would be his last call of the day, a simple *hivernage* (putting the pool into winter hibernation) and then it would be home to a warming cognac or something. What he hadn't expected as he tried to get through the gate was a seriously ill-looking horse acting as bouncer and clearly taking a dislike to the poor man. Junior was very obviously unwell and a shadow of his former size, but there was still enough residual hate in his veins for snorting maniacally at boiler-suited strangers who had the temerity to turn up unannounced.

I tried to move him myself but he was having none of it from me, and so the three of us just stood there awkwardly filling time, Junior very obviously not taking his eye off the increasingly nervous Monsieur DeFrenne. We tried to make small talk about the weather and so on, but each time one of us finished Junior would just let out a snort as if he was making derogatory remarks about our shallow and uneasy attempt at bonhomie. Natalie duly arrived and of course the old sod was immediately politeness itself, though as he was led away he would stop every few yards and turn his head back to the anxious and still unwilling-to-enter pool technician, just to let him know...

To be fair, Junior hadn't been behaving like this as often as he used to. To us it seemed obvious that he had cancer; the length of his illness and the loss of weight seemed to indicate that. We were guessing of course and no-one in the horse-related veterinary world seemed willing to commit to such a diagnosis. The tests, though why this is I still don't know, would have to be carried out miles away and at some absurd expense while all the while it was obvious that the poor horse was fading. I'm not sure then if the tests would have told us anything we didn't already know but instead just added to the distress of the poor animal. Ultime didn't know how to respond either; one minute she would be crying out for him when he was allowed to roam outside the paddock and would then give him something of a beating on his return, to the extent that she now had to be separated from him altogether.

Tallulah, the oldest hen, was still suffering too and her 'tonic' drops were becoming less and less effective as she croaked quietly away to herself, her crest now lying so limply across her head it was like a Bobby Charlton combover and her feathers on the face of it seemed paler. Vespa had now been missing for six weeks, leaving Natalie heartbroken. Vespa had gone missing before but never while the hunting season was on, she stayed close to home then, and not while we had a seeming epidemic of foxes in the area too. Monsieur Girresse, now apparently allowed back in the public eye by his watchful family, proudly announced to us that he had shot 52 foxes since September. Vespa, he therefore suspected, had been the victim of one of the 'red vermin'.

In all the time we have lived here I had only seen one fox and that was two miles away, so there was a nagging feeling, possibly and hopefully unfairly, but expressed by other neighbours too, that poor Vespa may have been the victim of

C'EST LA VIE

Girresse himself. But unless Vespa – in some form or other – turned up, who knew what had happened to her.

Either way, what with Junior's death and Vespa's disappearance, Natalie was taking it badly. I'm not one necessarily to pooh-pooh modern mental health disorders, we live in a relentless world and the pressures that come with it bring forward new issues, but it always struck me that seasonal affective disorder (SAD) was one of the woolliest of these new-fangled maladies. Maybe, and as a direct result of my job, it's that I spend so much time in darkened rooms or am out late at night that the idea of bleak, dirty grey, long winter days isn't that much of a culture shock. Also, I find it hard to credit that anyone born in the British Isles would possibly suffer from SAD as most years it's pretty much the one 'season' anyway.

I've changed my mind on this, though.

Natalie has always suffered from it. Her desire, need almost, to be outside in the garden is trampled on by the onset of harsh weather and the dark days, and her mood – and overall happiness – suffers accordingly as she's left cooped up like a songbird in a cage, unable to spread her horticultural wings. She's always hated the winter anyway, the weather is foul and keeps her indoors, but the sense that this new winter season very much marked the end of something was compounded by the fact that by the end of it there was a very real possibility that not only would we be without our first horse, but possibly our first cat and our first hen too, and that was a very depressing thought indeed.

Junior had looked awful when I had returned home on the Sunday evening. He was stood in the stable, facing the corner like a punished schoolboy, his head hung low and his mouth open, practically motionless, and there seemed that there was nothing we could do for him now. It being a Sunday the horse vet was unlikely to come out and we weren't at all sure that we would want her to anyway, fearing that a very painful decision would then have to be made. We decided instead to wait until the morning and call the vet first thing.

As is normal for a school day, on Monday, Natalie was up early with the boys and went out to see Junior. He was lying down and the end was near. He responded to her touch, again the closeness of their relationship offering comfort, even at this stage, to both of them. Natalie briefly returned indoors to call the vet and then went back out to be with him again. It was too late. You can read all manner of things into events like this, positives and negatives, but it really did seem that through some tremendous force of will he had been determined to hang on until morning to say goodbye to his mistress and, because of the Olympian levels of stubbornness he could call on, had managed to do just that.

Natalie was inconsolable. It didn't matter that this had been on the cards for weeks, if not months; it didn't make the end any easier to bear and while Samuel and Thérence kept their distance, a naturally curious Maurice wanted to say his goodbyes too. As a sensitive and emotional little boy it may not have been the right thing to do, and affected him for a good couple of weeks afterwards, but I honestly think he would have been more upset if we hadn't let him see Junior one final time. They stood there together in the cold stable, holding on to each other.

'Can't we bury him?' said a sobbing Maurice.

'We're not allowed to,' Natalie said.

C'EST LA VIE

'Even just a bit of him?' Maurice begged.

I took the boys to school while Natalie began the necessary process of registering Junior's death and therefore arranging for his body to be taken away. The website for the Haras Nationaux was the obligatory first step, but in order to begin Natalie had to set up a username and password, something which even the most frivolous of websites demand these days so that they can bombard you with spam later; but it's difficult enough to come up with an original and secure password at the best of times, when it's during the registration of the death of your horse your mind is naturally on other things.

Once that had been done, the particulars had to be filled in, name, address, cause of death and so on, which is all very well and can't actually be questioned but because the website was having serious problems, every time Natalie submitted the information she would be returned to the home screen and asked to start the whole process again. Things were painful enough as they were without having some technical Groundhog Day issues stretching the thing out, meaning Natalie had to repeatedly re-enter the raw details over and over again.

She composed herself and rang the helpline instead which helpfully suggested calling back later, when someone helpful would be there to help – all, unhelpfully, at a time that suited them.

We went back out to the stable while waiting for French bureaucracy to start its working week. I had had to move Junior's considerably heavy head in order to shut the stable door and keep Ultime and the goats out but Ultime was now nudging at the door trying to get in, knowing something was wrong. The vet, who we had rung for advice, suggested that it might be better to let her in to the stable so that she too could say her goodbyes but it wasn't that easy trying to move Junior aside again.

I've had to deal with quite a few animal deaths in the past few years but the sheer size of Junior put this on an altogether different scale and I couldn't see how he could possibly be moved at all, assuming we eventually got through to the bureaucrats who could sign this off. I got the door open enough to let Ultime in and she moved in gingerly and quietly and nuzzled, kissed even, Junior's lifeless head and neck. Their relationship had been fraught for the past few months, but there was genuine affection once again in his death it seemed.

'Congratulations! You're eligible for a discount!' The horse department *fonctionnaire* wasn't quite as jolly as that but even so, it was a bizarre start. Why we were entitled to a discount on our horse corpse removal needs was unclear, maybe it was the beginnings of a nascent loyalty scheme and while €120 is clearly better than €200 it wasn't, unsurprisingly, our most pressing issue. We were given a job number, and an email containing a docket would be sent shortly which we would then have to print out and 'leave by the animal'. It was all so cold. I know these people deal with these things all day every day but the bedside manner left a lot to be desired.

The *équarrisseur* – I looked up the translation and did not like what I found, '*équarrisseur*: noun (m) – squarer, butcher, hewer, knacker' – arrived late morning in a massive lorry which wasn't even going to get through the gates, never mind up towards the stable where Junior lay. We had explained this to him on the phone but he wanted to come by anyway, he said, to see just what the situation was. A young-looking, wiry man, he showed the kind of compassion and understanding which had hitherto been lacking in the whole process and despite, you would have thought, having become quite desensitised to these things, he dealt with a difficult situation with real warmth and sympathy.

That did not detract from the very real problem, however, of how we were going to move Junior's body. The *équarrisseur's* lorry, which had a large grabber on the back like one of those fairground arcade games, would have to stay out the front and Junior be brought to it. I'd had trouble just moving his head, in fact I had trouble moving him when he was alive, so lifting his dead body would be impossible and even if we could do that there was no way that we could carry him the sixty or so metres to the front gate. It was all very stressful and Natalie, keeping remarkably calm, rang the farmer Monsieur Rousseau for advice.

Rousseau, unfortunately, was in hospital, though he didn't reveal this information until, with his usual patience and good humour, he said to Natalie that he'd love to come and help but things were a little difficult at the moment. That was the measure of the man though, and a mark of just how different he was to Girresse, our other farmer neighbour, was that he asked two of his farm hands to go around and help us, something neither he, nor they, had to do at all. The *équarrisseur* pointed out though that in order to move Junior at all, and that was assuming that we could, we would have to dismantle the stable walls because the door gap would be too narrow even if we could lift him. Natalie took the man inside and gave him a coffee while I set about the stable in the presence of Junior's lifeless body. The amount of times that I'd had to rebuild this stable wall because of his escape attempts or simple aggressive peevishness meant that you could have driven a car at the thing now and it wouldn't have collapsed, but here in one final act of massive inconvenience he had me working on it again, taking it down for his smooth passage to who knew where. He would have loved that.

Rousseau's colleagues arrived and the *équarrisseur*, with a now wilting Natalie, came back to the stable; Manuel had arrived too but seemed reluctant to get involved. With the stable wall down, the horrible next step was to move Junior's body to the gate by attaching tow ropes to him and dragging him behind a heavy jeep. It would, the farmhands said, clearly having some experience in the matter, be pretty awful and Natalie and I should go inside and they would call us when it was over.

Natalie didn't want to leave him but recognised it was for the best while I said that I'd remain with Junior. 'Are you sure?' the men asked again. 'The sound is awful.' I knew about the death groan and was expecting it, it even sounded like Junior was having one last scornful dig at me and I didn't mind that, but I'm not sure why I didn't just do as I was told and stay inside with Natalie. I wasn't trying to be heroic or look manly in front of these people, any look at what I was wearing had already made their minds up in that regard, I just wanted to be with him.

We had had our run-ins, he never hid his contempt for me but I wanted to be there for him not just leave him in the hands of strangers; I admit though, I had trouble holding it together as his body was pulled unceremoniously to the gate. The force of resistance from the ground kept dragging his head back as he was pulled along making it look once again like he was fighting any attempt to make him obedient or to pacify him; one final futile battle fought for his own benefit, the head held arrogantly high just for the sake of dignity. The grabber picked him up and placed him, thankfully gently, into the lorry. The roof closed noisily behind him and with that, Junior was gone.

JUST THE BEGINNING...

'You must wake up every morning, look out of your window and just pinch yourself?'

Yes, well, you'd think so, wouldn't you? But to anyone who knows me, who knows what a neurotic, pessimistic doom-monger I can be then they wouldn't waste their breath asking that question, which is why it was something of a surprise that it came from my sister-in-law, who knows me better than most. So the answer is 'no'. No, I do not wake up every morning, count my blessings and go about enjoying the experience, because usually I've woken in the middle of the night, in a cold sweat and have been fretting over whether it's in any way sustainable.

I don't know what role performing stand-up in French will play in the grand plan, if any at all, but the first gig would be a strong gesture of intent and so there was an awful lot riding on it. But since I had booked it in June, largely at the boys' behest, it had hung over me like a dark cloud, like I'd set the date for my own professional execution. And as the date approached so my nerves got worse, and the many, many reasons I could come up with for cancelling it got more and more compelling and more and more tempting to use. My nerves made Natalie and the boys nervous too; I said to Natalie a week before the show just how anxious I was about the whole thing and she had replied, 'I know! It's making me sick just thinking about it!', which was hardly the vote of confidence I was fishing for. And it wasn't just close family who feared for me either: Cendrine, my hairdresser in France, asked me how I was practising, specifically who I spoke French with, considering she knew that we don't speak the language at home.

'You're the only person I speak French with on a regular basis,' I pointed out to her in what, even for me, was bad French. She went silent, avoided eye contact and hurriedly changed the subject, quite rightly making the assumption that our six-weekly vocabulary struggles with my fussy, mod hairstyle needs were hardly the stuff of performance articulacy.

It wasn't that people thought it would go badly; it's just that anybody who I spoke to about it couldn't really understand why I was doing it at all. Even I was a little hazy about the whole thing. Like moving to France in the first place, the reasons for doing so were numerous – if it went well. If it didn't go well, then professionally it wouldn't make any difference – stage confidence can be a fragile thing, but dying on my hole in French would have little or no effect on my 'English' performances. However, as far as my self-confidence goes, in the country in which we've chosen to live, it would have been a crushing blow. And not just for me, but for Natalie, Samuel,

Maurice and Thérence too, who would be doomed to a life of translating for the thickie in the corner.

When I first started doing stand-up I had no great ambitions in the industry – far from it. I can honestly say that for almost the first ten years of being a stand-up comedian I was so shocked that I was being paid for it at all that I almost tried to hide myself away, convinced that at some point someone would tap me on the shoulder and tell me my time was up, that I'd gatecrashed the party for long enough, off you go. This was different. If I could crack this I could potentially be at home far more than I currently was; I could actually leave for a gig and return on the same day, a luxury that was the only thing I missed about not still living in England. Also, I desperately needed to improve my French and I thought if I gave myself a deadline I would stop hiding behind Natalie and the children and actually do something about improving my language skills. Cockily, I'd always convinced myself that I already had the language skills but somehow they were suffering from some kind of locked-in syndrome and that this gig would act as a plunger and suddenly the dormant linguist would spill forth.

Yes. I was wrong about that.

When I sat down to write the French set with Natalie it became apparent, very early on, that my French skills were, in a word, *merde*. I had a certain level of vocabulary, but my grammar and sentence construction were pathetically weak, which made our joint writing sessions somewhat fraught. I would tell Natalie what I wanted to say and she would come up with a sentence that looked so complicated it was like the work of a French Chaucer. For Natalie, correct grammar and sentence construction is almost an evangelical obsession, sometimes she'll just stare angrily at social media on the computer for hours, shaking her head and on the verge of tears at the 'crimes' perpetrated by grammar nihilists. In the end we had to call in Samuel to help with the writing, just so that we could find some acceptable middle ground between my laissez-faire attitude to accurate syntax and Natalie's Académie Française wordiness.

Strangely enough, I was never that concerned with whether what we were writing was actually funny or not. By choosing to do the gig in London to a French audience and talking about how embarrassingly pitiful my French is, I was essentially preaching to the converted. My logic being that they live and work in England, they are therefore, the majority at least, Anglophones and linguists, so it was going to be a subject they knew about. What worried me most, apart from learning the lines themselves, was the complete lack of skills I would have as a performer in a language I'm not comfortable speaking. Chatting to the front row, reacting to heckles, ad-libs, asides – all vital weapons in a stand-up's weaponry – these were going to be unavailable to me, or so I thought. It was going to be like my first gig all over again, only with a lot fewer words than I had at my disposal then.

The show was to be on a Monday night and I spent the weekend in monk-like solitude in a hotel in King's Cross, eschewing all offers of sociability. I read and re-read my script. It was important that I knew not only *what* I was saying, but *why*. There was no point, nothing to be gained linguistically, if I just learned it by rote. I was like a school pupil before an important exam, too scared to move with any fluidity in case some of the recently gained knowledge fell out of my ears.

On the Sunday, Armistice Day, I went for a walk in Regent's Park. It was a glorious, sunny morning and the park was busy with people taking advantage of the weather, though some were perplexed by the sight of a suited mod, walking the paths, waving his arms about and reciting French very loudly and to no-one in particular. I'd gone there for a bit of peace, but after 20 minutes that peace was violently broken. It sounded like a huge gathering of angry hornets and suddenly the tranquillity of the place was ruined by the incessant, and to me glorious, whining of about three hundred mod scooters! I had inadvertently become encircled by the annual Remembrance Rideout and all of a sudden this mod, deep in his own anxiety and fearing for his immediate future, was surrounded by 'brothers'. I took it as a sign.

I went to The Comedy Store early on Monday evening, nervous as hell. The brilliant staff there, most of whom I've known for years, could tell at once I was dreading the show. I was visibly shaking with nerves, carrying my script around with me as though at this late stage that would make any difference at all. I was introduced to the two French acts who were the main attraction on the bill and they were friendly, even concerned as my fragility was tragically obvious.

The lights went down, the music stopped and the French headline act, Le Comte de Bouderbala (which translates as 'Lord of the Ghetto'), gave me a warm introduction to the stage.

I walked on to the famous Comedy Store stage, like I'd done hundreds of times before, took the microphone out of its stand

and promptly forgot everything I'd planned to say. I shuffled about a bit, said *'Bonsoir'*, pretended to look at my hand for the next bit – in my head desperately trying to remember what the hell I should be talking about. I had said to Simon, the stage manager and a good friend, before the gig that what I really needed for my set to be a success was the audience to buy into it, to buy into the 'character' of an Englishman out of his comfort zone, struggling in a language totally alien to him. And eventually, once I had actually begun to speak, they did, thankfully they did. Partly, of course, because this 'character' that they thought was being acted out in front of them was not a comedy character at all; this act had integrity, honesty and pathos because I really was that struggling Englishman, it was about as authentic as I've ever been.

My time on stage absolutely flew by, so much so that in the end, by the time I'd regained a grip on my script, I had to cut things out as I went along, surprising myself with my ability to mentally edit a foreign-language script while still performing. I did my time, the red light came on signalling that it was over and I left the stage to a thundering ovation, a packed Comedy Store house all cheering and whooping, and walked into the dressing room and the warm congratulations, and relief, of the other acts.

As a mark of how well it had gone the French comedienne who followed me on stage opened her set by asking the audience how on earth they had managed to understand me, 'what with that accent of his'. They didn't like that at all, some even booed her. They had very much taken 'their' Englishman to their hearts.

JUST THE BEGINNING...

Everybody else in the building seemed almost as relieved as I was and then the talk was all about when I'd be doing my next one, come back and do a full set next time, have you thought about touring? I felt like crying. The relief was almost too much to bear and the exhaustion was suddenly overwhelming too.

I returned home the next day on a massive high, I undertook the journey not in my usual state of mute fatigue but with a newfound confidence. Suddenly I was that annoying bloke on public transport, the one who wants to chat, but I didn't care, I felt good and I was going home too.

I was tired, though. Seventeen days I'd been gone, and during that time I had occupied seven different beds, it was time for some serious, and hopefully prolonged, home duvet action.

I really am naive at times.

I don't remember specifically volunteering to become a dinner lady, though I have no reason to doubt Natalie at all on this. Maybe she's become a hypnotist and has me 'volunteering' for all sorts of things without my knowledge, maybe the constant, round-the-clock diet of *Star Wars* films has taught her Jedi mind tricks or maybe, and this is far more likely, I was lulled into it while away and over the course of a late-night phone call was caught up in a fatal mix of 'trough of despond' and 'misty-eyed homesickness' during which, in all honesty, I'd volunteer for anything if it meant being nearer to her and the boys.

The result, however, was rather than have a lie-in at home for once; I was up at the crack of dawn armed with my apron, a catering-sized bottle of HP Sauce, a hundred teabags and a whisk. Maurice's primary school were involved in a project about 'foods of the world', not just specific foods themselves but eating habits and meals and the like, and as part of this project planned to cook the entire school a full English breakfast, the FEB. The full English breakfast holds quite a fascination for the French: firstly, they think we all eat it, *all* of us, and every day. I have pointed out before that this isn't the case and that if it were then life expectancy in the UK would be about twenty-seven and no Calais-bound ferry would ever leave Dover, and would just sink instead.

They really don't know much about it, so it was suggested that maybe some hands-on knowledgeable supervision in the kitchen would be appropriate, in other words some cooking. Natalie and I had discussed the 'menu' with the school already, mushrooms were out, they said, too unpopular with kids; sausages and bacon were a given; baked beans (an American addition but as long as tomato ketchup was to be added to the rather insipid locally bought stuff, I was prepared to tolerate it); black pudding, though a local delicacy, was decided against too, and no tomatoes; I can't remember why, but as I'm allergic to the things I wasn't fussed. Hash browns were suggested, at which point I threatened to throw a full-on Gordon Ramsay hissy fit if anyone threatened to 'further Americanise my culinary heritage'; fried bread on the other hand, once explained, nearly scuppered the entire venture. Which left eggs: fried or scrambled? Well, it's a personal taste thing isn't it? Personally, I like a poached egg, but seeing as I was 'the egg department' and would be cooking the things for over a hundred seven- to eleven-year-olds, it was going to be scrambled as anything else would be far too difficult to get

JUST THE BEGINNING...

right. Anyway, the main thing to remember about an FEB once you've decided on the make-up of the plate, is that the food must all be touching each other. This isn't haute cuisine and this may be why it's so very English; this isn't about quality, this is all about quantity. But to give it a French twist, there was absolutely no vegetarian option on offer.

I arrived to find the other 'volunteers' already in the school kitchen waiting for me – only they weren't volunteers at all, they were fully paid-up dinner ladies and the headmistress; *I* was the only 'volunteer' on the cooking side of this project, and while they had already got the bacon, sausages and beans under way they were awaiting egg-based instructions. I don't like sharing a kitchen at the best of times, so when I said I'll be fine to just get on with it myself, I meant it. 'You'll wash your hands first!' said the headmistress, a fussy little woman who I suppose had every right to be so as perhaps suddenly the idea of inviting some oddly dressed stranger into her school kitchen and just letting him get on with things was beginning to seem a little dicey.

'I'll take my coat off first,' I replied, just letting her know I can compete in the prissy stakes.

'Well how many eggs do you want? Shall I break them?' And then she added wistfully, 'We did a French breakfast for the pupils last year.' I could see that she thought this effort might all be a bit complicated and maybe it would be, but this is a full English breakfast, love, I thought, not just a vat of hot chocolate and skip load of croissants.

The thing is, I've never been all that good at scrambled eggs; I never get the balance right, or the timing, and I wanted it to be just right this time, it had to be. Too often hotel breakfast buffet scrambled eggs, for instance, are either like chewing on a memory-foam mattress or characterless dollops swilling about in too much liquid. So I'd done a little mental prep and had things worked out nicely, though I was a little thrown when I was told that they don't use wooden spoons, which to me are vital in the cooking of scrambled eggs. Honestly, if this had been a gig at that point I'd have walked, citing 'intolerable working conditions'.

I made do and, even if I say so myself, they were the best scrambled eggs I'd ever made: slightly creamy with a good light – it's all in the pre-whisk – texture. I was very proud and therefore not a little upset to see that they would now be put in the oven to keep warm, the oven in which the sausages and the bacon were still cooking. (I know they should be fried but I think 'arteries' are an issue for young kids so I was overruled).

While my eggs were in the oven being turned into polystyrene, I paced the kitchen anxiously just like I had done at The Comedy Store a couple of days before, expectant and nervous. The press arrived too, adding to the pressure of the thing. I say press; it was a very old man from the local paper who was brandishing, in shaky hands, one of the early digital camera prototypes. Eventually the food was served and my eggs, though now not at their best, were still pretty good and I waited for the response. There was a book out a few years ago called *French Children Don't Throw Food* about why French children are such good eaters and so on; it's another one of these ridiculously generalised books that draw massive, nationwide conclusions based on middle-class assumptions and coffee-morning conversations, but French children are better at the table, largely because they eat with their parents every day, parents who ate with their parents every day and all the way back. Food is still part of the curriculum, hence my dubious presence, but it's France for Heaven's sake – food is very much an issue and not just as a basis for gossamer-thin scare stories that newspapers use solely to frighten people.

That being said, my 'audience' were eyeing their plates with a certain level of distrust. Collectively they looked like a stag night the morning after, full of bravado about the FEB until confronted by the reality itself. Slowly, they began to tuck in, Maurice leading the way, obviously, and eventually they even began to like it. To us, the full English breakfast is such a part of our culture it seems almost surreal to think that these kids – and most of the adults – in the room had never even seen a plate like this before. And though I personally wouldn't have accepted 'French toast' as a fried bread substitute, nor refused brown sauce on the grounds of it being 'too spicy', and frankly would never drink PG Tips tea without milk (I served it under duress believe me, one little girl even asked me what flavour of *tisane* it was, '*PayJay*' I replied, like it was an exotic fruit), it was all a great success.

Also, I very much like the idea that while food education is quite rightly all about nutrition and balance these days, here I was in rural France showing the kids a full English breakfast, like a saturated-fats missionary. I even, and for the second time that week, got a round of applause from a French crowd.

Natalie and I walked arm in arm the short distance back into the centre of the small town. On the way we were greeted by the *boulanger*, the *garagiste*, Cendrine the *coiffeuse* and even our postman. *Bonjour! Ça va? Fait beau, eh?*

C'EST LA VIE

'It's so lovely,' Natalie said as we strolled along in the early winter sunshine, 'we really are a part of this community. It really feels like home.'

Then she pinched my arm.

'Ow!' I said, taken completely by surprise. 'Why did you do that?'

'Because,' she replied, stopping as she said so, 'sometimes *you* need reminding.'

RECIPES

Medlar Jelly

They really are an odd little fruit, medlars, and about as unappetising to look at as fruit gets. Occasionally Natalie has grabbed one off a tree and just stuck a spoon in it, but she can get a bit Bear Grylls when the mood takes her. If picking the fruit from your own trees, the important thing to remember, and certainly for this recipe, is let them 'blet', or rot, first. They shouldn't be harvested until after the first frost, and then should be left until they are dark brown and slightly mushy.

Ingredients

A quantity of nicely bletted medlar fruit
Sugar (an equal quantity to the fruit)
Lemon juice
Jelly bag
Sterilised jars

Method

- Take a 'quantity' (I never measure these things out), halve the fruit, add some lemon juice or divide a lemon into wedges (not too much, approximately one lemon per kilo of fruit) and cover with water in a large pan. Bring to the boil, stirring occasionally, and leave to simmer for about an hour, or at least until soft.

- Empty the softened fruit into a jelly bag suspended over a large bowl – I use two fire pokers hung across the bath to do this. The idea here is that your juice will drip into the bowl. It's important that you resist the temptation to hurry the juice through; don't press the jelly bag or your jelly will be cloudy and nobody wants cloudy jelly.

- Leave it where it is for a day or so.

- Empty the juice into a pan and bring it to the boil, then add an equal quantity of sugar and boil again until the sugar has dissolved and then boil for a few minutes more. Spoon into sterilised jars, seal and leave it to cool.

- When it has done so, stand back and wonder how a fruit so ugly could produce something so golden and pure!

C'EST LA VIE

Plum Leathers

I'd never even heard of these before but they are great to eat, and are especially useful for kids' lunchboxes and picnics. You can also cut them up and put the strips on desserts or even use them as Christmas tree decorations.

Ingredients

A quantity of plums
Baking parchment
Greaseproof paper

Method

- Preheat the oven to its lowest setting, about 60°C, and line a baking tray or two with baking parchment.

- Stone the plums (though any stone fruit or berry can be used, really) and boil on the hob until you have a thickish pulp, or compote.

- Once the pulp is ready, push it through a sieve, or a mouli, and spread the purée really thinly with a palette knife until the baking sheets are covered.

- Place in the oven overnight, 12 hours minimum. The purée should be completely dry and peel easily off the parchment.

RECIPES

- Roll the leathers up in greaseproof paper, cut to the required length for storing in a large airtight container (we use medium-sized, airtight jars) and either nibble on for the next few months or sell to Lady Gaga as material for a future dress.

ACKNOWLEDGEMENTS

I'd like to think that the classic 'difficult second book' scenario was skilfully avoided by virtue of my own sangfroid, coolness under pressure and ability to operate in a bubble. This would of course be entirely wrong and so heartfelt 'thank yous' are due all over the place.

Firstly, thank you to those good people at Summersdale: Claire Plimmer, Amy Hunter and Dean Chant, and especially to my ever-patient and brilliant editor Chris Turton. A special thanks also to Jennifer Barclay for precious hints and tips.

I am also indebted to Nicky Ness and Georgina Smith at SSVC and Cdr Susie Thomson at the MoD: their help and advice while writing about the sensitive issue of the armed forces decompression tours was both invaluable and generous.

As always there are good friends, particularly those who thought that my paranoid and neurotic ways would end when the first book was published, but who were kind enough to offer patience during the second; thank you then to Charlotte Phillips, Paul Thorne and Sonja Van Praag.

ACKNOWLEDGEMENTS

A special thank you to my lovely wife Natalie who still, after all these years, puts up with my grumpiness with astonishing good humour.

And lastly, to the millions of people who cleverly ducked out of attending our writing school and forced me back on to the keyboard coalface, your input was priceless!

Ten years on and this all feels slightly surreal. It's fun to see where we were and where we are now. Thanks again to all those at Summersdale, Rebecca Haydon and Jasmin Burkitt, and to my agent Bill Goodall who keeps me going!

ABOUT THE AUTHOR

Ian Moore is the best-selling author of the Follet Valley crime series which began with *Death and Croissants*. He is also the author of *The Man Who Didn't Burn* and *Dead Behind the Eyes* in the Juge Lombard series. Ian is a well-known stand-up comedian on radio and TV in the UK and a husband, father of three boys, farmhand and chutney-maker in France where he owns a writers' retreat.

Have you enjoyed this book?
If so, why not write a review on your favourite website?

If you're interested in finding out more about our
books, find us on Facebook at **Summersdale Publishers**,
on Twitter/X at **@Summersdale** and on Instagram and
TikTok at **@summersdalebooks** and get in touch.
We'd love to hear from you!

Thanks very much for buying this Summersdale book.
www.summersdale.com